Restructuring a Traditional Industry

Edited by **Helen Rainbird and Gerd Syben**

Construction is a large industry, accounting for a sizeable sector of employment. The site- rather than factory-based organisation of production limits the application of principles of scientific management and new technology with the result that there is a continuing demand for on-site craft labour alongside new specialist trades and recombinations of skills. However, the creation of a single European market in 1992 will result in the internationalisation of industries and a more competitive environment. Technological change will therefore also be of great significance for the construction industry.

This collection of original papers examines contemporary restructuring within this industry. It brings together research carried out in four countries: France, Denmark, Britain and West Germany, and focuses on the implications of organisational and technological change for work organisation, employment skills and training. Developments in the individual countries are set against the wider European context.

Helen Rainbird   Industrial Relations Research Unit, University of Warwick

Gerd Syben   Hochschule Bremen

Restructuring a Traditional Industry

Construction Employment and Skills in Europe

Edited by
HELEN RAINBIRD and GERD SYBEN

BERG

New York / Oxford
Distributed exclusively in the US and Canada by
St Martin's Press, New York

First published in 1991 by
Berg Publishers Ltd
Editorial Offices:
165 Taber Avenue, Providence R.I., 02906, USA
150 Cowley Road, Oxford OX4 1JJ, UK

© Helen Rainbird and Gerd Syben, 1991

British Library Cataloguing in Publication Data

Restructuring a traditional society: construction
employment and skills in Europe.
1. Europe. Construction industries
I. Rainbird, Helen II. Syben, Gerd
338.47624094

Library of Congress Cataloging-in-Publication Data

Restructuring a traditional industry: construction employment and
skills in Europe / edited by Helen Rainbird and Gerd Syben.
p. cm.
1. Construction industry—Europe—Technological innovations.
2. Construction workers—Europe—Effects of technological
innovations on. I. Rainbird, Helen. II. Syben. Gerd.
HD9715.E82R47 1991
338.4'5624'094—dc20   90–362
                                                                                        CIP

ISBN 0–85496–585–8

Printed in Great Britain by
Billing & Sons Ltd, Worcester

Contents

Contents

Tables, Figures and Insets

Tables

Figures

Insets

Contributors

Jacotte Bobroff Centre d'Enseignement et de Recherche Techniques et Sociétés, École Nationale des Ponts et Chaussées, Paris

Sten Bonke Department of Construction Management, Technical University of Denmark, Copenhagen

Elisabeth Campagnac Centre d'Enseignement et de Recherche Techniques et Sociétés, École Nationale des Ponts et Chaussées, Paris

Stephen Evans School of Industrial and Business Studies, University of Warwick

Elsebet Frydendal Pedersen Department of Construction Management, Technical University of Denmark, Copenhagen

David Gann Science Policy Research Unit, University of Sussex

Josef Hilbert Institut Arbeit und Technick, Wissenschaftzentrum, Nordrhein – Westfalen, Gelsenkirchen

Jürgen Koch GJW Europe, Brussels

Joachim Reus Industriegewerkschaft Bau-Steine-Erden, Frankfurt

Helen Rainbird Industrial Relations Research Unit, University of Warwick

Wolfgang Streeck Department of Sociology, University of Wisconsin, Madison

Gerd Syben Hochschule Bremen

Michèle Tallard Institut de Recherche et d'Information Socio-économique - Travail et Société, CNRS

Ursula Weis Department of Architecture, University of Karlsruhe

Graham Winch Institute for Management Research and Development, University of Warwick

Acknowledgements

The idea of producing an edited collection of papers on the European construction industry came out of an international conference held at the University of Warwick in April 1988. The theme of the conference was 'New Technology in Construction: Employment, Skills and Training' and it was organised to develop and deepen our understanding and analysis of recent changes in the construction industry, which began with a conference on 'CAD/CAM in Construction' in March 1987, hosted by the Technical University of Denmark in Copenhagen. Approximately half of the papers reproduced here were originally presented at the Warwick conference. The remaining papers fall into three types; those that were commissioned specifically for publication in this book, extracts from longer reports, and translations of papers not otherwise available in English.

Producing a collection of paper is, by definition, a collective enterprise and we would like to recognise the help and collaboration we have received from many people. Firstly, we would like to acknowledge the financial support we have received. The Nuffield Foundation provided a grant for the preparation of the manuscript for publication; the British Council in Hamburg provided funding for editorial meetings and contributed towards translation costs; and the West German construction union, Industriegewerkschaft Bau-Steine-Erden (IG BSE) also contributed towards the cost of translating some of the German papers. Secondly, we are grateful to our respective institutions, the Institute for Employment Research at the University of Warwick, in particular to Margaret Birch and Rosalie Edkins for administrative and secretarial support respectively, and to the Hochschule Bremen, where Annamarie Beneke provided support. Thirdly, we would like to acknowledge the cooperation we have received from all the contributors to the book, who have succeeded in meeting deadlines despite the constraints imposed, in a number of cases, by research conducted on short-term contracts.

We would like to give special recognition to the following: David Gann of the Science Policy Research Unit at the University of Sussex for his contribution to our early discussions on the structure and contents of the book; the members, past and present, of the Construction Industry Studies Group at Warwick for contributing to a congenial work environment; and Graham Winch for his persistence in unravelling the intricacies of the French construction industry.

We also acknowledge the intellectual stimulation provided by all the participants, both academics and trade unionists, at the Danish and British conferences, as well as at other international meetings on the construction industry in Dortmund and Paris in 1987 and 1988. We would like to thank Louise Gibson and Nicki Le Feuvre of the Department of Modern Languages at the University of Aston for translations of chapters 3 and 4, and 7 and 12 respectively, and to Ulrich Bingel for help in translating chapters 5 and 14. Finally, Helen would like to record her gratitude to Francisco Salazar, for his support and understanding.

HELEN RAINBIRD
GERD SYBEN

Abbreviations

AEU	Amalgamated Engineering Union (Britain)
BDA	Bundesvereinigung der Deutschen Arbeitgeberverbände: Federation of German Employers' Associations
BEC	Building Employers' Confederation (Britain)
BTS	Brevet de Technicien Supérieur – higher professional certificate (France)
CAA	Computer-aided architecture
CAD	Computer-aided design
CAD/CAM	Computer-aided design and manufacturing
CAE	Computer-aided engineering
CAM	Computer-aided manufacture
CAP	Certificat d'Aptitude Professionel – certificate of vocational aptitude (France)
CAPC	Computer-aided production control
CAPM	Computer-aided production management
CAPP	Computer-aided production planning
CEDEFOP	European Centre for the Development of Vocational Training
CEN	European Committee for Harmonising Standards
CENELEC	European Committee for Harmonising Electrotechnical Standards
CGT	Confédération Générale du Travail
CIM	Computer-integrated manufacture
CITB	Construction Industry Training Board (Britain)
DIY	Do-it-yourself
DoE	Department of the Environment (Britain)
DUT	Diplôme Universitaire de Technologie – university diploma of technology (France)
EC	European Community
ECU	European Currency Unit
EDC	Economic Development Committee – sector com-

	mittee of the National Economic Development Office (Britain)
EDP	Electronic data processing
EFBW	European Federation of Building and Woodworkers
ETUC	European Trade Union Confederation
EVMB	Emploi et Valorisation des Métiers du Bâtiment – committee for the employment and development in the construction trades (France)
FMB	Federation of Master Builders (Britain)
FRG	Federal Republic of Germany
GDP	Gross domestic product
GNP	Gross national product
HDB	Hauptverband der Deutschen Bauindustrie: Association of the German Construction Industry
IG BSE	Industriegewerkschaft Bau-Steine-Erden – the West German construction union
ILO	International Labour Organisation
IT	Information technology
PPS	Project planning systems
R&D	Research and development
SMIC	Salaire Minimum Interprofessionel de Croissance: index-linked minimum wage (France)
TA	Technology Assessment (Denmark)
VLS	Voluntary Labour Service (pre-war Germany)
ZDB	Zentralverband des Deutschen Baugewerbes: Central Association of the German Building Industry
ZDH	Zentralverband des Deutschen Handwerks: Central Association of German Artisans

1

Introduction

Helen Rainbird and Gerd Syben

If industrial sectors of national economies are judged on the basis of volume of production, and proportion of total production and employment, then the construction industry must rate as one of the most important economic sectors in Europe. Despite its significance in terms of volume of economic activity, employment and training, construction has attracted relatively little attention from social scientists compared to more glamorous sectors such as motor vehicles, steel and engineering.[1] We believe that the construction industry's image as a traditional, technologically backward industry may have contributed to this, although the image is not entirely warranted. Rather, a major process of modernisation has been occurring in the 1980s which, in principle, is not different from that of industry as a whole. The construction industry, as all other industries, has had to respond to a crisis of profitability. Three main factors have characterised this crisis in construction. First, the general economic crisis has led to a general decline in the demand for buildings. Second, the housing sector, in particular, has registered a sharp decline in investment. Third, the state has been a major client for construction goods. The economic crisis has produced public expenditure cuts on the one hand, and policies aimed at reducing the contribution of the state to gross national product on the other.

Under these conditions, competition in the construction industry has increased and companies have been forced to introduce measures to increase productivity. This process has created some new developments which we refer to as 'restructuring'. We use this term to indicate the ways in which the industry has confronted the crisis of the 1980s. Attempts to increase productivity and maintain profits

1

have not occurred primarily through the introduction of automation and new technology. Rather, the emphasis has been on rationalisation and the reorganisation of the production process. The papers in this collection focus on four major aspects of this process of change: the role of the state in encouraging certain forms of restructuring; management strategies towards increasing profitability at a time of crisis and retrenchment; the consequences of new technology for the organisation of work; and the implications of these changes for skill requirements and training policy. A final paper looks forward to assess the likely implications of the completion of the European market for the construction industry.

The Construction Industry in Europe

Even though the construction sector experienced an acute crisis in many countries of the European Community in the early 1980s, investment in building was still substantial. In 1985 building investment amounted to £200 billion (338.5 billion ECU) in the twelve member states. This constituted slightly more than 10 per cent of combined gross domestic product in the European Community (Table 1.1) and 53 per cent of all investment. Between them, France, West Germany, Great Britain and Italy accounted for nearly 80 per cent of all EC building investment.

Construction influences all sectors of economic activity and private life. It includes civil engineering, commercial building, housing, and repair and maintenance. It is common to make the distinction between structural work – the work involved in raising the superstructure of a building, which accounts for the greater part of turnover and employment – and the finishing trades, many of which are specialist or craft traders such as roofing, tiling, plastering, painting, heating and ventilating, electrical work. Although public sector construction investment has been severely affected in the recession, this is also true of work for private sector clients. In this respect, construction activity is closely related to levels of activity in other sectors of the economy which affect the volume of commercial building. Even housing has been affected: in the mid 1980s about one-quarter of construction investment was spent on housing, but this figure is an average of levels of investment in different European countries and represents a 15 per cent decline in investment between 1983 and 1987. The overall level of investment

Table 1.1 Gross domestic product, building investment and productivity in construction, 1985

	Gross domestic product (bn ECU)	Building investment (bn ECU)	Building investment as % of GDP	Building investment as % of EC total	Building investment per employee (ECU)
Belgium	105.2	9.1	8.7	2.7	43.500
Denmark	76.7	8.3	10.8	2.5	50.600
Irish Republic	24.2	2.0	8.3	0.6	23.800
France	690.6	65.5	9.5	19.3	43.000
West Germany	822.8	92.8	11.3	27.4	50.300
Great Britain	595.5	46.2	7.8	13.6	30.900
Greece	43.6	4.7	10.8	1.4	13.100
Italy	556.5	64.7	11.6	19.1	40.100
Luxemburg	4.7	0.6	12.8	0.2	37.500
Netherlands	165.9	16.1	9.7	4.8	48.900
Portugal	27.0	3.2	11.9	0.9	8.100
Spain	216.1	25.3	11.7	7.5	33.700
EC	3,328.8	338.5	10.1	100	38.500

Source: Hauptverband der Deutschen Bauindustrie, *Die Bauwirtschaft in der Europäischen Gemeinschaft*, Bonn, 1988, S. 36.

Table 1.2 Construction investment by sector in six EC countries, 1987

	% of total construction by sector					Total (bn ECU)
	Housing	Commercial	Public	Civil engineering	Repair maintenance	
Belgium	27	36	9	18	9	11
France	24	12	4	22	37	67
West Germany	22	15	5	15	43	124
Great Britain	20	24	6	6	44	50
Italy	27	11	3	14	44	63
Netherlands	26	11	5	16	50	19

Source: Euro-construct Conference, Vienna, 1989 (our calculations).

in construction varies considerably between countries, as does its distribution between public and private sectors (Table 1.2).

Table 1.3   Employees by sector of EC industries, 1985[a]

Industry	Employee numbers
Oil industry	119,700
Production and distribution of energy	1,031,700
Chemical industry	1,682,800
Mechanical engineering	2,646,300
Electrotechnical industry	2,683,700
Car industry	2,545,700
Food industry	2,570,800
Construction	5,563,900
Industry total	31,904,000

(a) 9 countries – without Greece, Portugal, Spain.
Source: Statistical Office of the European Communities, *Statistische Grundzahlen der Gemeinschaft* (Statistical basic data), Luxemburg, 1988, p. 120.

Construction is also a major sector of employment and in the European Community it employs 8.8 million people. This constitutes 7.2 per cent of all employment and in this respect makes construction the largest single industry (Table 1.3). Within each country the proportion of construction employment varies according to levels of investment in building on the one hand, and levels of productivity on the other (Table 1.4). The number of people employed in the industry is proportionately lower in countries where productivity is higher, as in Denmark, West Germany and the Netherlands.

Construction: A Traditional Industry?

The popular characterisation of the construction industry as technologically backward is correct only if technological progress is equated with the automation of production processes. Automation is rarely found in the construction industry itself, though it may be found in the building materials sector, especially in prefabrication. In this respect, it is found at the limits of the production process. Likewise, new technologies based on electronic data processing are being introduced slowly and only in certain parts of the production process, and in this respect their full potential has yet to be realised (see chapters 6–9). Specific features of the construction industry

Table 1.4   Employment and unemployment in construction, 1985

	Total employment	Employment in construction employees and self-employed	% of total employment	Unemployed construction workers (1987)
Belgium	3,662,000	206,000	5.7	38,200
Denmark	2,553,000	164,000	6.5	17,800[a]
Irish Republic	1,056,000	59,000[b]	7.4[c]	43,300
France	21,397,000	1,524,000	7.1	231,300
West Germany	25,482,000	1,846,000	7.2	124,500
Great Britain[d]	23,818,000	1,494,000	6.3	437,000
Greece	3,589,000	170,000[b]	9.6[c]	17,000[e]
Italy	21,151,000	1,612,000	7.6	230,700[e]
Luxemburg[f]	158,000	16,000	10.1	–
Netherlands	4,561,000	329,000	7.2	46,100
Portugal	3,906,000[g]	393,000[g]	10.1	19,000[d]
Spain	10,500,000	751,000	7.2	367,500[e]
EC	121,813,000	8,782,000	7.2	1,572,000

(a) 1985   (b) employees only   (c) % of all employees   (d) 1984   (e) 1985
(f) 1982   (g) 1981
Source: Hauptverband der Deutschen Bauindustrie, *Die Bauwirtschaft in der Europäischen Gemeinschaft*, Bonn, 1988, p. 35.

have influenced this. In particular we would emphasise two important differences with manufacturing industry in general.

Firstly, construction production is bound to a particular locality, the construction site, where the product will be used. Transportation of the product is impossible. As a consequence, plant and equipment must be mobile. There is a technological barrier to technical progress inasmuch as it is more important that the machinery should be robust than that it is capable of performing sophisticated functions. These conditions of production have consequences for the labour process itself. Whilst in other industries the problem of efficient production is one of organising the flow of material through the factory to optimise use of machinery, in construction the problem is to optimise the flow of inputs in the form of materials, equipment and labour around the product as it is constructed. Therefore it is appropriate to have machinery and tools which can be adapted to a variety of tasks rather than for performing only specialised functions. This normally requires a skilled labour force which has a high level of knowledge about handling materials and tools. In addition, variations in physical conditions mean that the workforce must have sufficient knowledge of the labour process as a whole in order to be able to react to unforeseen problems. In this respect, relatively high levels of worker autonomy are found.

The second major feature distinguishing construction from manufacturing is that production is not normally for a generalised market but to meet the needs of a specific client. As a result, production is organised in such a way as to produce a high level of variability in the product, normally referred to as 'one-off' production. So the standard means of rationalisation applied to production processes in other industries, such as the standardisation of goods, the use of assembly lines, single-purpose machinery and the subdivision of tasks, cannot be applied. There is thus also an economic barrier to technical progress in so far as there are few economies of scale to be gained. The concentration of capital, which is normally considered to be a precondition for the development and implementation of technological progress, does not confer any special advantages in production techniques.

Because there are few economies of scale affecting production processes, firm size does not influence the technical level of the construction process to nearly the same extent as in manufacturing industry. As a result, another characteristic of the industry is the wide variety in firm size. The number of construction firms in the European Community is estimated to be 1.1 million, of which approximately one million have less than 10 employees. The largest companies have between 20,000 and 30,000 employees. However, it is not generally the case that advanced technology is used in large firms and more backward production equipment in smaller firms. Observations of construction sites show no such correlation between technology and firm size. The technology employed in different countries is also similar, although levels of concentration, in terms of turnover and numbers of employees, varies considerably (Figure 1.1).

Firm size has a greater bearing than the technology employed on the types of construction projects the firm is engaged in. In other words, economic power and technical know-how affect the segments of the construction market in which firms operate. In broad terms, the biggest firms work on large projects for which considerable amounts of capital and technical know-how are required,

Figure 1.1 Concentration in the European construction industry

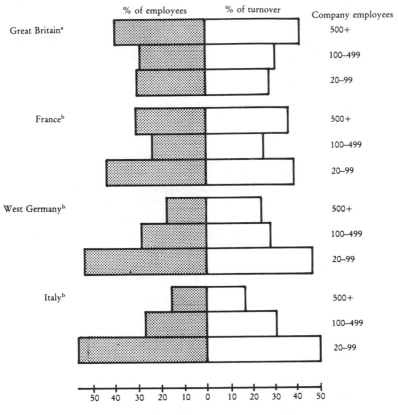

(a) Establishments   (b) Enterprises

Source: Statistical Office of the European Community, *Survey 1983.*

whereas smaller firms work on lesser projects such as housebuilding, domestic repair and maintenance, which can be produced with less equipment and do not burden them with heavy overhead costs.

Although there is empirical evidence to support the concept of a segmented construction market, this requires further theoretical and empirical study. Nevertheless, the segmentation of the market appears to be part of the modernisation strategy of the industry as a whole and the outcome of restructuring processes. These processes of modernisation are very similar to those observed in other industries, which have sometimes been referred to as 'flexible specialisation' (Piore and Sabel 1984). The concept of flexible specialisation has been used to denote new methods of organising the labour process in mass production industries. Before the economic crisis, the Fordist production paradigm was geared towards the production of single products for mass markets using highly specialised, single-purpose machinery. Newer production technologies have been introduced to respond more flexibly to changes in product type, with consequences for the organisation of the labour process.

In contrast to the manufacturing industry, there have always been limitations in the extent to which single-purpose, automated machinery can be employed in construction. The nature of construction markets has always required flexible production methods and the consequence of this has been its dependence on a relatively skilled labour force. It had to obtain productivity objectives on the basis of unspecialised, multi-purpose machinery. So the method of organising the production process has always had those elements now considered to be 'new' in manufacturing industries, as they attempt to resolve the objectives of being highly flexible and highly automated at the same time. Therefore, in construction, when we speak of restructuring, we are not referring to new methods of reorganising the production process, but rather to the extension and development of existing ones.

Three major forms of reorganising production processes can be identified:

1 Production processes on site are restructured not by the use of more or new technical means, but through changes in work organisation. Rationalisation is achieved by speeding up processes and removing interruptions in the continous flow of work. In manufacturing, this is known as 'just-in-time' management.

2 Firms have been restructured in such a way as to reduce costs of maintaining workers and equipment when they are idle. In this way, some of the factors of production which are normally owned by the company are simply hired when they are needed. As a result there has been a growth in the numbers of plant-hire companies and specialist subcontracting. In some instances, large corporations have set up plant-hire companies as separate operating units within their overall structure.

3 Patterns of cooperation between firms have been restructured. Overall subcontracting has increased. Some of this represents an increased reliance on specialist techniques and materials. In many instances, however, it represents a strategy of passing economic risks onto smaller companies and onto construction workers

themselves, as in the case of labour-only subcontracting.

These general processes of restructuring in the construction industry occur in varying forms under different political and societal conditions, as the authors in this volume show. Along with Campinos-Dubernet (1984 and 1988) we believe that the specific characteristics of the construction industry arise from the central problem of mastering variability in the production process. This refers to the uncertain nature of the workload in an industry which does not produce for an undifferentiated market, but to meet special demands as well as uncertainties, which arise from the physical variability of site conditions, in the production process itself. Campinos-Dubernet argues that firms respond to this uncertainty using two types of strategy: the externalisation of variability (*extériorisation de la variabilité*) whereby risk is passed on to other firms and workers through subcontracting; and the internalisation of variability (*intériorisation de la variabilité*) whereby firms attempt to adapt to the uncertainty of market conditions by increasing their internal domination of the factors of production and making them more adaptable (1988: 15) These strategies are influenced by the regulatory framework provided by the state and different patterns can be observed in the countries discussed in the contributions to this volume.

Summary of Articles

Evans's paper on the British construction industry examines how the state has encouraged certain types of restructuring. He shows that policies of deregulation pursued by the British state have not encouraged the adoption of new technologies, but have created an environment in which labour-intensive production methods and, within this, strategies of labour intensification are pursued. The framework of employment law and the Conservative government's industrial relations policies have contributed to the promotion of a short-term strategy towards the industry rather than one which is based on investment in technology and human resources which will lead to long-term gains in labour productivity. Ironically, deregulatory measures have not achieved the objective of reducing labour costs. Rather, they have rebounded in the emergence of a pathology of labour-only subcontracting, casualisation, a sharp reduction in apprenticeship training, the encouragement of narrow, specialist skills, and in trainees failing to complete their training. More recently, the deregulation of financial markets produced a construction 'boom' in London and the south-east of England, exacerbating skill shortages. Moreover, whilst self-employment and labour-only subcontracting may reduce labour costs for employers during a recession, the emergence of skill shortages has had the opposite effect of producing high informal wages, which are not regulated by collective agreements. Evans concludes that despite policies of privatisation and non-interventionist policy stances taken by the Conservative government, there is a considerable degree of interdependency between the state and construction capital. Policies pursued in recent years have favoured the interests of the largest construction firms, but in promoting short-term gains at the expense of labour and smaller contractors, have militated against investment in new production technologies and skills training. In this respect, long-term advances will be frustrated.

In contrast to the British state, Tallard examines how the French state has promoted policies of social innovation since the late 1970s, and in particular the effect of the 1982 Auroux laws promoting workers' participation in companies. These have not been of a philanthropic nature, but were introduced by the French Socialist government as a means of increasing companies' abilities to adapt and rationalise. First introduced in large companies, these measures were later implemented in smaller ones, and resulted in a shift from sectoral level negotiation to that of the firm. Compared to other sectors, the French construction industry demonstrates a number of specific characteristics; weak unionisation combined with strong and long-established bipartite structures concerned with specific issues, such as pension funds, and the preponderance of small companies, with a strong, paternalist management. Because the Auroux laws are based on the assumption of unionisation, weak unionisation in construction – estimated to be at between three and five per cent of employees – effectively means that the laws have not been applied. Despite this, since 1985 policies of social innovation have flourished, especially those linked to the training and motivation of employees. They have usually been adopted by firms which are attempting to integrate constraints related to the variability of the construction process. A study of one company which introduced these experiments on three sites demonstrated how this type of modernisation works. The greatest productivity gains were not achieved by reducing labour costs, but by basing production on the principles of workers' autonomy, responsibility for quality control and the training of operatives and supervisory staff alike.

Nevertheless, it is difficult to introduce policies of social innovation in the construction industry as a whole. They must take account of the discontinuities of site production on the one hand, and the significance of professional and trade identity on the other. Therefore connections are needed between the different levels of negotiation so that macroregulations, for example those governing recruitment, dismissals, occupational grids and insurance schemes, can be determined at sectoral level whilst the company becomes the focus for negotiations linked to work organisation and the adaptation of rules agreed at sectoral level.

Historical evidence suggests that there is no inevitable logic of technological development from lower to higher levels and that employment policies determined by the state can have a significant effect on wages, skills and the type of technology adopted. Weis demonstrates this in examining the dialectical relationship between technology and the social relations of production with respect to developments in Germany between 1919 which marked the period of working-class gains under collective labour law, and 1934 when the fascist labour law was introduced. In the 1920s the political and economic strength of the German construction union was sufficient to enable skilled workers to resist compulsory labour schemes, and innovations were introduced in concrete work and in the transportation of construction materials. However, by the 1930s, union power had been eroded by mass unemployment and these new techniques had been replaced by more labour-intensive methods, using only hand tools and human labour power for transportation. The decline in the level of technology was reflected both in the level of social assistance paid to workers and in the quality of housing that was produced.

Weis argues that the quality of labour, whether it is skilled or unskilled, affects the pattern of technological development. She points to a relationship between the system of social relations regulating the value of labour, patterns of reproduction of the labour force and the form of technology. However, the exact form of the wage and the social wage are linked to the history of social conflicts and their resolution. Though the analysis refers specifically to the 1920s and 1930s in Germany, these types of developments can also be observed in more recent times, for example in many of the schemes such as the Community Programme, the Youth Training and the Employment Training Schemes introduced for the unemployed in the recession of the 1980s in Britain.

In the second part of the book, the strategies of construction capital towards restructuring are considered in more detail. Continuing some of the themes highlighted by Evans, Syben considers how construction capital achieves productivity gains by organisational means in the absence of real technological change. Compared to manufacturing plants, there are limitations to the introduction of new technologies on construction sites. This is because 'self-acting machines' cannot be programmed in practice to work under the high levels of variability encountered in construction production. Increases in productivity can be achieved through prefabrication off-site, which allows certain economies of scale to be made, and organisational changes which result in increasing levels of specialisation through subcontracting. Both these strategies require greater emphasis on planning and coordination by construction firms, which develop and extend existing methods of production which are flexible by nature. So to some extent construction is a very modern industry in so far as it has always operated a form of 'stockless production', and is now developing more formal systems of just-in-time management. In the same way the nature of the labour process has required a skilled labour force and high levels of worker autonomy, characteristics not unlike the skills sought by employers in multi-skilled workers, who are encouraged to take more responsibility for their own work and the quality of the product and to identify with the objectives of firms through methods such as quality circles. Finally, he argues, fragmentation and decentralisation of production require new responses from workers' organisations, so that they can bargain successfully with the real seats of decision-making.

Some of these developments are examined by Gann in his discussion of new management strategies and technical change in the British construction industry. Like Syben, he identifies mechanisms for reducing costs; organisational change, the use of new materials and components, the shifting of production off-site through prefabrication and the use of more capital equipment. He examines factors affecting technical change in different phases of the production process: product innovation is most likely to be initiated by designers and component producers, and process innovation by builders. Specialisation militates against the diffusion of new techniques and technologies, whilst speculative building may be less open to innovation than contracting due to the weight of land development gains in profits.

A case study of fast-track construction techniques shows how new management techniques are being developed to improve the quality of work on very large office development sites. The aim of this management method is primarily to increase the rate of capital turnover and returns on it through the speeding up of the construction process. This occurs through the overlapping of the design and construction phases, allowing site work to commence before the design is completed, and also allows clients to make a faster return on their investment by allowing occupation of part of the building before it is fully completed. Whilst requiring higher levels of skill and coordination amongst professionals, the overall effect is for a reduction of labour requirements on site, with greater emphasis on specialist skills on the one hand, and 'limited skills' for assembly-type work on the other. Though reduction in production times may make union organisation harder, there have been indications that time and quality constraints, alongside health and safety considerations, may predispose site management to encourage unionisation as a means of regulating employment and workers on site.

Some rather different methods are employed for overcoming these same problems of quality control and meeting completion dates in France. Campagnac examines developments in management strategy in the French industry, focusing on the place of information technologies in the achievement of the goal of integrating the cycle of production. She argues that there is not a straightforward relationship between technological change and changes in the labour process. Rather, new technologies allow a global reorganisation of the production process, though different actors, such as construction clients and site management, seek to use it in different ways. A significant development has been the greater cooperation of private contractors with large public sector clients. In this way, competition is reduced through emphasising product quality and guarantees on completion dates and contractors are able to offer services to the client which enable them to negotiate contracts rather than to compete purely on price. A major consideration of management strategy has been to obtain greater control over costs through exerting control over all stages of the production cycle. As a result, large companies are increasing their emphasis on design and in achieving flows of information between different phases of the production process, to the extent that one can speak of general computer-aided design (CAD) systems, as opposed to specific software used by different professions.

A major feature of an integrated CAD system is its ability to break down the functional divisions between different actors and different stages in the construction process. This is linked to firms' strategies towards the reduction, transfer or integration of the variability of production. Like Gann, Campagnac argues that a major objective of firms is the reduction of the duration of site work, and that the key to doing this is through the management of the interfaces between different tasks. Organisational developments and new strategies towards the management of the labour force, including increased emphasis on training and work autonomy (discussed in more detail in chapter 12) are the major factors behind productivity gains.

The third part of the book examines technological change in more detail. The problem of the integration of new technologies is also analysed in a paper by Winch on the application of computer-aided draughting and project planning systems. He compares the organisational obstacles to the introduction of fully-fledged CAD systems in construction compared to manufacturing industry. Although technologies based on microelectronics are 'integrating' technologies, the division between the design and production phases in the British construction industry, that is between independent architects and consultants on the one hand, and the contractor and subcontractors on the other, inhibits their full application. This is because the design and production phases are carried out by different organisations so that flows of information about progressive stages of production are not transmitted in the same way as when the entire process is carried out by a single company. This raises problems relating to the interfaces between different systems, as well as how data collected at one stage in the process can be made useful and transmitted to other stages. Compared to developments amongst the largest French companies reported in the previous chapter by Campagnac, this contribution demonstrates how a particular technology operates in different ways under different organisational conditions. Even new contract forms, such as management contracting, are unlikely to overcome these problems of integration. However, in theory, speculative housebuilding and design and build firms should have significant advantages in implementing CAD systems since they combine design and execution phases of production within the same organisation and so do not experience the same obstacles to establishing information flows between different parts of the system. However, as Gann also notes, speculative housebuilders are little inclined to technological innovation since a major source of their profit comes from land development gains. In contrast, Winch suggests that greater progress has been made in implementing CAD and project planning systems in design and build firms. He argues that through this, they will eventually gain competitive advantages over firms operating within both the traditional and more modern variants of the contracting system, possibly leading to a restructuring of the industry towards the design-and-build type of organisation.

The comparison between the applications of electronic data processing (EDP) in construction and manufacturing is also examined in the contribution by Reus and Syben. They point to the lack of microelectronic controls on site in West Germany and, in particular, to the relative lack of mechanisation of horizontal and vertical transport and assembly operations. Nevertheless, they argue this should not be seen as evidence that processes of rationalisation and applications of EDP are absent in the design phase and in commercial processes. Empirical evidence suggests that the application of EDP is largely restricted to commercial operations and to design work in engineering offices and is resisted by project managers on site. Although currently it affects mainly technical and commercial staff, potentially it will affect all employees. This points to the advantages for construction workers of union organisation based on industrial sector, as in the case of the Industriegewerkschaft Bau-Steine-Erden, the West German construction union. Policies directed towards EDP can provide a means of uniting members in different occupations and may form a means of involving and empowering sections of the workforce in the union who traditionally have not seen many benefits to unionisation. In doing this, the union recognises that the introduction of EDP is not just a technical problem. Rather, it facilitates organisational rationalisation and supports the decentralisation strategies of firms. This reinforces the case for industrial unionism and in particular the strategy of seeking industry-level national agreements on new technology.

Turning to the Danish construction industry, Bonke and Frydendal Pedersen show that there is not a mechanistic relationship between technology and conditions on site. Rather, there is a degree of choice, and the objective of their research project was to link the introduction of new technology to improvements in working conditions and to the involvement of construction workers and decision-making processes at site level.

Computerisation tends to focus on formal, legal channels of communication which are linked to the division of labour between firms in the construction process. In contrast, at site level, informal methods of communication are necessary so that construction workers can make adjustments to plans as they encounter variations in site conditions. This flexibility is a major source of work autonomy and has the result that methods of management control normally found in manufacturing are not appropriate to site conditions. Rather, indirect forms of control over the labour force are sought, for example through the operation of piece-work and bonus systems and the use of casual employment. High levels of unionisation (100 per cent) and the high level of skills of construction workers have allowed the Danish trade unions to pursue a policy of building on the autonomy of workers on site as a means of strengthening their power base. The complexity of communications structures and the form of information generated in construction production militate against the introduction of computers in construction compared to other sectors.

The Danish trade unions see new technology as a means of improving working conditions on site, of democratising computer use and as a means of increasing skill levels. Management has also recognised the need to motivate staff as a means of obtaining an efficient use of computers. The research project sought to develop a proactive strategy towards new technology as part of a future development process. It aimed to demystify technology for site workers and sought to identify and build on the positive aspects of construction work.

The fourth part deals with modernisation strategies as they are developed through the policies of the state, employers and unions towards technology and skills training in different countries. Rainbird examines the effects of labour market deregulation and firms' strategies of externalisation of variability on skill formation in Britain. She argues that the growth in numbers of very small firms and the self-employed in the recession does not represent the growth of independent small businesses. Rather, it constitutes a form of disguised wage labour, which has the effect of intensifying labour exploitation rather than increasing its productivity. These developments which have been widely recognised as being antithetical to skill training, in combination with the operation of a training system in which the number of trainees fluctuates according to employers' demand, have produced major skill shortages as the British industry has moved from slump to boom in the late 1980s.

Although there is a clear relationship between the decline in training and the growth of labour-only subcontracting and self-employment, little is actually known about the ways in which self-employed workers operate or if, and how, they train. Rainbird refers to the findings of a research project which provides some clues to the relationship between self-employment and the ability of the self-employed to train. The findings demonstrate that the working conditions of the self-employed militate against training in general and against quality training in particular. Policies designed to encourage the self-employed to train are misdirected since they are likely to result in a dilution of training standards, and they fail to tackle the real seat of the problem which lies in the failure of large employers to employ workers directly and provide pay and conditions to make the industry attractive. As a consequence an industrial strategy to improve long-term performance needs to be based on improvements in wages and conditions alongside investment in training, rather than on reducing labour costs through deregulation.

A strong contrast with the British situation is presented by Bobroff, who examines how some of the leading French firms have reassessed their policies towards human resource management. Firms have adopted a range of policies in the face of increased competition and reduced contract size; some involve rationalisation through specialisation and prefabrication, others rely on traditional craft skills and subcontracting of specialist trades, whereas others depend upon the development of these new approaches to human resource management. The latter reverse the erosion of the skill base of the industry which had been occurring over the previous two decades and attempt to rejuvenate the age profile of the labour force.

The French state has played a major role in supporting these new developments through programmes linked to its role as a major construction client. It has involved consultations on new curricula and the development of links between educational institutions and firms. However, Bobroff points out an important contradiction: many of the qualities now sought by firms as 'new competences' are precisely those which characterised traditional craft skills, especially the ability to act autonomously on site. The appropriation of the concept of autonomy by management marks a shift in emphasis from strategies linked to the control and discipline of the workforce to those aimed at establishing a higher level of trust and the identification of the worker with the firm.

The West German training system is also embedded in an industrial strategy based on the development of workers' skills and responsibility for production. Streeck and Hilbert focus on the institutionalised involvement of employers' associations and the construction union in training policy, arguing that the West German state delegates authoritative decision-making to these organisations through neo-corporatist arrangements. However, the institutions of training policy cannot be separated from other features of the West German political system. The unions and employers' associations are centralised, monopolistic organisations. They are involved in the management of the economy and there is also a high level of regional decentralisation. They point to the interdependence of the system of industrial relations, the organisation of works councils at company level and government policy towards the labour market. They emphasise, in particular, the 'density' of these institutional arrangements.

The authors discuss recent developments in training in the West German construction industry. These have been linked to efforts to maintain training volumes in the recession and the need to make the industry attractive to young workers. The West German construction union is highly supportive of training, since it is viewed both as a means of improving security of employment and as a means of securing commitment to the union. In the coming years emphasis is likely to shift increasingly towards retraining as the West German employers seek to increase the flexibility of existing employees in the face of demographic shifts in the labour market.

Finally the effects of the completion of the internal market in the European Community on the construction industry need to be considered. We agree with Koch that there will be far less impact than expected, or feared, today. Koch emphasises how the specific features of the construction industry impose limitations on the economies of scale to be achieved through the completion of the internal market though, given the size of the sector, relatively small cost savings will be significant at the European level. These are expected to be found mainly in border regions, in technologically advanced operations and where there are different levels of activity between adjoining regions. Liberalisation will significantly affect public procurement markets as these are increasingly opened up to Community-wide tendering processes, but existing guarantees for competition in public construction orders have been circumvented by contractors and governments alike and this is likely to continue rather than stop.

However, the largest construction companies operate not just in Europe but throughout the world and patterns of international operations develop and change over time. In the 1970s West European construction firms attempted to recycle petrodollars by sending equipment and employees to large construction projects in the Middle East. Now they have changed their strategy to one of exporting capital. They enter foreign markets in cooperation with national firms or by buying shares in overseas companies. It seems that this is likely to be the pattern of development within Europe and represents the strategy of the largest corporations, though it may eventually extend to medium-sized firms as well. Smaller firms are more likely to be affected by factors affecting labour. International patterns of labour mobility are already well established and European harmonisation will consolidate this process. In trying to assess these developments, we distinguish between mechanistic and political perspectives.

From a mechanistic point of view, the liberalisation of frontier controls may allow labour to be sold at the lowest price. It is possible that workers will move from site to site and this may have the effect of undermining wages and conditions of employment. On the other hand, there is already considerable mobility of labour within Europe and it has not had this effect. Site work requires a skilled labour force, and so long as there is a connection between high skill levels and productivity under given technological conditions, this is unlikely to change. In other words the large construction projects on which the multi-national construction corporations are engaged are precisely those projects which are most dependent on skilled labour to meet quality standards and completion times. In this respect a highly skilled work force is 'cheaper' than an unskilled one. Although mobility may continue to increase, this will not automatically result in the substitution of skilled labour by unskilled labour, and the undercutting of wages and conditions of employment.

Two further factors will impede the undercutting of workers' conditions, according to Koch. First, there is the directive which states that tenders must be based on the wage levels of the region in

Helen Rainbird and Gerd Syben

which the project is being built. So a firm originating in a low wage
country, such as Portugal, will be obliged to tender on the basis of
West German wage rates for projects in West Germany, rather than
Portuguese rates. The second factor will reflect the policies and
strength of the construction unions at a European level. If union
objectives are attained, firms which operate on the basis of undercutting the rules of fair competition will be excluded from tendering
processes. These objectives include the elimination of labour-only
subcontracting. Therefore the completion of the European market
may have less impact on the construction industry than has sometimes been argued. The extent to which wages and conditions of
employment are 'levelled up' rather than down will depend on the
determination of the construction unions to implement their policies, rather than directives from Brussels. As we have argued here,
the maintenance and improvement of wages and conditions are the
means for ensuring the maintenance of a highly skilled labour force,
essential to achieving quality construction products.

Note

1. Exceptions to this have been the work of Hillebrandt (1974 and 1984), Ball
(1983 and 1988) and Briscoe (1988) in Britain. In France the Centre d'Études et de
Recherches sur les Qualifications has coordinated a major comparative project on the
construction industry, the findings of which were presented at the Colloque 'Europe
et Chantiers' in Paris, 28–30 September 1988, and are due to be published shortly.
See, for example, Campinos-Dubernet (1984) and the special edition of the journal
Formation/Emploi on the construction industry, No. 22 (1988). The French Ministry
has also sponsored research through the programme Emploi et Valorisation des
Métiers du Bâtiment. Bobroff, Campagnac and Tallard have all produced reports for
this programme. Villa (1986) has examined the Italian construction industry, whilst
Janssen and Richter (1983) have written on the West German industry.

Bibliography

Ball, M. (1983), *Housing Policy and Economic Power: the Political Economy of Owner Occupation*, Methuen, London
—— (1988), *Rebuilding Construction. Economic Change in the British*

20

Construction Industry, Routledge, London

Briscoe, G. (1988), *The Economics of the Construction Industry*, Mitchells, London

Campinos-Dubernet, M. (1984), 'La Rationalisation du travail dans le BTP: un exemple des limites du Taylorisme orthodoxe', *Formation/Emploi*, 6, April–June

—— (1988), 'Des rigidités de la flexibilité: le BTP dans quatre pays Européens', paper presented to Colloque Europe et Chantiers, Paris, 28–30 September

Hillebrandt, P. (1974), *Economic Theory and the Construction Industry*, Macmillan, Basingstoke

—— (1984), *Analysis of the British Construction Industry*, Macmillan, Basingstoke

Janssen, J. and W. Richter (1983), *Arbeitsbedingungen der Bauarbeiter*, Campus, Frankfurt/New York

Piore, M. J. and C. Sabel (1984), *The Second Industrial Divide*, Basic Books, New York

Villa, P. (1986), *The Structuring of Labour Markets. A Comparative Analysis of the Steel and Construction Industries in Italy*, Clarendon Press, Oxford

Part I

The Role of the State in Restructuring

2

The State and Construction Performance in Britain

Stephen Evans

Introduction

The long-term dynamic potential of an economy is unlikely to be enhanced by an economic and industrial relations environment which encourages enterprises to rely on raising productivity and profitability from existing resources. It is arguably along such a path of pursuing short-term gains by intensifying work within traditional production technologies that contemporary as well as historical conditions have propelled British construction firms.

Evidence of construction performance is contradictory. Prais and Steedman (1986) cite a variety of sources which, for instance, show that comparison of labour inputs in the 1960s saw the British measure more unfavourably against the US; output per employee in French construction was estimated between a quarter and a third higher than in Britain in 1980; and British construction was 'exceptionally costly'. Yet other evidence suggests that British construction firms have lately achieved impressive improvements in cost control, productivity and completion speeds, and output levels per employee reached a par with the US (Flanagan et al. 1986).

Construction occupies a strategic role in providing infrastructure, housing and employment, thereby ensuring its importance for the economy at large. Continuing along the 'short-term' path, above, may be logical and expedient as well as profitable for construction capital. But it will put in jeopardy recent performance improvements to the long-term detriment of construction users and the wider economy. The state has been central to the industry's development, and its relation to these issues of construction performance provides the focus of this chapter.[1]

Stephen Evans

State Policies for Construction in Britain

The relationship between the construction industry and the state is crucial and complex. Points of convergence and divergence can be identified between the objectives of government and those of the industry's various interest groups. A consistent feature of the state's role throughout the period since 1945, under Conservative and Labour governments, has been its failure to provide sufficient stimulus to restructuring, inadequate attention to intervening in and guiding accumulation except on a piecemeal basis, and always subordinating industrial policy to the priorities of managing aggregate demand. 'Stop-go' policies in the 1960s and deflationary monetarist cuts since 1976 were one of a piece (Fine and Harris 1985: 14–18). State planning for construction has been of a limited, indicative and voluntary kind, handicapped by weaknesses of the state-planning apparatus and employer and union organisations, and by its domination by the Treasury and Bank of England (Jessop 1980: 40–1).

Central government's efforts to improve productivity and performance in the 1960s were hampered by shortages of labour, materials and managerial expertise, and by its own small central staff and inadequate control mechanisms. It briefly experimented with restructuring along 'Fordist' lines, providing for economies of scale by giving contractors incentives through select tendering, serial contracts and approval of proprietary systems to rationalise, merge and invest in industrialised technologies (Dunleavy 1981: 178). This was short-lived, falling victim to deflation and the disrepute attaching to cost and poor design and workmanship.

Labour market considerations, such as decasualisation, were also always subordinate to macro-economic concerns, and remain so. State policies tried only to steer the industry's own institutional mechanisms in the direction of broader governmental goals. These policies were largely uncoordinated, reflecting the often conflicting objectives of different government departments. The shake-out of labour that followed the application of Selective Employment Tax to construction in 1966, for example, only pushed labour from direct into self-employment. All governments, however, consistently accepted advice to regulate rather than eradicate one of the most prevalent forms of casual employment, labour-only subcontracting on a self-employed basis, and avoid compulsory or statutory registration of firms and workers as a means of decasualisation

(Austrin 1980: 311; Evans and Lewis 1989).

The Conservative government elected in 1979 inherited a crisis whose character was acutely political as well as economic. Among the peculiarities of the ailing British economy were its declining competitiveness in the domestic economy alongside thriving indigenous multi-national firms operating in international markets. Low levels of investment generated low productivity and a low social wage. Conflict over the wage–effort bargain was poorly controlled on account of the decentralised character of collective bargaining, and remained relatively immune to external labour market changes. These dilemmas for government were aggravated by the post-war commitment to full employment which brought continuing expansion of social expenditure and public sector employment, thereby underpinning unions' albeit subordinate influence within the process of political exchange.

The Conservative programme for resuscitating the spirit of enterprise since 1979 aimed at reducing the resources channelled through the state and expanding the base for private investment. In fact, from the mid 1970s at least, construction became a central target for state policies of reducing public sector borrowing and expanding the base for private accumulation. Cuts in real terms of almost 50 per cent of public expenditure on housing, roads and other construction between 1976 and 1986 mark the industry out from virtually all other capital expenditure programmes (Thompson 1986: 2). These were accompanied by commodification of previously state-produced utilities and services, shifting reliance for housing to the private sector, selling off council houses, and extending compulsory competitive tendering. At the same time, construction's labour-intensive technologies continued to offer government a handy means of soaking up labour market surpluses, especially among youth.

Deregulation of land usage, planning and development, and freeing of labour markets were essential corollaries of the Conservatives' privatisation agenda for construction. Because of local government's crucial role in supplying these regulatory functions in construction, it was vital, in turn, that the balance of power was rearranged within the state itself. Central government introduced a range of financial disciplines and legal controls aimed at inducing a market rationality into local government management and services, and at restructuring local authorities as market support mechanisms (Loughlin 1986; Young 1986: 234–52).

Labour market policies were premised on creating the conditions for employment growth by lowering the costs and risks of hiring labour or, alternatively, by releasing the enterprise of skilled workers through encouraging them to set up in business on a self-employed basis. This complemented the policy shift from collective and public to individual and private welfare provision, supported by tax changes and other administrative measures to foster small firm growth, including government intervention through job and training schemes.

Deregulation, Destructuring and Construction Performance

Construction slumped in 1976. New orders fell by 40 per cent overnight and total construction output declined by 15 per cent over the next decade. The state's role in this was crucial. State-sponsored construction averaged 45 per cent of total volume between 1945 and 1976, when it peaked at 52 per cent before falling below 32 per cent in 1985. Workload fragmented spatially and by size. The annual number of new, large projects halved between 1971 and 1981 (Hillebrandt 1984). Office-building schemes were mainly of small to medium size, and heavily concentrated in south-east England. Shop-building, the fastest growth sector, followed retailers' decentralisation away from urban centres. Newer manufacturing sectors had similarly smaller space requirements (Turner 1987: 16–23). 'Parcelling' of work into smaller values was also a feature of growth markets like management contracting.

Slump in domestic markets was only temporarily relieved by expansion of international contracting opportunities in the mid 1970s. The British share of this market was dominated by five top firms, but markets contracted and competition intensified with the entry of other foreign and indigenous firms. Competition for contracts at home also tightened up, as did contractual conditions, with a movement from fluctuating to fixed price contracts and from lump sum bidding to management-fee arrangements, preselection by interview of contractors suitable for tendering and lengthening of public authority tender lists, reversing public policy of select rather than open tendering. Competitive tendering remained the norm for awarding subcontracts unless nominated by architects.

Intense competition affected profit performance and industrial structure. Real average rates of return on capital employed (adjusting for inflation) fell from 8.4 per cent to 4.8 per cent over the decade from 1970, the burden falling hardest on medium-sized firms (Turner 1987), squeezed by the proliferation of very small firms and by large contractors moving down-market. Firms with seven or fewer employees more than doubled and single person firms increased in number by 150 per cent, while the number of firms with more than 600 employees halved between 1975 and 1985. Over the same period, the share of employment by specialist trades firms' rose by 10 per cent to 45 per cent while that of large general contractors fell by 11 per cent to 22 per cent; the latters' share of workload fell from 33 per cent to 20 per cent, small firms raised theirs from 15 per cent to 26 per cent, and specialist trades' share increased from 33 per cent to 45 per cent. Growth of repair and maintenance work explained only part of the apparent process of fragmentation. The rest was due to an expansion of subcontracting. Most recent industry-level data show that large contractors' sub-contracted gross output rose from 37 per cent to 44 per cent between 1979 and 1981. Other evidence, from one of a sample of a dozen national and regional contractors, suggests a further steep acceleration. The proportion of site labour forces in the main contractor's own employment between 1982 and 1985 fell from 35 per cent to 20 per cent, supply and fix subcontractors' labour fell from 46 per cent to 35 per cent, and labour-only subcontractors increased from 19 per cent to 45 per cent (Evans and Lewis 1989).

These shifts obscure other fundamental changes in industrial structure and caution against any simple characterisation of frag-mentation. Inflation and other pressures led clients to seek faster build times and more rapid return on investment, together with a more unified construction process, single-point managerial responsi-bility and greater client involvement and customised service. This stimulated new markets in management contracting, design and build, etc., and new contracting arrangements and management control systems such as 'fast-track' tendering (McKinlay 1987). The largest construction firms now dominate these sectors and the rapidly expanding private housebuilding market. In 1984, manage-ment contracting output was estimated to have accounted for 10 per cent of new, non-housing construction, and this has undoubtedly increased since then. The top five firms secured over half of this work, and the top sixteen almost 90 per cent (CCMI 1985). They now probably control a higher volume of workload than ever before, albeit mediated through a new hierarchy of contractors and subcontractors.

These new contractual forms and management controls brought changes in production, too. Detailed, integrated financial controls entailed in fast-track tendering together with reduced architect autonomy through design and build, greater attention to managing design teams and increased liability pressure on designers, all enhanced managerial controls over the work process, above and at site level. This facilitated further systematisation of design and standardisation of components, making production increasingly a process of simple assembly and allowing more effective allocation and coordination of labour in the different phases of the work programme. It seems most probable it is this set of developments that provided the basis for recent productivity improvements.

It seems unlikely that these changes would have occurred as they did without the shock effect of slump and mass unemployment in softening up construction labour markets. Employment in the industry declined by one quarter of a million to just under 1.5 million between 1975 and 1985. Unemployment rose from 11 per cent in 1979 to 24 per cent in 1982, with some much higher regional levels, and voluntary and involuntary labour mobility increased generally. While employed manual workers declined by 31 per cent, this contrasted with just a 9 per cent fall in administrative, professional, technical and clerical staffs who constitute a major fixed cost which contributed to the pressures to casualise on-site labour.

Casualisation took two main forms, neither of them new to the industry. First, there was an increase in casual hiring on and off the books to supplement nuclei of regulars. Second, there was a resurgence of labour-only subcontracting from the late 1970s, spreading deeper and more pervasively among main trades (its traditional home) and into specialist trades like electrical contracting where previously it had been marginal (Evans and Lewis 1989; Cathcart 1986). Recent estimates put the number of labour-only subcontractors at around 600,000, more than half the manual workforce in contracting (DoE 1988). The overwhelming majority of these work on self-employed contracts.

Within production, labour is deployed in various ways to suit specific project conditions. In some cases it is interchanged and work gangs organise themselves around different tasks, in others workers are allocated to specific tasks by foremen or site management. The trend is to narrow specialisation, however. The form of employment – contract of employment for direct employees and contract for services for self-employed – gives few pointers to the real substance of the employment relation. Most firms tend to retain a nucleus of regulars supplemented by casual hirings. For some workers who benefit from skill shortages this represents more of a formal rather than substantive change of employment status. As it spreads, however, the labour force comprises an ever growing number of workers trapped in casualised, narrow skill-based jobs. Moreover, by providing employers with numerical rather than functional (multi-skilled) flexibility, resort to casual engagement only relieved pressures to modernise production technologies and update skills training.

Employers' efforts to impose order on these forces have suffered from failure to develop strong, representative institutions, ambivalence towards the state, and preference for preserving the autonomy of their own voluntary organisations. At a representative level, employers' associations long warned of the dangers of unregulated labour markets, for instance. But adherence to collective agreements by individual firms was weak, and their associations lacked cohesion and disciplinary authority. As a rule employers resisted proposals for compulsory registration of firms and workers as conditions of entry onto tender lists, for example where these threatened to restrict their access to specialist, ready-skilled labour, deprive them of the flexibility of customary casual wage and hiring policies, or encourage union controls, the closed shop and site militancy (Evans and Lewis 1989). Employers complemented this *laissez-faire* approach, nevertheless, with demands that the state buttress self-regulation by guaranteeing and taking responsibility for enforcing legal controls over excess union power (Strinati 1979).

Construction unions, in fact, are on the whole weak and marginal. Like the employers, unions have been institutionally fragmented by competition and internal divisions, and express a similar ambivalence towards more detailed state regulation of the industry. Union controls within production are undermined by labour-market skill hierarchies that reproduce themselves largely outside the spheres of union influence, and by the dominance of the employers within the collective bargaining system (Austrin 1980; Evans and Lewis 1989).

Employers have, nevertheless, reacted to the depression since the mid 1970s by demanding labour-market deregulation, accompanying this with appeals for higher state expenditure on construction, more contracting-out of public authority work to private firms, and removal of regulations over land, planning and development. The

Conservative government declined to reflate on anything like the scale sought by the industry, but state and construction firms' objectives converged, first, in releasing foreign exchange controls to allow massive export of construction capital overseas and, second, in privatising increasing volumes of domestic construction work previously sponsored or undertaken by public authorities. This has cast the largest construction firms more and more in the role of funding and managing private ventures, shifting away from their traditional contracting role.

Deregulation, Technology and Labour Market

Labour-market deregulation and changes in employment legislation also provided important, if subsidiary, support for privatisation policies, especially in sectors like construction characterised by labour-intensive technologies and relatively favourable employment standards in the public sector enforced by state regulation, collective bargaining and trade union organisation. The Conservative government's aim has been to lower the cost of labour to employers and, thereby, to the state. In construction, this required forcing as well as enticing employers along the path. In 1980 the Department of Environment (DoE), the main sponsoring department, temporarily reimposed fixed-price tenders and denied reimbursement for wage increases agreed under national bargaining and previously allowed under fluctuating cost clauses. In the same year, the repeal of Schedule 11 of the Employment Protection Act 1975, and in 1983 the rescission of the Fair Wages Resolution, both had the aim of frustrating the wider application of recognised terms bargained at national level or, where these were absent, of general terms equivalent to the 'going rate' in the locality or trade (Bercusson 1978). Self-employment was encouraged when the DoE withdrew support for direct employment as the preferred form of engagement by its contractors and the Treasury introduced tax changes reducing the insurance liabilities of self-employed labour-only subcontractors.

Legal moves against the practice of tying employers into collective agreements by making contractors responsible for ensuring that their subcontractors complied with those agreements, a key component of labour regulation in construction, were initiated in Employment Act 1980 s. 18. This made it unlawful to use or threaten industrial action to compel workers to belong to a particular union.

Next, Employment Act 1982 ss. 12–14 rendered void clauses in commercial contracts which require work to be done exclusively by union members or by a recognised union. Employers enforcing such clauses are liable to commit a tort against the party who is excluded from tendering or is refused or removed from a contract, and unions lose their immunities for industrial action taken to uphold these practices. Employment Act 1982 left untouched a variety of 'labour clauses' in public contracts, especially. It was still open to local authorities, for instance, to harness their contracting power to ensure their contractors observed collectively bargained pay rates and other terms and conditions of employment, including engagement of directly employed labour in preference to self-employed. Local Government Act 1988 Part II closed off this gap. It imposes a statutory duty on public authorities to exclude 'non-commercial matters' from consideration when inviting tenders, selecting for or terminating contracts. The list of non-commercial matters includes the contractor's terms and conditions of employment, composition of workforce and promotion and training policies, and form of engagement (Evans and Lewis 1988).

Privatisation, deregulation and other measures of government intervention brought a mixed response from construction employers. Treasury opposition to increased public expenditure obstructed several large private development initiatives dependent on underwriting by the state, and without such subsidies it remains unclear whether private consortia can be enticed to fill the gap left by state withdrawal except in the most lucrative locations. Compulsory competitive tendering gave firms a growing share of public authority work (Ramsdale 1985), but they still accused local authorities of unfair competition by parcelling public contracts in such a way as to deter contractors from tendering. Where protection of shrinking local authority direct labour organisations and risk of litigation for enforcing labour clauses did indeed combine to induce some local authorities to parcel work out in smaller values, one reason was the difficulties encountered in practice in terminating contracts when they were breached for poor performance by subcontractors (Evans and Lewis 1988). It is worth noting how these developments, in turn, reinforced the casualisation of labour standards. Without a wider range and volume of work, local authority direct-labour organisations lost capacity and skill resources to support more extensive training programmes, and firms offered smaller work packages had less incentive to develop long-term employment commitments.

Employers criticised government's fixed price tendering, withdrawal of support for direct employment and rescission of the Fair Wages Resolution for encouraging firms to undercut tender prices by cutting wages. But they were pleased to secure the outlawing of union labour only, union recognition and other labour clauses. The impact of these measures varied. Fair wage principles continued to be widely retained in practice (IRRR 1985) and, since collectively agreed rates are minima rather than standard in most cases, these measures were unlikely to have much of a depressive effect independent of the market for labour. But by removing all statutory support for collective regulation, the government abandoned any direct means of arresting upward movement in wage rates, other than relying on the 'stop-go' policy of depressing demand by further limiting spending or increasing interest rates, so criticised by employers in the 1960s.

Most significantly, whereas public clients are prohibited by Local Government Act 1988 Part II from making any reference to non-commercial matters in contracts, private-sector clients and contractors remain free to continue their widespread practice of vetting firms and labour before admitting them onto approved lists and awarding contracts or employment. Despite demanding state regulatory intervention, the prohibition of non-commercial contract clauses leaves construction employers in a contradictory situation. The legislation was only secured after efforts to persuade unions to extend the scope of joint regulation and recognise the self-employed in collective agreements from which they were previously excluded (Evans and Lewis 1989). They wanted, first, to remove one source of unpredictable union militancy and, second, to regulate the labour market more efficiently by bringing labour-only subcontracting more closely under the scope of the industry's training programmes. Recently employers and union in electrical contracting have agreed to bring the self-employed within the scope of their collective agreements, and a similar development seems imminent in the building trades (IDS 1987: 2–5). Local Government Act 1988 Part II now makes it unlawful for public clients to enforce such an agreement. This will inevitably weaken its application in the private sector as well since many firms operate in both sectors, and this will thereby place in jeopardy the benefits of wage stability and technological development to construction consumers and the wider economy.

The impact of these policies on labour in the construction sector were even more severe. The distinctive characteristics of construction's economic and social organisation will not be rehearsed here (for example, see Ball 1988; Hillebrandt 1984). For many commentators, however, these are essentially natural and harmonious (Fleming 1977 and 1980; Phelps Brown 1968). Accordingly, specialisation by trade or task, fragmented industrial structure of contractors and subcontractors, range of firm size, and high levels of labour mobility are all seen as logical responses to demand uncertainty. This uncertainty arises variously from fluctuating demand at the macro-level, spatial fixity of final product, variability of product type and labour process (including climate and geography), and opportunity maximising behaviour of typically individualistic and mobile construction labour. These forms of work organisation are held to complement the diverse markets by product and location, enhance firms' flexibility, and minimise management control costs, working capital and non-productive time. Specialist trade subcontracting similarly stabilises work opportunities for firms and, since they work largely within local markets, for workers alike.

Because of its relatively labour-intensive methods, wages are a key factor in the productivity/technology equation in construction.[2] Unlike countries such as the USA where high construction wages helped secure wider adoption of new technologies (Lange and Mills 1979; Flanagan et al. 1986: 9), wage policy in British construction has been characterised by short-term adjustments to a low wage norm through 'spot' supplements, depending on the state of trade (NBPI 1968a; 1968b; 1968c; 1969). Labour-only subcontracting epitomises this short-term approach. Savings over direct labour of 20–30 per cent are claimed (Evans and Lewis 1989). Labour-only workers work faster and earn more than direct labour, motivated by a simple incentive calculated on an all-in basis, sometimes by the piece, sometimes by the hour or shift, and enhanced by attractive tax advantages for the self-employed. Since the price is fixed only for the duration of the particular task or contract, employers can avoid consolidation under collective agreements. Legally, labour-only workers occupy a 'twilight zone between employment and independent status' (Chesterman 1982: 38), and since most lack a contract of employment they automatically lose their statutory rights to notice, redundancy pay and protection from unfair dismissal. Employers avoid obligations to pay for 'stamps' under the industry's various holiday pay schemes and for national insurance contributions, and they are subject to less onerous obligations in respect of accident compensation and insurance.

The contracting system itself, however, is a source of uncertainties neglected in such accounts as those above (Ball 1980). Separation of managerial responsibilities for design and production between architects and other professionals and contractors generates conflicts within control systems and contributes to higher costs, inefficiencies, quality problems, and longer completion times (NEDO 1983). Difficulties predicting tender prices generate pressures to realise profit by maximising extra claims against clients. As a consequence, improving productive efficiency is subordinated to avoiding risk and maintaining flexibility of financial assets for investment wherever is most profitable, in construction or elsewhere. Risk is devolved by subcontracting and casualising employment, and relations between main and subcontractors and between employers and labour are antagonistic, at root, so that all parties endeavour to exploit the others' dependency as far as market conditions and other bargaining resources allow.

Recent studies have underlined some of these problems. Nomination of specialist trades by architects, for instance, leaves them outside contractors' direct control systems. Subcontractors, generally, are poorly integrated into design and planning stages, and invest insufficient resources in management skills and training in new technologies (Flanagan et al. 1986; Prais and Steedman 1986). Market control over subcontractors via competitive tendering can be weakened when demand is buoyant, and contractors may be induced to guarantee them work or concede higher prices in order to gain access to their supplies of labour and other resources.

Training policy, or lack of it, is also recognised as a major factor behind current shortages of skilled labour. It has been argued that high wage rates for young workers, relative to adult rates, have been a disincentive to employers taking on apprentices and a major reason for the low proportion of craft trainees in British construction (Prais and Steedman 1986: 50–1). However, high youth rates are more symptom than cause of the contradictions between employers' wage and training policies, revealed most clearly in the growth and impact of labour-only subcontracting. Employers' efforts to ensure an adequate supply of skilled labour have been frustrated by their encouragement of narrow specialisation in an expanding range of standardised tasks, offering high wages when demand allowed or required to workers with continuous work histories and ready-trained to go straight onto production work

(Winch 1986). Employers indulged substitution of informal, on-the-job, narrow skill-acquisition for broader craft-training and, not surprisingly, younger workers responded by foregoing apprenticeship or quitting before completion after acquiring some experience in order to exploit diminishing market opportunities for stable employment.

The effects of training policy have rebounded on wages, too. In many areas, skill shortages are so acute that self-employed labour-only subcontractors are the only available source of labour. They are increasingly able to command their own terms and, unconstrained by collective agreements, sustain their bargaining all year round in what effectively remains a 'local going rate', a process stimulated if not foreseen by government deregulatory measures (Evans and Lewis 1989; IDS 1987; 2–5).

Finally, the 'train drain' has also restricted diffusion of new technologies. There is a distinct lack of congruence between the processes of skill formation and work reorganisation. In the most dynamic areas of the contracting sector, among the largest firms where use of labour-only subcontracting has been expanding most prominently, labour-only workers become trapped with little chance of widening their skills (Winch 1986). Slump and competition, meanwhile, forced specialist subcontractors to travel further afield and, like main contractors, to subcontract more of their work to labour-only subcontractors, reproducing the phenomenon on an ever wider scale. Workers' capacity to adapt to new techniques was retarded and with it the incentive for suppliers and contractors to innovate.

Conclusion

State policies in the 1980s have been predicated on leading a way out of the crisis, which has been a crisis of political and social as well as economic relations, and establishing the basis for a new expanded cycle of accumulation. This involved commodifying social welfare and utility provision and required substantial reductions in public expenditure on construction. The industry's capacity to bargain with government for reflation was weak. Indeed, recent developments reinforce just how dependent the industry is on the state. What is particularly striking about these developments, however, is the mutual dependency they reveal between the state and the construction industry and, so long as the industry has to operate within a capitalist economy, the inescapable 'logic' of the state underwriting the profitability of construction firms, even if at the expense of wider economic and social interests. Construction firms play a key role in the Conservative government's privatisation agenda, and government has gone a long way to promote a future environment conducive to the largest of those. But doubts must remain about the capacity and willingness of private capital to fill the gap left by reduced state expenditure, sufficient to avoid a piecemeal and unplanned pattern of demand so criticised by the industry in the past.

Promotion of the interests of the largest firms has, nevertheless, left in place many of the characteristic deterrents to innovation among the fragmented lower order firms. One effect has been the mismatch between deficient labour supply and changing skill requirements in an increasingly systematised production process. Here, too, the state has been obliged to intervene more directly in coordinating and subsidising training programmes, because of the private sector's incapacity and to meet the threat to its own objectives. It is quite possible that such interventions will alleviate some of the immediate pressures. But the record suggests that limited interventions of this kind, preserving the essentially voluntarist, self-regulation of the industry's training programmes in the interests of construction employers, will only serve to frustrate longer-term advance. What is needed is a plan for the industry and its integration into the wider economy.

Notes

1. The analysis is based on the literature and on empirical inquiries into the construction industry which were part of a wider project on the theory and practice of the right to associate. The research was supported by the Leverhulme Trust and undertaken at the Industrial Relations Research Unit, University of Warwick, by the author and Roy Lewis. It involved site-based studies among twelve national and regional contractors, and over 140 interviews with managers, workers and representatives of employers' associations, trade unions and local government in Britain. It also included a strong comparative element with research undertaken by interviews with over 40 representatives of employers and unions, as well as labour law and industrial relations academics, in the USA. The author wishes to thank Professor Roy Lewis of the Faculty of Law, University of Southampton, Peter Nolan of the

Industrial Relations Research Unit, and the editors of this volume for helpful comments in preparing this chapter. For a more elaborate exposition of many points contained herein, see Evans and Lewis 1989.

2. Measuring productivity and relative advantage of different technologies is hazardous, not least in construction. A given level of performance and work organisation are shaped by a multiplicity of forces: market and industry structure; business strategies and managerial competence in using plant, labour and other factors of production to minimise unit labour costs; social structures and accumulated industrial relations practice; and the regulatory environment set by the state (see e.g. Fine and Harris 1985 ch. 1; Hall 1986 ch. 2; Nichols 1986; Nolan 1989).

Bibliography

Austrin, T. (1980), 'The "Lump" in the UK Construction Industry', in T. Nichols (ed.), *Capital and Labour: A Marxist Primer*, Fontana, Glasgow, 300–13

Ball, M. (1980), 'The Contracting System in the Construction Industry', Birkbeck College Discussion Paper No. 86, Department of Economics, Birkbeck College, University of London

—— (1988), *Rebuilding Construction*, Routledge, London

Bercusson, B. (1978), *Fair Wages Resolutions*, Mansell, London

Cathcart, R. (1986), 'Labour-only Subcontracting and Flexible Working Practices in the Electrical Contracting Sector of the Construction Industry: A Study of the Incidence of Self-Employment and Flexible Working in the Greater London Region', MA Dissertation, University of Warwick

Centre for Construction Market Information (CCMI) (1985), *Survey on Management Contracting*, CCMI, London

Chesterman, M. (1982), *Small Businesses*, Sweet and Maxwell, London

Department of Environment (DoE) (1988), *Housing and Construction Statistics*, HMSO, London

Dunleavy, P. (1981), *The Politics of Mass Housing in Britain, 1945–1975*, Clarendon Press, Oxford

Evans, S. and R. Lewis (1988), 'Labour Clauses; From Voluntarism to Regulation', *Industrial Law Journal*, 17, 209–26

—— (1989), 'Destructuring and Deregulation in the Construction Industry', in S. Tailby and C. Whitston (eds), *Manufacturing Change: Industrial Relations and Restructuring*, Blackwell, Oxford

Fine, B. and L. Harris (1985), *The Peculiarities of the British Economy*, Lawrence and Wishart, London

Flanagan, R., G. Norman, V. Ireland and R. Ormerod (1986), *A Fresh Look at the UK and US Building Industries*, Building Employers' Confederation, London

Fleming, M. (1977), 'Bogey of Fragmentation in the Construction Industry', *National Builder*, 58, 134–7, 284–6

—— (1980), 'Construction', in P. S. Johnson (ed.), *Structure of British Industry*, 231–53

Hall, P. (1986), *Governing the Economy*, Clarendon Press, Oxford

Hillebrandt, P. M. (1984), *Analysis of the British Construction Industry*, Macmillan, London

Incomes Data Services (IDS) (1987), *Building Workers' Pay*, Study 396, London

Industrial Relations Review and Report (IRRR) (1985), 'Fair Wages Clauses', Report 342, 2–6

Jessop, B. (1980), 'Transformation of the State in Britain', in R. Scase (ed.), *The State in Western Europe*, London, Croom Helm, 23–93

Lange, J. E. and D. Q. Mills (1979), *The Construction Industry: Balance Wheel of the Economy*, Lexington, Mass.: D.C. Heath

Loughlin, M. (1986), *Local Government and the Modern State*, Sweet and Maxwell, London

McKinlay, A. (1987), 'Management of Diversity: Organisational Change in the British Construction Industry, 1960–1986', *Production of the Built Environment* 8, Proceedings of the 8th Bartlett International Summer School, University of London

National Board for Prices and Incomes (NBPI) (1968a), *Pay and Conditions in the Civil Engineering Industry*, Report No. 91, Cmnd 3836, HMSO, London

—— (1968b), *Pay and Conditions in the Building Industry*, Report No. 92, Cmnd 3837, HMSO, London

—— (1968c), *Pay and Conditions in the Construction Industry Other than Building and Civil Engineering*, Report No. 93, Cmnd 3838, HMSO, London

—— (1969), *Pay and Conditions in the Electrical Contracting Industry*, Report No. 120, Cmnd 4097, HMSO, London

National Economic Development Office (NEDO) (Building Economic Development Committee) (1983), *Faster Building for Industry*, HMSO, London

Nichols, T. (1986), *The British Worker Question*, Routledge and Kegan Paul, London

Nolan, P. (1989), 'Walking on Water? Pay, Productivity and British Manufacturing Performance Under the Conservatives', *Industrial Relations Journal*, Spring 20 (2), 81–92

Phelps Brown, E. H. (1968), *Report of the Committee of Inquiry Under Professor E. H. Phelps Brown Into Certain Matters Concerning Labour in Building and Civil Engineering*, Cmnd 3714, HMSO, London

Prais, S. J. and H. Steedman (1986), 'Vocational Training in France and Britain: The Building Trades', *National Institute Economic Review*, 116, 45–55

Ramsdale, P. (1985), 'Evaluating the DLO Legislation', *Public Finance and Accountancy*, 13 September, 6–10

Strinati, D. (1979), 'Capitalism, the State and Industrial Relations', in C. Crouch (ed.), *State and Economy in Contemporary Capitalism*, Croom Helm, London, 191–236

Thompson, G. (1986), *The Conservatives' Economic Policy*, Croom Helm, London

Turner, D. (1987), 'The Construction Industry in Britain', *Midland Bank Review*, Autumn, 16–23

Winch, G. (1986), 'The Labour Process and the Labour Market in Construction', *International Journal of Sociology and Social Policy*, 6, No. 2, 103–16

Young, S. (1986), 'The Nature of Privatisation in Britain, 1979–85', *West European Politics*, 9, No. 2 (April) 234–52

3

Context and Limits of Policies of Social Innovation in Small and Medium-sized Construction Firms in France

Michèle Tallard

Introduction

Since the end of the 1970s social innovation policies, based upon policies to promote the motivation and involvement of salaried employees in company plans, have developed in the main sectors of industry. They rely upon a number of instruments of participatory management aimed at ensuring the flexibility of companies, whilst developing new areas where employees can demonstrate their initiative and express their views in order to promote their self-development and have a greater control over their working conditions and terms of employment. These measures were generally designed to restructure work organisation, establish participatory structures and modify the structure and composition of pay. These policies have either been implemented on the initiative of company managers concerned to establish direct contacts with employees, or have followed negotiations with the workers' representative bodies within a company. Although initially implemented in large companies, they have become widespread in medium-sized firms (200–500 employees) or even smaller companies in recent years, with the result that there has been a tendency to associate dynamic industrial relations with the small and medium-sized companies.

This process has led to a revival of negotiations at company level, whereas in the previous decade they had been held predominantly at industry level. In the main industrial sectors collective agreements had been negotiated regarding the classification of wage scales and minimum wages, working conditions, conditions of employment and dismissal. These rights were usually more comprehensive than the minimum rights laid down in legislation.

This revival of the company as the level at which negotiations are held was given a boost after 1982 by the Auroux laws. These included an annual obligation to negotiate wages and the number and organisation of hours of work, and an obligation to negotiate the means for employees in companies with over 200 employees (over 50 since 1985) to express their views.

On a more general note, the Auroux laws were, for the first Socialist government at that time, a symbol of their willingness to establish a real 'citizenship' at company level by extending the rights of the employees' representative bodies in management and by giving employees the opportunity to express their views on working conditions. This last law was also aimed at providing a framework for policies to motivate employees, which at that time were developed with more regard to increasing productivity than to improving working conditions. In practice, management participation and rights to expression either developed in tandem, or the former developed at the expense of the latter.

What has been the significance of these policies in the construction industry, where the system of production is dominated by small companies and where industrial relations have always demonstrated a number of specific characteristics? This article will concentrate upon this one question, whilst bearing in mind on the one hand the collective agreements behind the development of these policies, and, on the other, the forms adopted by these policies, so that they can be directly seen within the framework of the law on the right of employees to express their views and that designed to increase their motivation.[1]

The Specific Characteristics of Industrial Relations in Construction

Industrial relations are characterised by a combination of the following factors: the strong influence of joint institutions, the undermining of collective rights laid down in sectoral agreements, and the weak organisation of trade unions in companies.

Employers in the construction industry have traditionally viewed trade unions as the organisers of social funds, such as pension and provident funds, which are not directly related to the work process. Their determination to confine trade unions to this role is reflected in the formal recognition of the role of unions in the management of social insurance schemes, and in the fact that they are willing to negotiate on improvements to the functioning of these schemes, whilst they refuse to put other subjects on the agenda for negotiation.

According to this view, the company is the exclusive province of the company manager. Managers therefore find it difficult to accept either trade union presence in the company or state interference in relations between management and employees. Indeed, all the activities which come under the aegis of the joint commissions have helped the employers form an image of a type of 'corporatist institution', whose task is to regulate most of the relations between workers and management arising from the social insurance schemes in the name of professional values. Work organisation and the management of the workforce is, however, to remain the prerogative of the company manager. Employers tend therefore to reject all forms of state intervention, seen here as an 'omnipresent institution', by pointing to these sector-specific institutions. This is particularly the case when the state tries to intervene directly in the relations between management and employees on site.

This paternalistic concept of the relations between employer and employees is particularly prevalent in the small- and medium-sized companies, which account for most of the production in the construction industry. Table 3.1 shows that there are few companies with more than 10 employees (slightly above 5 per cent) and more than half (53 per cent) of the workforce is employed in companies of this size. Furthermore, 90 per cent of the firms with more than 10 employees have less than 50 employees.

Social innovation policies in small and medium-sized construction firms can not be analysed unless they are placed in the context of industrial relations in this industry. This is essential to understanding the obstacles to the implementation of these policies.

Since the beginning of the 1980s negotiations have been conducted to improve social insurance schemes (and, by extension, the functioning of the joint institutions) on the one hand and, on the other, agreements have been reached in line with legal obligations, for example on youth training.

Given this stagnation in the negotiation processes, collective

Table 3.1 The structure of companies and the workforce in the construction industry, 1986

	Companies			Employees		
	Total	%	% of firms over 10 employees	Total	%	% of firms over 10 employees
1–10	278,817	94.2	–	688,770	53.05	–
11–19	9,028	3.05	52.8	129,121	9.9	21.2
20–49	6,377	2.1	37.3	191,768	14.8	31.5
50–99	1,030	0.3	6.0	73,889	5.7	12.1
100–199	449	0.2	2.6	61,794	4.7	10.1
200+	224	0.1	1.3	152,936	11.8	25.1
Total	295,925	100	100	1,298,279	100	100

Source: Enquête Annuelle d'Entreprise, 1986.

rights, like those laid down in the national agreement for manual workers, have tended to become less significant in terms of their content, in the face of legislation or other collective agreements. This places the sector in an unfavourable position in the competitive labour market.

Joint Commissions

Although most of the joint employer–worker commissions were founded after the Liberation or in the years following the conclusion of collective agreements or the legislation on vocational training, they should be seen as following in the tradition of the mutual aid associations set up at the end of the nineteenth century, which were organised on an occupational basis. The durability of these organisations seems, even today, to demonstrate the strength of employees' identification with their occupation. Moreover, the predominance of small firms and the mobility of the workforce have both led to the founding of institutions which bypass the firm. These manage social insurance funds which are managed by firms in other sectors.

The main joint commissions are responsible for pension and provident funds, training, the prevention of accidents at work, profit-sharing schemes and, more recently, an insurance scheme.

These organisations have the following in common: first, a joint administration system at national level (OPP–BTP, GFC, CCCA), regional level (AREF–BTP, safety commissions) or, where necessary, at local (department) level (GDA). Second, the state has the right to regulate them. These bodies are either supervised by government, or a state representative with consultative powers sits on the board of directors. Furthermore, the state often plays a role in defining the actions of these bodies (particularly where training is concerned), on the basis of cooperative agreements.

If one excludes the Training Fund Insurance which has existed in many sectors of economic activity since 1979, the majority of these joint commissions and the occupational schemes which they organise are peculiar to the construction and public works sector and rarely exist in other industrial sectors. There are, several contradictory tendencies.

1 A strong formal identification with and recognition of the occupation, to which company managers delegate tasks which are not indirectly or immediately connected with the production process.
2 A tradition inherited from the guilds, including their concepts of solidarity and of mutual recognition based on occupational values.
3 A desire to confine the activities of the union to this sphere, in order to prevent its presence in the company.

The crisis in the building sector and the concomitant large number of job losses and company closures have jeopardised the resources of the joint decision-making bodies at a time when collective bargaining is weak in the construction industry. Despite this, the joint decision-making bodies remain a forum for discussion between employers and workers. This forum has sometimes proved useful where social welfare matters are concerned. Four agreements, all of them universally applicable and aimed at reforming the CNPO, have been concluded since 1979. They are widely considered to be established bodies which guarantee some employees a wide range of social benefits, although, as we shall see below, their collective status is relatively weak. The status quo will probably prevail, both in terms of the functioning and of the range of activities covered by the joint decision-making bodies, even if the logic behind their functioning now tends to be less founded upon the original principle of solidarity and upon social consensus.

Joint Commissions

CNPO: Caisse Nationale de Prévoyance des Ouvriers – National Provident Fund for Workers (responsible for health insurance)

CNRO: Caisse Nationale de Retraite des Ouvriers – National Pension Fund for Workers

OPP–BTP: Organisme Professionel de Prévention (Bâtiment- et Travaux Publics) – Professional Body for the Prevention of Accidents at Work

GFC–BTP: Groupement de Formation Continue – Group for Further Training (manages the compulsory contributions from firms to training funds)

AREF–BTP: Association Régionale d'Enseignement et de Formation – Regional Association for Education and Training (regional structure of the GFC)

CCCA: Comité Central de Coordination de l'Apprentissage – Central Committee for the Coordination of Apprenticeships

GDA: Groupements Départmentaux d'Apprentissage – Departmental Apprenticeship Groups (structure of the CCCA at department level)

Collective Guarantees

The mechanisms which regulate the collective status of salaried employees in the construction and public works sector are very complex and heterogeneous: one can attempt to summarise a few principles:

1 National collective agreements specifically for each grade of manual worker, for technical and supervisory staff (ETAM) and scientific, administrative and managerial staff (IAC), none of which is universally applicable.[2]

2 Similar, but distinctly different arrangements for the three sub-sectors, building, craft and public works, and in some of the subspecialisations of the latter.

3 Universally applicable national agreements together with additional clauses which have set up mutual aid schemes (supplementary pensions, provident funds) for manual workers and ETAM in the three subsectors.

4 National agreements often stemming from agreements concluded

Grades of Employee

ETAM: employees, technicians, supervisors
IAC: engineers, administrative and managerial staff
OS: unskilled workers
OQ: skilled workers
OHQ: highly skilled workers

The classification scale of construction workers comprises two grades of unskilled worker (OS2 and OS3), three grades of skilled worker (OQ1, OQ2, OQ3), one grade of highly skilled worker (OHQ) and two foreman grades (CE1, CE2); a third grade of very highly skilled worker (MO) on the same level as CE1 was created in 1979. The following point system applies: OS2 = 150; OS3 = 160; OQ1 = 170, OQ2 = 180; OQ3 = 200; OHQ = 215; CE1 = 225; CE2 = 240; MO = 225.

Qualifications

CAP: Certificat d'Aptitude Professionel (certificate gained after the first level of vocational training)
BTS: Brevet de Technicien Supérieur (higher professional certificate gained after two years of higher education)
DUT: Diplome Universitaire de Technologie (the same level as the BTS but with a bias towards management studies)

Other Abbreviations

SMIC: index-linked minimum statutory wage: basic salary periodically laid down and revised by the state. No real salary paid by companies may fall below the level of the SMIC. When the minimum salaries agreed in negotiations fall below the SMIC, they are automatically made null and void by the SMIC.

APE: Activité Professionelle des Entreprises. This is a code given by the national statistical organisation (INSEE) which makes it possible to identify the economic activity of firms, and therefore the collective agreement which binds them if the collective agreement is universally applicable.

between professions, affecting one or several grades of worker and the three subsectors in general. These are, for the most part, universally applicable.

5 National agreements in the public works sector concerning all grades of worker or only manual workers, some of which are universally applicable.

6 A large number of collective agreements (approximately 140) concluded equally between regional and department levels, of which none is universally applicable except that for the construction industry in the Paris region, and those for the overseas departments and territories.

Therefore, unlike many other industrial sectors, the construction and public works sector is characterised by a fragmentation in the regulations for various grades of employee, by the non-application of the overall mechanism (but the application of many of its clauses), and finally by the important role of its infranational mechanism. Since it is impossible to study the content of the overall mechanism, I will only examine here the development of the National Agreement for Manual Construction Workers and the additional clauses implemented since its conclusion.

The national agreement defines its field of application and specifically the principles and content of its negotiations at national and local level (either regional or departmental). At the latter level it outlines the framework of the arrangements which should be included in the collective agreements made at departmental level and only leaves questions relating to bonuses, extra pay for night shifts, minor travelling expenses and the overall level of salaries to be negotiated at this level. It was not until the adoption of a national grade scale in 1972 that only point-values relating to wage differentials were discussed at infranational level (see Box – Grades of Employee). This overall mechanism (the national agreement plus the agreements concluded at departmental level) is similar to a collective agreement in the sense of the provisions of the 1950 law. When it was concluded in 1954, the unions considered the agreement to be a 'good' one. The comments made at the time by the signatory unions underlined the benefits which they had gained in terms of public holidays, holiday pay, days off in exceptional circumstances, period of notice, definition of seniority, youth training, and even guarantees regarding union rights and the protection of elected representatives or candidates in elections. By taking into consideration the 'effective' hourly salary this agreement was one of the few to go beyond existing legislation on issues such as the pay of young workers, the securing of a holiday bonus and overtime pay.

If one makes the same comparison with current legislation or other collective agreements, one finds that a number of the concessions initially won, such as the decrease in tax contributions for young workers, have lapsed since they were subsequently overruled by legislation. Others, such as the protection given to electoral candidates, have been incorporated in the legislation. Moreover, on a number of important points such as the period of notice, dismissal procedures, redundancy pay and leave of absence, the agreement partially represents a step backwards *vis-à-vis* legislation and employees therefore only benefit from the legal minimum.

The fact that legislation has caught up with the tenor of agreements is particularly highlighted if one examines the links between the index-linked statutory minimum wage (the SMIC) and wage minima in the industry. The latter are calculated by multiplying the index by the point-value attributed to job grades, which comes from agreements or unilateral decisions taken at regional or departmental level.

In theory, the SMIC should be the bottom level of the wage scale. In other words, it should correspond to the minimum wage for labourers. In fact, given the rise in the level of the SMIC, the system of point-values has developed very differently from the SMIC. In the Paris region the SMIC is equivalent to the salary of the OS3. In effect the scale begins at this level, and at the other extreme in Provençe and Côte d'Azur the SMIC is higher than that of the OQ2 and the wage scale only begins at the level of the OQ3. This 'erosion' (if not 'raking') effect of the SMIC calls into question the fundamental relevance of grade classification as a reference table of wage minima for the establishment of actual salaries. Actual salaries have also fallen behind in comparison with those of other economic activities. There is a gap of about 17 per cent between annual net salaries of workers in the construction and public works sector and salaries in other sectors in 1985.

To go beyond the content of these agreements and ask questions about the collective rights contained in agreements which are not universally applicable, the number of employees affected must be examined.

Great progress has been made in terms of the number of salaried employees covered by agreements in this branch of industry since the beginning of the 1980s: in 1984/5 84.5 per cent of salaried employees were covered by a collective agreement or alternative settlement. However, it is the lowest rate of coverage of all industrial sectors. This situation can be linked to the large number of small firms in the sector, for it is usually firms employing less than 50 employees which do not implement collective agreements.

In a number of sectors negotiations at company level supplement or reinforce those concluded for the sector as a whole. In the construction and public works sector, since 1981 there has been a large increase in the number of employees covered by agreements at company level, but it still remains the lowest of all economic sectors. Consequently, the vast majority of employees are only covered by an industry-level agreement.

In 1981 12 per cent of salaried employees in the construction and public works sector were still not covered by an agreement concluded at sector or company level; this figure dropped to 3.4 per cent in 1985. How can one explain this extraordinary development which bolsters the overall cover afforded to the workforce? Beyond welcoming this general trend, one is forced to ask whether there is not some link with the large number of job losses and company closures during the period 1981–5. It is possible that the firms which have gone paid little attention to collective guarantees. It seems that the largest percentage of uninsured employees is to be found in firms with 10 to 49 employees. The worsening of the crisis has therefore had the unexpected effect of enforcing stricter moral standards upon the profession by eliminating those firms which dragged their feet over protecting their employees.

The Efficacy of Legislation at Company Level

Since the 1982 Auroux laws, legislation has been implemented with a view to improving relations between management and the workforce at company level both by imposing upon management an annual obligation to negotiate wage levels, the length and organisation of working hours and by giving employees the right to express their views.

The efficacy of this system depends, however, upon the presence of trade unions in the company. As we shall see, there is a weak trade union presence here and these laws are therefore rarely enforced. Although social innovation policies are rarely based upon these laws, they have nevertheless acted as a positive stimulus.

Many questions regarding social innovation policies can be asked. What is the true scale of these policies? What proportion of firms in a given sector is affected by them?

According to studies by IDEA–CITERA (1985), it seems that not more than a third of small and medium-sized firms are likely to implement social innovation policies, and even these experiment with new forms of management and organisation on only one or a few construction sites. Given that these firms play a major role in the formal structures for negotiations between employers and employees, it is important to consider if they are in a minority in so far as actual practice is concerned, or is it rather the case that the majority of firms use archaic management methods? Given that there is no standard policy for the sector as a whole, what is the substance and limitations of these policies? Whilst many policies are implemented in the name of social innovation, some tend to be based upon the training and retraining of the workforce, and others upon promoting and obtaining an enterprise culture.

All trade unions recognise that they have a weak foothold in construction and public works. They widely agree that between 3 and 5 per cent of employees belong to a union, but this is difficult to verify. However, indicators such as the number of trade union representatives, or the results of the elections for representatives of the workforce or for representatives on the works council, provide more accurate information regarding the level of trade union representation in the sector.

If one examines firms with more than 50 employees in all economic sectors, 57.4 per cent have one trade union representative compared with only 43.2 per cent in the construction and public works. This places the latter in the small group of industries which have trade union representation in less than 45 per cent of its firms; the corresponding figure is almost 80 per cent in the chemical industry.

Construction and public works is one of the sectors where employees have least representation and where their representatives are most frequently non-union. The 1985 study on firms with more than ten employees shows that only firms in the leather and shoe industries have fewer representatives than those in construction. Of construction employees in 1985 who worked in firms with more than 50 employees, only 18 per cent voted in the works council elections and almost 40 per cent of these, the highest level for any industrial sector, voted for non-union lists. Only 11.1 per cent of salaried employees in firms with more than 50 employees therefore voted for trade union lists.

These figures indicate an environment not conducive to the implementation of laws which presuppose the existence of a union which plays a full role in the organisation of the company. The annual obligation to negotiate with a union is rarely put into practice: almost 40 per cent of firms bound by the obligation (firms with more than 50 employees) did not enter negotiations in 1985 and overall less than 38 per cent finished up with an agreement. These are the lowest percentages to be found in all sectors. They can partly be explained by the structure of the sector in terms of the size of its firms; the larger firm tends more often to fulfil its obligation to negotiate, and in a more comprehensive way. However, one must note that, irrespective of company size, when negotiations take place they are more comprehensive than in other sectors. The construction and public works sector holds the most frequent negotiations on salaries, on length and organisation of working hours and, more rarely, on salaries alone. This seems to be a characteristic of the sector which probably reflects work organisation rather than size of the company. Despite these specific and significant features of settlements, there remains the salient fact that only 3 per cent of the workforce in the branch is covered by these union agreements. The only economic sector to have a worse record in this respect is the garage sector. One can therefore say that this law is almost totally ineffective.

The right of employees to express their views, which was one of the major innovations of the Auroux Laws, has effectively never been realised in practice, although it established for all employees except public servants 'a right to the direct and collective expression of views on the content and organisation of their work and on the definition and implementation of measures designed to improve working conditions in the company' (extract from the law on employees' rights to expression).

By giving employees a say, the Auroux laws were intended to be the mainspring of a new concept of industrial relations at company level, in that they attempted to provide a framework for the policies aimed at participatory management first established at the end of the 1970s. Employers in firms with more than 50 employees were obliged to implement these laws and employers in firms with more than 200 employees were obliged to negotiate ways to implement them. Therefore, the social innovation policies which have developed in the construction industry for some time now could have made use of this particular law, but a number of observations show that this has rarely been the case.

Several factors must be considered in determining the effectiveness of putting employees' rights to expression into practice: the demarcation and stability of work units (hence the possibility of putting together a collective group report), the frequency of meetings, paid day-release, the type of organisation of meetings, the method of preparing reports, the substance of the views expressed by employees, the deadlines for and the quality of the responses to these views and their realisation.

Two studies are particularly revealing on the implementation of employees' rights to express their views in the construction and public works sector. Firstly, a statistical analysis by the Ministry of Employment of 3,000 agreements notified to the Regional Boards of Employment before 15 April 1985, makes it possible to construct a profile of the agreements concluded in the different economic sectors. The second is a study by CREDOC (1986) on the basis of a survey of nine construction firms in the Paris region which had signed the agreements. These firms were differentiated according to size (200–500, more than 500 employees) and by subsector of activity (construction, public works, highways). In looking at the difficulties experienced in putting the right to expression into practice, this study tried to distinguish between factors which are based upon the specific features of the production process in the sector and factors resulting from the strategies and practices of employers and employees (Campinos-Dubernet, 1984a and 1984b). The study indicates a more or less deliberate rejection of the law.

'The economic sectors where the legislation passed on 4 August [1982] has had the least impact are primarily the construction industry and public works and, to a lesser extent, the textile, clothing and distribution industries'[3] (CREDOC 1986, Appendix, 7). The construction and public works sector is indeed the sector where the least number of agreements on employees' right to expression have been concluded; they make provision for the least frequent and the shortest meetings (one to two one-hour meetings per year) and they are most frequently initiated by training personnel. Moreover, it is also the sector with the highest percentage of agreements concluded without union agreement. Finally, scarcely 6.3 per cent of the total workforce in this industry are affected by these agreements.

The survey of the firms shows that little consideration has been given to the specific features of the production process; the agreements make provision for meetings on a fixed date, whatever the stage of development of the site. There is often a delay of between three and six months before management responds to employees' views. The response is, in effect, announced at the next meeting and it is most unlikely, given the instability of workteams, that the same collective which originally expressed its views will obtain a response some months later. In addition, the large proportion of immigrants in the workforce (particularly in the Paris region) has not been considered in the choice of method for publicising management responses. Indeed, even if they have been resident in France for a sufficient time to make themselves understood, immigrant workers find it more difficult to read French and hence the written reports of meetings of noticeboards. Meetings where reports could be presented orally have hardly ever been organised, even if it has been recognised that they could play a useful role. Finally, most of views expressed by employees concern problems relating to work materials, organisation and conditions and are treated as complaints by management. The organiser, who is a member of the company hierarchy or management, gives the management response, but employees are not collectively involved in the solution-finding process.

Therefore, at best there has been the more or less formal respect for the law, at worst the inertia or paralysis of a meaningless procedure.

Social Innovation Policies as a Productive Concept

Formal social innovation policies seem to have flourished since 1985. However, this umbrella term covers very heterogeneous policies, both in terms of their scale and content. Although they all appear to refer to training, flexibility, motivation and the ability to adopt responsibility, it has been shown elsewhere that the various policies can be distinguished in terms of their actual content according to whether firms have reduced, integrated or optimised external variability. This is defined 'both in terms of the reduction of the size of operations, the diversification of demand and in terms of the non-repetitive nature of the product' (Campagnac et al. 1985: 119). The small and medium-sized firms which implement social innovation policies are primarily those which integrate or optimise variability. They therefore need to implement policies which will motivate, involve and integrate the workforce. They have to develop the autonomy and responsibility of polyvalent teams, to expand the role of the intermediate hierarchy to include business functions, on the one hand, and the functions of organising the work collective and of overcoming the division between management and site, on the other. They do this by encouraging communication between management and employees in both directions, particularly in order to improve information flows on the discrepancy between design and production and the ways of adapting to subsequent risks.

In construction firms industrial relations are often characterised by the weakness of active trade unionism and the strength of the paternalism traditionally found in the sector. However, other firms, which have had to take into account the existence of trade unions and a tradition of industrial relations which is more based upon agreements, have implemented experimental policies which were primarily concerned with providing employees with more information and improving working conditions.

Experimentation Based on Dialogue

These firms have negotiated with representative bodies the experimental implementation, on some sites, of policies aimed at developing the process of informing and involving employees. However only one firm has actually tackled the question of work organisation (see following section).

In these few small and medium-sized firms with 200–400 employees the legislation passed on 4 August 1982 on the right of employees to express their views served as a legal pretext to impose upon trade union sections an experiment in employee participation on a 'laboratory site'. Indeed, in at least one of the firms known to have taken this kind of action, the trade union sections which had the right to inform the workforce about union activities within paid working hours (45 minutes per month for each organisation), were afraid that the widespread implementation of the law would threaten these meetings. In their view, these provided a forum where workers could express their views. Furthermore, they believed that the right of employees to express their views could be manipulated by management given the lack of trade union involvement here. However, because they were unable to confront the law head-on, they accepted with goodwill an experiment which, from their point of view, contained a number of guarantees.

These included the involvement of a consultant acting on behalf of ANACT, which as a paragovernmental body of the Socialist administration aroused little suspicion, who was to be responsible for the setting up of a follow-up to the experiment and for the organisation of meetings. The involvement of representative bodies in the operation was through a presentation to the works council and the attendance of delegates of each organisation at on-site meetings, but no agreement was concluded within the framework of the legislation. The company hierarchy and the consultant jointly organised the meetings.

Other Organisations

ANACT: National Office for the Improvement of Working Conditions (promotes and subsidises actions to improve working conditions in all economic sectors)

EVMB: Employment and Economic Development in the Construction Trades (the committee which finances research and experiments on the construction trades)

H.88: Habitat 88 (committees set up by the Ministère de l'Equipment responsible for promoting technological developments which can lead to a decrease in the construction costs of housing)

These experiments were more concerned with providing employees with information than giving them autonomy. This involved providing information on the progress of the site every two or three months, and the attendance of staff from the engineering and design office to overcome the division between the design process and site production and to respond to questions immediately.

From the point of view of management, this circulation of information was positive in that it allowed for 'an improvement in the industrial climate' and 'the discovery of minor problems on site and the measures taken to compensate for them' (Lajoinie, 1984). However, the trade unions, whilst recognising the improvements in working conditions and in safety at work, demanded that workteams should be made autonomous as quickly as possible and that the role of training personnel should be critically examined.

These experiments therefore incorporated a dynamic element which pushed towards a more fundamental redefinition of work organisation on site. This dynamism came up against the traditional practices associated with the established pattern of work organisation.

From Experimentation to Implementation

Boulin (1986) provides a detailed report of an experiment in social innovation in one firm. This firm, a medium-sized construction firm with about 400 employees, has chosen the path of industrialisation and differs from other firms in several respects.[4] Firstly, parallel to experiments with a new construction module designed to cut production costs, the firm reorganised work on three construction sites within an experimental framework defined in conjunction with the EVMB programme. It divided the operation into macro-sequences and established two workteams overlapping for four days, each of them working 35 hours per week. Secondly, this experiment has led to the establishment of a protocol covering the experiments (EVMB–H.88). It was preceded by the drawing up of a social contract with the works council, which stipulated that the shortening of the working week from 39 to 35 hours would only be offset in the wage packet if there was a 10 per cent rise in productivity, 40 per cent of any rise in productivity above that level would financially benefit the work team. Employees would review the progress made towards realising these productivity targets at monthly meetings.

The follow-up to this experiment has revealed a number of dysfunctions: the division of the operation into macro-sequences has been abandoned and there has been very little communication with the workforce. The fulfilment of productivity targets has only been achieved on one site where the team was made up of older employees in the firm, most of French origin and with a higher level of qualification than on other sites. These characteristics, the new organisation of work (two people working on the same task) and of working hours, associated with a proposed profit-sharing scheme, explain the strong motivation of employees on this site and their satisfaction with this experiment. On other sites where teams were not as well qualified and were hired to do only labouring work, employees were given little information and had less motivation to participate in the experiment, with the result that the targets were not fulfilled.

Elsewhere, these sites have had to suffer because of their experimental nature; the quality of components supplied by the prefabrication factory, where employees were not involved in the experiment, often proved to be faulty. The experiments therefore had limited value because of their non-integrated application.

After reflecting on this first phase, the company management decided, on the one hand, to extend the reduction of working hours to all sites of the main office. On the other, they began a new experiment more oriented towards training and towards the participation of employees in the process of increasing productivity, using the team which had successfully completed the first phase.

At the time of the previous experiment, the management signed a protocol agreement with the works council which allowed for the interlocking of the new phase with the first phase. The new protocol outlined in detail the central goal of the second phase: the development of functions, the evolution and modification of the role of the production workforce. This goal was to be achieved through making production workers more autonomous, flexible and responsible: each team was to be responsible for all of its materials and to construct the whole shell of a building. Employees therefore had to accomplish the complete range of tasks.

In order to attain this goal quality circles were established on sites and a clerk of works was appointed as a quality control coordinator. In addition, a training programme was aimed at the supervisory staff and site management, as well as production workers. The establishment of a three-year training programme has led to a quadrupling of its training budget.

A protocol on the experiments negotiated with the EVMB provided for the implementation of and the follow-up to these arrangements on three sites.

Finally, this firm began to modify its recruitment policy. The management has seized the opportunity provided by the measures to promote the employment of young people with a higher level of general education to renew its workforce, both labourers and supervisory staff. The majority of young people recruited on the basis of these agreements have the CAP and some of them have the BTS or the DUT. Although the latter tend to be managers or administrators, the former have employment-training contracts for 12–18 months, comprising 1,200 hours of training, 500 of which are external training, in the course of which they successively take on jobs preparing the site (quantity surveyor), jobs on site (highly skilled worker and foreman), and finally the post of assistant site foreman. This is lowest level of the technical and supervisory grades on site and opens up for them a career as site foreman.

This recruitment derives from the rationale of a policy foreshadowed by the experiments in progress, which aims to change the content of site jobs. On the one hand, it is a question of making workteams more autonomous and more versatile by giving them, for example, responsibility for the completion of a building (thus eliminating the need for a team in the finishing trades). On the other hand, it is a question of using computers on-site to manage both site planning and materials. This management is undertaken by the new assistant site foremen who are more familiar with computer techniques than the present site foremen, who have generally worked their way up from the manual workforce.

In this firm the measures concerned with work organisation and with modifying the role of the employee are based on the initial goal of increasing productivity. From the point of view of management, the plan is ultimately to make the employee a 'contracting party' rather than an employee.

The Network of Innovatory Firms

A large percentage of the small and medium-sized firms implementing social innovation policies are part of a network of innovative firms, which have on average between 20 and 200 employees, and mostly less than 100. Its goal is to publicise innovations in technology and organisation. This network recently carried out a study within the framework of the EVMB programme, on the basis of four case studies using participant observation and a survey of managers and different grades of workers in about 20 firms in order to gain a better understanding of the substance, import and limitations of these policies (Thionville and Seidlitz 1987).

These policies are based upon a desire to improve communication within the company and are founded upon a principle of giving site workers autonomy and more responsibility. In order to apply this principle, these firms employ means which do not always simultaneously occur in a firm. They include

1 A re-emphasis upon the role of the middle management in both the business and technical spheres close to the site, with which they must be able to maintain 'a dialogue and permanent negotiations'.

61

2 The establishment of a structure to inform employees about progress on site.
3 The definition of areas where workers can develop their initiative and relative autonomy and where in particular they have opportunities to be involved in the planning process and in the definition of work organisation and material requirements.
4 Making the team responsible for time and delays, a process which has as its prerequisite the development of a spirit of enterprise based upon an improvement in the quality of collective work and a rise in productivity.
5 An expansion of the role of employees *vis-à-vis* their environment (clients).

The development of initiative giving the team more responsibility and the opening up of the environment should allow the emergence of a team leader as a 'worker-leader'. Quality control circles, review groups or other meetings of this kind have enabled some firms (about a third of the group) to attain these objectives.

The means used may well be diverse, but these firms all have in common the attempt to implement 'a regulation linked to the trade' based upon the traditional values of the construction trades: the search for greater solidarity, a hierarchical relationship based upon the method of organisation from above, a cohesion established upon the basis of seniority and trade associations, and the importance of personal wishes and reciprocal choices when forming workteams. Therefore, as one study observes, in the construction industry 'one cannot tackle the question of motivating workers without also looking at this culture' (Pillemont and Weisz 1985: 1).

The social innovation policies which have been examined here seem to be based upon both a model adopted from manufacturing industry and a model specific to the construction. Based as they are primarily upon the pursuit of progress, these policies do not escape what some writers have called an infatuation with quality control groups, 'these having the advantage of appearing to be a ready-made management technique' (Chevalier and Iresps 1986: 37). They attempt to foster an identification with and a culture based upon the company which, according to Tripier, 'is both the result of the interaction of groups within the company and of their cultural models for the production of norms and values, by means of their own system of socialisation' (1986: 375). This is occurring in a sector where identification with an industry is important and whose culture is still characterised by trade values and their concomitant social relations.

Conclusion

This analysis of the social innovation policies implemented by a number of small and medium-sized firms and the context of the sector in which they were carried out, highlights their limitations and the possibilities of a connection between regulation by the industrial sector and regulation by the firm.

Recent social innovation policies have come up against limitations arising from their experimental nature and from the shortcomings of collective guarantees.

The majority of current policies of social experimentation rely upon training, the acquisition of new organisational skills and motivating employees. These appear to have come up against the recognition of the greater importance attached to occupational values in terms of qualifications and wages. The study by Thionville (1987) together with the Centre of Managers in the Construction Industry (Centre des Dirigeants de la Construction) on social innovation in small and medium-sized construction firms shows in effect that, as far as policies aimed at the emergence of a 'worker-leader' are concerned, 'the recognition given to occupational values proves to be a problem. The negative aspect of autonomy is the removal of the worker from the direct supervision of the manager'.

For, despite the recourse to a number of palliatives (bonuses, days off, shareownership), the need to at least partially replace interpersonal evaluation by falling back upon a more stable and standard reference system appears to be all the more acute given that the instability of the instruments of recognition and their specificity put the posts on a more temporary basis. They therefore do not permit the planning of career development on the one hand, and act as a brake upon mobility on the other. Therefore, the failures of the guarantees secured for the industrial sector are likely to be a factor that promotes rigidity rather than flexibility. Here the problem raised by Eymard-Duvernay (1985), can be identified, who argues economic flexibility can be gained by using agreements which, through the commitment which they presuppose, lead to greater legality and, by this very fact, open up new opportunities for flexibility'.

The economic and social characteristics of the sector can not be ignored in any attempt to define the spheres which are respectively negotiated at sectoral and company level. The connection between the various levels of negotiation has been the subject of several recent studies which attempt either to isolate the factors which influence the choice of these levels (Sellier 1984), or to examine the indications for a new emphasis upon the company (Eyraud and Tchobanian 1984), or indeed for a transitional phase before a more complex transformation of the system of regulation (Jobert and Rozenblatt 1986). In the construction industry, factors such as the economic and social heterogeneity of the sector, the weakness of the trade unions and, in association with this, the relatively few possibilities for 'bargaining' at company level, the central importance given to trade values should be taken into consideration. Undoubtedly, consideration must be given to the system of connections between levels of negotiation which would give increased validity to the sector as the level of the negotiation of macro-regulations indissolubly linked with the durability of the trade system (the regulations governing recruitment, dismissal, long service, the classification of wage groups, insurance schemes), and would establish the company as the place for the negotiation of micro-regulations particularly linked to work organisation and to the adapting of the rules governing the industrial sector.

Notes

1. This article is based upon an attempted synthesis of the studies by the author in the period 1985–7 (see the bibliography) on the content of the statute concerning employees in the construction and public works sector and on the policies implemented by the sector and firms. It was first published in France in *Plan Construction Actualités*, no. 30. It also draws on the research and evaluation of social experiments by the Centre IRIS–Travail et Société and other research bodies within the framework of the EVMB (Emploi et Valorisation des Métiers du Bâtiment) programme in the construction industry.

2. When concluded, an agreement or convention is not universally applicable. In other words it only applies to those firms which are members of the employers' association which is signatory to that agreement. At the request of one or more signatories an agreement may be extended after approval by the national commission for collective negotiations. It is then legally binding upon all firms in the designated sector of the economy (identified by the APE code).

3. An extract from a report presented by the Ministry of Employment before Parliament finally voted on the legislation.

4. Here I am adopting elements of Boulin's description of this experiment.

Bibliography

Boulin, J. Y. (1986). 'Suivi de l'expérimentation d'une réduction–réorganisation du temps de travail', Research Report, *IRIS–Travail et Société/ Plan Construction*

Campagnac, E., M. Campinos-Dubernet, and M. Tallard (1985). 'L'Intervention des salariés dans le bâtiment: un enjeu dans les stratégies "économiques"', *Critique de l'Économie Politique*, 32

Campinos-Dubernet, M. (1984a). 'La rationalisation du travail dans le BTP: un exemple des limites du taylorisme orthodoxe', *Formation/ Emploi*, 6, April–June

—— (1984b). 'Emploi et gestion de la main-d'œuvre dans le BTP', *Dossier CEREQ*, No. 34, Documentation Française

Chevalier, F. and G. Iresps (1986). 'Cercle de qualité; une intégration problématique dans la gestion de l'entreprise', *Revue Française de Gestion*, November

CREDOC (1985). *L'Expression des salariés. 2 ans d'application dans les entreprises*, Ministère du Travail

Eymard-Duvernay, F. (1985). 'Modes de gestion de la main-d'œuvre et flexibilité du marché du travail', Communication au colloque 'Structures du marché du travail et politique d'emploi'

Eyraud, F. and R. Tchobanian (1984). 'Tendances et évolution des relations professionnelles en France: la tentation de l'entreprise', *Document LEST*, (Working Paper) 84–3

IDEA–CITERA (1985). 'Les PME dynamiques du bâtiment', *DAEI*, Research Report, Ministère de l'Equipement. January

Jobert, A. and P. Rozenblatt (1986). 'Les niveaux et les formes pertinentes de la négociation et de la concertation sociale', Research Report, Centre d'Études de l'Emploi, September

Lajoinie, G. (1984). 'Évaluation socio-économique des chantiers expérimentaux dans el secteur du BTP', Research Report *OPS–ANACT*, June

Pillemont, J. and R. Weisz (1985). 'Organisation du chantier et modes de communication', Conference paper presented to 'A partir du chantier', organised by Plan-Construction, 15–16 April

Sellier, F. (1984). 'La Problématique du niveau dans les négociations collectives', Communication to the round table organised by CNRS–INSEE 'Les outils de gestion du travail', 22–3 November

Tallard, M. (1985). 'Statut des salariés et politiques de gestion de la main-d'œuvre. De la croissance à la crise. Le cas du BTP', *Sociologie du Travail*, I

—— (1986a). 'Les grilles de classification du bâtiment: le métier, élément incontournable?', *Formation/Emploi*, 15

—— (1986b). 'Le statut des salariés du BTP: enjeux et stratégies', Research Report *LEST/IRIS–Travail et Société/Plan-Construction*, November

Tallard, M. and H. Oeconomo (1983). 'Travail précaire et politique de gestion de la main-d'œuvre dans le BTP', Research Report *CREDOC*

Thionville, R. and G. Seidlitz, G. (1987) 'Les innovations sociales dans les PME du bâtiment', Research Report *Plan-Construction*

Tripier M. (1986). 'Culture ouvrière et culture d'entreprise', *Sociologie du Travail*, III

4

Processes of Change in Historical Perspective: Technology and Technique in the Construction Process 1919–1933 in Germany

Ursula Weis

Introduction

Generally speaking, there has so far been very little empirical and historical research completed on technology in the construction industry in terms of the actual material production processes. This can equally well be said of the research on the development of construction technology as a science of the material forms of production which can be effectively applied to the production process. It is therefore not surprising that we have yet to see the development of theoretical approaches to explain the historical development of construction techniques and technology.

Many people make the assumption that construction technology has, like general technology, developed more or less independently of other factors. Others link the development of construction technology to the development of the demand for building services, or to its dependence upon a variety of topographic situations. It is impossible to develop this kind of rigorous theoretical approach in the framework of a study which examines a relatively short period. I certainly do not claim to do so in the following remarks. They will perhaps nevertheless call into question widely accepted views and point instead to the relationship between technology and the social development of labour, which is not only a product, but, first and foremost, a prerequisite of technological development.

No form of technique or technology can develop without human labour. Brick walling or reinforced concrete construction techniques presuppose that there are individuals who can invent and execute these techniques *before* they can develop. If these individuals do not exist, then reinforced concrete and brickwork cannot exist either. This was most evident during the period 1919–20 in Germany, when there was an attempt to return to clay building techniques in the construction of homes, following the production crisis in the mining industry and the resultant coal shortage and curbing of brick production. This move failed because there was an acute shortage of workers who could work with clay. The consequence was that numerous buildings collapsed or were weakened by the rain. At the time the Prussian Ministry of the People's Welfare pointed to this correlation, making the astute observation that this situation was not due to the clay-building techniques, but rather to the shortage of workers with the relevant skills.

It would, however, be incorrect to state that the mental and physical skills of individuals were the sole factor influencing the development and evolution of construction technology. The Imperial Society for Research into Efficiency in the Building and Construction Industry and Housing Sector (Reichsforschungs-gesellschaft für Wirtschaftlichkeit im Bau- und Wohnungswesen) was founded in 1927 in Germany. This institution had the combined objectives of researching the material work organisation in building production and the qualitative conditions for creating and maintaining a skilled labour force, and claimed to make the rational organisation of house keeping the criterion for the material development of building production. This reflects the concept that the use value of labour determines the form of production, just as the use value of the building product, the home, determines the organisation of its reproduction, a concept which was generally condensed into the metaphor of the 'living machine'. In this context the home is defined as productive capital.[1]

The Society was, however, itself a product rather than a condition of the social development which determined the actual development of housing construction. It was founded at a point where there was a really dramatic upturn in the construction of publically funded housing. When there was a downturn in the construction of this type of housing, the institution disappeared in 1931.

As far as the actual development of housing construction is concerned, it is however evident that the use value of the home does not only reflect the skills of the workforce. Somewhat simplified, one can say that during the period 1924–8 skilled construction workers, generally speaking, built good-quality functional homes for skilled or white-collar workers. In the following period unskilled construction workers increasingly built 'a home designed specifically for those on the minimum wage' (for unskilled workers). Finally, from the end of 1931 onwards primarily unemployed construction workers built pitiful accommodation for the unemployed. Many of these were the very same men, who, as skilled construction workers, had earlier built homes for other skilled workers.

Above all, this indicates a significant change in the form of employment. This, however, not only took effect at the level of reproduction, but was an equally strong influence upon the form of technology used. Whereas in previous years there had been an almost explosive development in construction technology, the above-mentioned housing schemes for the unemployed had to be built without the use of any kind of new technology.

The influence of intellectual and physical labour upon material production is itself, like the conditions of its reproduction, largely dependent upon the system of social relations, which regulate the value of labour. In capitalism these are not simply interchangeable with the exchange relations of the market.

In capitalism comparisons are made between inanimate products on the basis of a system of values which neither recognises the labour which has created those products, nor their use. This system makes no distinction between war or peace. In this system butter and cannons have equal value and validity. These value relations have, by definition, no connection with the process of material production itself. They do nevertheless influence this process by simultaneously determining it as the production of values, the components of which are recognised as values. In this sense labour power is also an abstract concept which is related neither to labour, nor to consumption. The value of labour power therefore does not correspond to the value of the products the worker produces, but his/her value is calculated according to another criterion in modern capitalism: time. The concept of time, however, is not used to compare inanimate objects or conditions, but processes. The concept of the hourly rate thus embodies a recognition of human labour, if only at an extremely abstract level, which makes it possible to establish a more conscious relationship between the manufacturing process and the process of consuming or destroying natural resources, the latter being inevitably linked with the former, and the process of their restoration.

History shows us that with the generalisation and development of the hourly rate an increasing proportion of the expenditure upon reproduction was excluded from the direct mechanism of value relations. Initially, this came about because individual employers themselves provided means of subsistence such as company-owned accommodation or pension funds, particularly for their longer-serving employees. Later, this was increasingly due to funds formed from specified wage-deductions, on the basis of which part of the social labour product above all not only represented, but also guaranteed the long-term securing of reproduction. The social labour product as such was embodied in these funds, rather than in goods. At the same time the social division between labour and consumption, which forms the basis for the exchange of goods, began to be eliminated. The labour product saved in this process was not exchanged, but redistributed according to need. As these welfare institutions were founded, the production of those goods which served to support rather than destroy individuals was also assured: namely, provision for the sick, educational facilities, housing and food.

When institutions disappear, guarantees disappear with them. The part of the product of labour represented in these institutions will be returned to the bargaining process between capital and labour. It is transformed into an abstract value, but this is a fiction, because it does have a concrete form: the social institutions which form part of the process of reproduction of labour. Within these value relations there can be fluctuations in the value of products, both as a result of increased productivity, for example an increase in the productivity of technology and of the labour force, and as a result of a decrease in the values invested in production. The reduced value of technology can represent both a decrease in the value of the machinery used on the basis of the increased productivity of its production, as well as a lower level of technology. The decrease in the value of labour can result from a decrease in the value of basic products, or from a lower level of material reproduction. Here it is irrelevant whether the values are created in the 'free market' or elsewhere.

From a purely logical point of view, it is quite correct to consider the development which led to the hourly rate, and thence to the social wage, as an element of Marx's concept of relative surplus value production and the actual subjugation of labour to capital. Historical observation indicates that the history of this development was simultaneously the history of critical social conflicts and of their resolution. This essentially means that the condition of its development was an expansion in the political and social power of human labour. The introduction of insurance against accidents and sickness and of pension schemes in Germany around 1890 followed the 'Law to counter the dangerous endeavours of social democracy'. There were calls in the German parliament for the introduction of universal social welfare for the unemployed when Germany first began to feel the effects of the 1917 Russian Revolution. It was eventually decreed in one of the first proclamations of the 'Council of the People's Representatives' on 13 November 1918 after the outbreak of the November revolution in Germany. At the same time the general revolutionary situation led to a significant expansion in trade union power.

A Perspective on Labour Law, 1918–1934

At the most superficial level, the development of construction technology during the period 1919–30 can be characterised as the qualitative development and the widespread use of construction techniques using concrete and reinforced concrete in all sectors of building production. Parallel with this technological development, the large construction firms, an increasing number of which were developing into joint-stock companies and financed by banks, became involved in all sectors of building production. This was particularly true of the housing sector, where they had had hardly any involvement before 1914. At the same time the form of management commonly known as Taylorism, and as 'scientific management' in academic circles, became increasingly widespread in the building and construction trade. Initially this was implemented in the large firms, then after 1925 it became clearly reflected in the development of the white-collar workforce, even in small and medium-sized firms, if only at a most basic level. The principal element of Taylorism is the separation of production into the preparation and business control of the material production process by a team of technical and business managers on the one hand and tasks of execution on the other. The centralised regulation of both these elements was found in large construction firms.

This development took place against a background of dramatic social and political developments, beginning in November 1918 with the implementation of collective labour law and ending in January 1934 with the legal enshrining of fascist labour law in the 'Law for the regulation of National Labour'. The collective labour law of 1918 meant the following in practical terms:

1 The recognition of collective agreements on working conditions and wages for all trades and sectors of production in the sense that no employee–employer relationship could be formed outside the collective contract of employment. One of the most important practical elements of the new wage legislation was the universal introduction of the 8-hour day.
2 The recognition of trade unions 'as the elected representatives of all male and female workers', that is the exclusive right of trade unions to negotiate wage agreements and to conclude wage contracts.

This implied the recognition of all production as social labour, not only production on a building site or in a factory, but also production between various factories and various sectors of production, in other words the formal inclusion of labour in the principle of socialised production.

With the 1934 'Law for the regulation of National Labour' all workers of the German Reich were classified as unemployed under the terms of the collective labour law. On this basis it was possible to develop scientific management into its most extreme and perverted form, so that it no longer constituted the (only) principle governing the material organisation of production, but it was primarily the constituent system of social relations in the production process, which determined the value of labour. The trade unions were annihilated and production declared to be in private hands. Workers had to obey unconditionally orders given by their superiors in the factory, following the principle of 'Gefolgschaft'.[2] Parallel with this development there was the transition from the parliamentary democracy enshrined in the Weimar constitution to the dictatorship of the Führer Adolf Hitler. It is, however, important to stress that the principles behind fascist labour law did not uniquely derive from the fascist dictatorship, even if it only formally became law under this regime. By 1931, at the latest, it was fomulated as a political programme in the speeches and writings of prominent representatives of industry, including the construction industry, both in terms of its thematic principles and its linguistic metaphors.

The development of building production played an important and specific role in this process of social and political change. In the following section I will attempt to offer a comprehensive analysis of the technological and social elements of this development in its most important stages.

Technology and Contracts, 1919–1923

In a parallel development to the demobilisation of the German army at the end of the First World War, the Reich and Land authorities increasingly began to undertake major civil engineering projects, some of which had been planned before the war. There were two major reasons for this: firstly, the exploitation of new sources of energy and new methods of transportation, primarily the sometimes large hydroelectric power stations and canal construction projects, and secondly, the suppression of revolutionary groups, particularly in the cities. There was also a shortage of building plant. For these two reasons hundreds of thousands of manual workers were employed on these projects. From 1920 there was increasing capitalisation, as can be seen in the orders for a large amount of heavy construction machinery on large sites.

This trend was also linked with changes in the conditions for contracts for tender and with changes in construction contracts. Whilst in the period 1918–19 the large construction firms had agreements with the state contractors whereby the firms provided them with services and the state undertook to pay wages and to provide building materials, during 1920 contracts based upon performance became increasingly common following pressure from the firms. This type of contract, unlike the above-mentioned prime costs contract, again gave firms the opportunity to make a profit. Since it was, however, impossible to award contracts on the basis of fixed prices given the rapid rise in inflation, flexible contracts were introduced, which made the realisation time measured in wage-hours rather than the cost of implementation the criterion for the assessment and payment of work. This was the reason for the rapid generalisation of 'scientific management' in large companies. This contractual basis required the most precise estimations of material

73

production in terms of temporal units rather than units of cost.

These developments, along with the occasional chronic shortage of skilled construction workers and the variety of often complex topographical situations in mountainous or coastal regions, led to the rapid widespread adoption of a new construction technique using cast concrete in large construction companies. The cast concrete was transported from high foundry towers to the place of use by means of channels or cable cranes, instead of on dump trucks pulled by men or by engines on rails as had normally previously been the case. This latter form of transportation had had to be constantly adapted to the variety of land formations, some of which could often only be foreseen with great difficulty. Apart from the fact that the new process saved a significant amount of time, it also made it much easier to find a general criterion by which to judge the time and manpower needed for a project on the basis of the estimation of the flow-speed/angle of inclination and the use of the same equipment (Hess 1922: 279–80). This same correlation was the reason for the first use of the 'separation method of construction' in Germany in wall construction, that is the separation of a massive wall into its constituent parts, i.e. arches, flying buttresses and flagstones. This meant that the transport, use and processing of the necessary building material could be reduced by 80 per cent and only approximately 200 workers were therefore needed instead of 1,000 (Bechtel 1926: 1–8).

The Social Development of Labour, 1919–1923

This important development in construction technology was accompanied by the increasingly public struggle of the employers – and not only in the building and construction trade – to have the collective labour law struck from the statute books, until this was formulated as a political programme and almost achieved in 1923 in the context of the debate about currency reform. Until then it primarily found its expression in the relationship between changes in the function of unemployment assistance and the latent changes in the social conditions of workers, particularly those in the construction industry.

In 1919 the German Association of Construction Workers (Deutscher Baugewerksbund) declared that their union would give priority to the following goals:

1 The complete unionisation of all construction workers. This was all the more pressing, given that many workers from outside the industry had been employed as construction workers on the largest civil engineering projects.
2 The general right of the unions to represent workers as their 'elected delegates' was to cover all construction workers. Actual wage agreements were also to be valid for all construction workers. This goal was achieved in 1919 with the very first wage agreement for civil engineering workers.
3 The eradication of piece-work.
4 The extensive erosion of wage differentials.

The unions made these four demands in order to realise the ideal of the collective labour law and the 8-hour day. The right of the union exclusively to represent the workers had to be put into practice in the organisation of all construction workers and their inclusion in wage agreements. The principle of the 8-hour day could only be maintained so long as the minimum wages in the agreement were paid or as long as high wage differentials were not offset by overtime working, on the one hand, and higher productivity, on the other. The health of workers was protected by the 8-hour day and was not allowed to deteriorate through the reintroduction of piece-work.

The union's programme reflected the political view that the social development of labour rather than changes in the relations of ownership was the strategy for transforming social conditions. This view only became rational and realistic with the introduction of universally applicable unemployment assistance in 1918, which, as the 1918 decree emphasised 'was not a type of alms'. For, in contrast to social welfare legislation before 1914, it did not merely ensure the conditions of reproduction, but it also directly reflected the repercussions of the conditions of reproduction upon working conditions. It not only prevented the unemployed from suffering material hardship and social disintegration, but it also protected the working conditions of those in work.

As early as 1920 significant elements of this trade union programme were again called into question: piece-work was explicitly declared legal on condition that it was regulated by the individual trade unions; the new national wage agreement introduced different wages for 'skilled' and 'unskilled' workers, that is unskilled workers from outside the industry. A proposed new national wage agreement for workers on civil engineering projects was not implemented and the trade union executive itself questioned the principle of the total unionisation of all the workers employed in the construction industry.

The public financing of 'relief projects', including many major civil engineering projects, from the budget allocated to unemployment assistance after 1920 had already led to a trend towards the exclusion of workers employed on 'relief projects' from the terms of the collective agreement. A government decree laid down that from January 1920 onwards these workers were to be paid on the basis of their productivity. This was in clear contradiction to the wages agreement then in force.

As a means of increasing the work rate, these measures undoubtedly went some way towards meeting the technological needs of companies. However, the debate about piece-work in connection with the general strike against the reactionary coup in March 1920 led by Kapp and Lüttwitz, the subsequent demands for the nationalisation of key industries and for a 'workers' government', the disruption of the general strike and its suppression by government troops in the Ruhr area all indicate that this was not the only goal of these measures. In this context piece-work was not only a question of the degree of excess expenditure on labour, but also a question of 'political power'. The rejection of piece-work was correspondingly seen as the 'sabotage of business life' or a 'security for the political rights' of the 'misled masses' (Wagner 1920). Up to a certain point this trend also influenced the German Association of Construction Workers, causing it to modify its wages policy and expel its communist members in 1921.

The next stage was reached in 1921 with the alignment of the wages of all construction workers employed on the 'relief projects' with the lower wages of unskilled workers from outside the industry, whether they were in work or not. Only individual skilled workers, foremen, members of the permanent workforce and master craftsmen were excluded from this measure. Gradually the wage differentials between skilled and unskilled workers were also increased on other projects than the 'relief projects'. On the one hand, this indicates the growing demand for skilled workers given the new technology, but it primarily indicates the trend towards excluding the labour of ever larger groups classed as unemployed from the collective agreement.

On 13 October 1923 a government decree made work the condition for claiming unemployment benefits. In other words, the work of the workers employed upon relief projects was no longer remunerated, but considered the condition for them receiving income support. At this point there were between 3 million and 3.5 million unemployed workers in Germany. To exclude all of them from the collective labour law was tantamount to excluding human labour from the relations which make up society. In practice, it was equivalent to excluding them from the civil right to ply their trade, from wage agreements, from the right to strike and from the representation of their interests at company level.

The above debate demonstrates the close relationship between economic considerations and the social order. Long before the promulgation of this decree, plans for a 'increase in production on the basis of unemployment' (Potthof 1923) were formulated both at a theoretical level and in practice, constituting conclusive programmes for a new organisation of the German economy in conjunction with the currency reform. The reasoning was basically as follows: the production process was burdened by a surplus of unproductive labour. The result was a low level of productivity because of an excessively slow work rate. If production was relieved of its burden of economically damaging labour, the remaining labour would produce more than the larger number of workers did previously. Planned unemployment was both the precondition for the lowering of reproduction costs, the intensive exploitation of current resources through the use of remnants for food, clothing and housing, the new establishment of agricultural estates, and the construction of roads and canals by unemployed workers.

The Social Development of Labour, 1924–1925

This programme, however, could not be realised, or at least only partially realised, during the period 1924–5. Construction workers were the group initially hardest hit by the increase in production on the basis of programmes for the unemployed. In February 1924 72 per cent of the members of the largest construction workers' trade union alone were out of work, the workers employed in the construction industry on relief projects accounted for approximately 70 per cent of those still regularly in work, and there were further plans for relief projects in the housing and railway sectors. However, unionised skilled construction workers refused to work on relief projects. In so doing, they helped to bring about a measure which was supported by some members of the government, namely the financing of new housing from a new tax. At least part of building production was therefore excluded from relief labour. This enabled the construction workers not only to block the use of skilled workers on relief projects, but also to transform the subsequent lock-outs into one of the major strikes of the 1920s. They emerged triumphant from this strike in the sense that overall they achieved substantial wage increases.

This industrial action was not first and foremost a confrontation between employers and workers in the construction industry, but, from a quantitative point of view, merely a small element of the wider struggle of German industrialists against the trade unions. It took place against a background of a colossal wave of lock-outs, with 22.78 million working days lost as a result in 1924 alone, over half of which were in the coal and steel industry. As can be seen from the reports of trade unions and employers in the construction industry, most lock-outs were implemented following pressure from industrial clients and a united front of associations representing businessmen, bankers, industrialists and employers fought the 1925 strike of construction workers by submitting several petitions to the government and conducting a widespread public campaign against the 'assault troop of the trade unions'.

At least at national level the successful industrial action taken by the construction workers prevented an increase in production on the basis of large-scale unemployment. Their action once again strengthened the position of the trade unions and rescued the collective labour law, despite the currency reform. The construction workers' unions nevertheless had to accept as an outcome of their industrial action, which was suppressed by the government in August 1925, a significant expansion of the wage differential between skilled and unskilled workers, which was finally fixed at 17 per cent in the 1927 national wage agreement, and the complete exclusion of workers on civil engineering projects from the negotiated wage rates.

The Development of Construction Technology, 1925–1930

If one takes a purely superficial view of the development of construction technology after 1925, one is immediately aware of the increasing emphasis upon structural engineering projects and of a large increase in the volume of production from 5.82 thousand million Reichsmarks in 1925 to 8.91 thousand million Reichsmarks in 1928. This fell back only slightly in 1929 and did not fall below the 1927 level until 1930. At the same time concrete and reinforced concrete technology was also introduced in these sectors. This, however, does not mean that the process, which was introduced on large civil engineering sites in 1920, was simply transferred as an entity to the structural engineering sector. A significant change took place above all in basic contractual conditions, which after 1925 were again adapted to fixed prices in all sectors of construction production.

Both the empirical sources which provide information about the struggles within society and those which reflect the development in technology portray a range of subjective experiences and viewpoints, based upon the respective positions of their authors in the production process and society. If one reads the accounts of engineers, technological development appears to be almost exclusively the result of their labour. The practical and material labour of construction workers is only mentioned in a peripheral way in their accounts and they appear completely unaware of the significance of their social position. By contrast, changes in technology are often only reflected in the experiences and projections of those executing tasks, when they constitute a new threat to their health or to life on site, or a threat to their livelihood. This type of subjective experience has greatly contributed to the prejudice that technology is the source of social development, whereas social development can equally contribute to the type of technology applied.

In the general debate on the increase in production of German industry, which grew particularly intense during 1922–3, other models of interpretation also become evident, which suggest a different experience (Hertz and Seidel 1923; Brentano 1923). Central to the discussion was whether the 8-hour day should be maintained or abolished. Broadly speaking, the employers argued that productivity could only be increased by forming new capital on the basis of the reintroduction of pre-war working hours. In contrast, the trade unions argued that productivity could only be increased by maintaining the 8-hour day and increasing wages. For only this could lead to capital investments, which in their turn would promote productivity.

More recently, economic historians have tended to interpret the general development of technology in Germany during the period 1920–3 in line with the second position outlined above. Productivity grew slowly as the result of a real wage constantly depleted by inflation, which allowed the export industries to maintain their competitivity on foreign markets without improving production levels and on the basis of extremely cheap labour (Blaich 1985). It was a completely different situation in the most important sectors of construction production. The large construction companies had made significant progress in terms of increasing productivity during the period 1920–4. Real wages were also low in the building and construction trade, but, unlike the export industries which were able to exploit inflation, the construction companies were operating under conditions which made this impossible. This was because their profit opportunities were linked to real increases in productivity (the saving of wage-hours) instead of international differentials in currency values.

When calculations of time and output were again made subject to cost or value calculations in the building and construction trade as well, two opportunities were open to them. They could increase productivity through substituting labour by technology, or by substituting skilled labour by unskilled labour, given the high wage differentials between the various wage groups. As far as concrete technology was concerned, the relatively high wages of carpenters initially played a significant role, particularly given that the carpenters' trade union had consistently refused to work for piece-rates. In the technological discussion this is evident in the fact that one of the companies' central concerns was the economising on shuttering and scaffolding. One of the most important successes was the development of the various forms of the cylindrical shell. This was a design which had previously not even been imagined, and whose invention in its initial stages went back to the period of inflation. It was first used on a monumental scale in building projects during the period 1926–7, thereby replacing the traditional steel constructions. The increasing significance of technology based upon finished concrete parts both on site as well as in permanent works and the introduction of sliding shuttering contributed to a real increase in productivity.

This was, however, only one of the many reasons for the success of concrete technology. The bulk of the labour force using the new concrete and reinforced concrete technology were badly paid unskilled workers or structural engineering workers, whose wages were subject to strong regional variations, sometimes up to 35 per cent below the wages for unskilled labour and occasionally below even the legally recognised minimum living wage. In particular, they were no longer only employed as labourers in ground work, but also as workers using concrete technology.

As the development of unemployment in the building and construction trade and its distribution amongst the various trades shows, these components primarily determined the development of construction production. After 1927, relief projects were finally put on a equal footing with other projects and their number sharply reduced in a short period. At the same time, numerous workers who had formerly been employed on relief projects flooded the ordinary labour market. This development also influenced material production: from about 1930 onwards civil engineers observed that even large building firms were using porters and men pushing wheelbarrows instead of transporting equipment and that concrete and mortar were once again being mixed by hand.

Technology as a Weapon against Trade Unions and Skilled Workers

The social factors of technological development are most apparent when technology is consciously used as an instrument to bring about changes in the social position of human labour.

When it became clear that the lock-outs in the building and construction trade had not been such a complete success as they had been in the coal and steel industry, the employers' associations persuaded the relevant ministries to decree that planning authorities should 'encourage wherever possible semi-skilled and unskilled workers from other industries, and to make extensive use of such building materials as will make it easier for unskilled and semi-skilled construction workers to be employed in the building and construction trade' (Deutscher Baugewerksbund 1925: 39; Deutscher Wirtschaftsbund für das Baugewerbe 1924–6: 133). After the construction workers' strike, concrete technology was valued more because it generally did not require a skilled labour force than because its use led to increased productivity. This trend is particularly obvious in the discussions about the construction of publicly-funded housing as the sector which had promoted the success of the construction workers' action during the period 1924–5. The efforts to prevent its expansion beyond 1924 levels were almost always based upon the argument that there was a shortage of skilled labour. In 1926 the Imperial Association of German Industry (Reichsverband der Deutschen Industrie) made its agreement, elicited under political pressure, conditional not only upon the use of cheaper materials, but also upon state regulation of the wages of construction workers. Moreover, several ministries organised surveys amongst the chambers of commerce about the effects of housing construction upon the wages of construction workers before approving the release of public funds for this purpose. This finally led even the leader of the Christian trade unions to plead in the Reichstag for the use of alternative construction techniques using steel and cement instead of brick, in order to overcome the opposition to a more major housing construction programme. The unemployment of skilled construction workers, particularly of bricklayers, which was caused by this policy, increased during the period 1928–9. This had a major impact on the construction trade unions, whose core membership was made up of skilled workers.

Unemployment and the Transition to Fascism

The world economic crisis after 1929–30 led German industry into one of its most critical slumps in production and was also the condition for a significant increase in the power of the employers, which found expression in the 1934 Nazi legislation on the regulation of labour.

Just as building production had been an important factor in hindering this goal during the period 1924–5, it played a pioneering role in the restructuring of the social and political order in the period 1931–3.

> From the legislative point of view the current situation is the following: the relief worker does indeed have work, but no form of pay. Indeed he does not receive a wage, but financial support. He must, however, largely finance this support through his own contributions made previously whilst in work. . . . We will doubtless have a major surplus from the workers' contributions to unemployment assistance funds. As in the case of other forms of social insurance, thousands of millions of marks will accumulate, which can be later used to pay the productively unemployed a wage, which is nevertheless not a real wage. (Deutscher Baugewerksbund 1924: 438–9)

Given the developments after 1931, this almost prophetic forecast made by construction workers in 1924 points to the close parallels between the situation in the period 1923–4 and the period after 1931. Whilst construction workers were successful in rejecting these developments as far as the majority of unionised construction workers were concerned in the period 1924–5, they offered no opposition to the same proposals in the period 1931–3, because no sector of building production remained totally reliant upon their labour.

The period from late 1928 onwards was marked on the one hand by wide-scale industrial action, particularly in the metal industry, which was primarily about the general validity of the wages agreement rather than solely about wage levels, and on the other by controversial debates about unemployment assistance which in 1930 finally brought the fall of the coalition government and with it also the democratic practice of parliamentary decision-making. Industrial action regarding insurance against unemployment particularly affected those construction workers who had already been excluded from the normal assistance schemes in 1928 and had been included in alternative special assistance schemes offering worse conditions. Taken as an annual average, 29 per cent of the members of the largest construction workers' trade union were unemployed in 1929, 47.6 per cent in 1930 and 68 per cent in 1931. In 1932 there was no period where less than 78 per cent of all unionised construction workers were unemployed. At times over 90 per cent were unemployed.

During the period 1930–2 the level of the standard unemployment assistance sank and the length of period during which it could be claimed continually shortened. On the one hand, this meant that a growing number of the unemployed increasingly received support from the public welfare funds of local authorities, rather than unemployment assistance from the state. On the other hand, it led to the accumulation of significant amounts of capital in the unemployment insurance scheme. At the same time compulsory labour of the type found during the period 1923–4 was reintroduced, but generally under the new name 'Voluntary Labour Service' (Freiwilliger Arbeitsdienst).

The resources of the unemployment assistance scheme were primarily used to promote 'Voluntary Labour Service'. In January 1932, 4,968 people worked on the VLS programme, in June 70,444 and in September 206,665. As can be seen from archive documents and trade union reports, the VLS programme, unlike former types of unpaid work, employed a large number of skilled construction workers. Only public bodies were at first permitted to make use of VLS labour. This situation changed with the government decree of 15 October 1932, which laid down that private firms, and specifically those of the building and construction trade, should be integrated in the VLS programme. In this way, the social form of labour which was to be enshrined in a universally applicable labour law in 1934 was initially implemented in the building and construction trade.

The publications of the German Institute for the Technical Training of Labour (Deutsche Institut für Technische Arbeitsschulung (DINTA)) make explicit the economic background to this policy. It was initially implemented in the coal and steel industry in 1925 and later applied throughout Germany with a network of training workshops in all branches of industry, including the building and construction trade. One can see from these publications that from the outset the VLS was considered to be merely the very beginning 'of a healthy movement of great significance for the education of the population' with the aim of implementing compulsory labour and of 'creating compulsory workshop labour' (DINTA 1931: X1).

The stagnation of a highly capitalised and sometimes highly indebted industry brought about by the crisis seemed likely to lead to a kind of self-destruction of fixed capital. This could only be offset by maintaining production with minimal labour costs, for example by using compulsory labour on 'projects which are useful, from the point of view of capital and technology' (Arnhold 1932: 106):

> Today our factories are barely working at 50 per cent capacity. If one could however use compulsory labour to ensure the second half of the production of, for example, a cement works working on prime costs, then no losses would be incurred. On the contrary, there would be additional advantages for each factory, given that the unavoidable fixed costs could be spread over a wider base. (Arnhold 1932: 107)

The reasons for the transition to the production of absolute surplus value in 1932 were diametrically opposed to those of 1919:

> If it were possible . . . to win over employers to using compulsory labour . . . then one could begin to tackle major projects such as a

cross-country canal to connect existing canal systems, the building of dykes along the North Sea coast, dams and river control. (Arnhold 1932: 107)

Conclusion

I cannot fully explain here what part the VLS played in the job-creation measures taken by the fascist government, for example the construction of the national motorways. Mason's observation that a change in the unemployment statistics largely accounted for the reintegration of the unemployed in the production process after 1933 (1978: 126–7) indicates that the VLS was probably an important factor. Before 1933 those who voluntarily worked on National Labour schemes and workers on compulsory or relief projects were classed as 'unemployed'. After 1933 they were removed from the unemployment statistics. The essential role played by the building and construction trade in this restructuring of production did not lie in the production of the energy and transport infrastructure so urgently needed for the reconstruction of industry, as it had done in the period 1919–20. Rather, it lay primarily in the production of goods, the value of which could be realised outside the sphere of consumption. The standard of the housing settlements for the unemployed, which had largely been built by unpaid labour before 1933, shows the extraordinary contradiction between the policy of minimal labour costs and the production of consumer goods: the value of a family home was not permitted to exceed 3,000 Reichsmarks. This was equivalent to about 25–30 per cent of the costs of a newly-built flat in the period 1927–8. The home was to have between 40 and 45 m of total usable floor surface, but no form of sewerage system or plumbing. Firms were not permitted to use construction machinery for the construction of these homes. This was certainly not because this machinery did not exist, as was the case in 1919, but because this would have transferred excessive value to the product.

Ursula Weis

Notes

1. These concepts derived from a general understanding in the 1920s that modern society and all its subsystems were subject to the same rational organisation and planning as they were in industrial production in the factory. In this context even housing was understood as a kind of machine-like process and the metaphor of the 'living machine' became quite common for a certain type of large, uniform housing. In this instance, not only was the dwelling mass-produced, but living in it was also a mass process. It is in this context that the home is defined as capital, which could be used productively as a means of reproducing labour power.

2. This term cannot be translated into English. In the terminology of the Nazi system it reflects the idea that the whole of society should be constructed according to the leader principle. This meant that every social subsystem had to be governed by a leader and that the relationship between the leader and followers was one governed by unconditional obedience.

Bibliography

In order to keep the bibliography as concise as possible only the most important sources are given. For more details see Weis 1988a and 1988b.

Arnhold, C. (1932), 'Arbeit als Dienst am Volk', *Arbeitsschulung*, 4, 99–109

Bechtel, K. (1926) 'Uber den Bau der Talsperre Vöhrenbach in Baden'. *Sonderdruck aus Beton und Eisen*

Blaich, F. (1985), *Der Schwarze Freitag. Inflation und Wirtschaftskrise*, DTV Verlag, Munich

Brentano, L. (1923), 'Der Ansturm auf den Achtstundentag und die Koalitionsfreiheit der Arbeiter', *Soziale Praxis und Archiv für Volkswohlfahrt*, 19, 419–24; 20, 451–6; 22, 499–502, 23, 515–51

Deutscher Baugewerksbund, (1925), *Niederschriften über die Verhandlungen des ersten ordentlichen Bundestages abgehalten vom 3.–6. September 1924*, Verlag des Deutschen Baugewerksbunds, Hamburg

—— (1926), *Jahrbuch 1925*, Verlag Deutscher Baugewerksbund, Hamburg

Deutscher Wirtschaftsbund für das Baugewerbe (1924–6). *Geschäftsbericht über die Jahre 1924–1926*

DINTA (1931), *Tätigkeitsbericht für die Zeit vom 1. Juli 1930 – 30. Juni 1931*

Hertz, P. and R. Seidel (1923), *Arbeitszeit, Arbeitslohn und Arbeitsleistung*, Verlagsgesellschaft des ADGB, Berlin

Hess, E. (1922), 'Betreib und Wirtschaftlichkeit der Betonbaustelle', *Beton und Eisen. Internationales Organ für Betonbau*, XXI. Heft IX, 263–264; Heft XX, 279–280

Mason, T. W. (1978), *Sozialpolitik im Dritten Reich. Arbeiterklasse und*

Volksgemeinschaft, 2nd edn, Westdeutscher Verlag, Wiesbaden

Potthof, H. (1923), 'Produktionssteigerung durch Arbeitslosigkeit', *Soziale Praxis und Archiv für Volkswohlfahrt*, 7, 39–42

Wagner, M. (1920), 'Der Akkordlohn im Baugewerbe', *Volkswohnung*, II, 6, 77–80

Weis, U. (1988a), 'Unemployment and the Organization of Building Labour in Germany in the Period 1919–1933', Working Paper, presented at the 9th Bartlett International Summer School, University of London

—— (1988b), 'Arbeitslosigkeit und Organisation der Arbeit zwischen Novemberrevolution und Faschismus. Die Rolle der Bauarbeit in Deutschland 1919–1933', *The Production of the Built Environment* 9, Proceedings of the 9th Bartlett International Summer School, University of London

Part II

Construction Industry Strategies towards Restructuring

5

Strategies of Growth of Productivity in the Absence of Technological Change

Gerd Syben

Introduction

Technical progress is often thought to be the main means of increasing productivity. In this paper, an examination of the construction industry will be used to demonstrate that in the post-war period in West Germany, the development of technology is only responsible to a small extent for increases in productivity. Rather, increases in productivity have resulted not so much from the mechanisation of the construction process, but from changes in work organisation. In this respect, the construction industry, although often thought of as a 'traditional' or 'backward' industry demonstrates surprising modernity. Many of the features of these rationalisation processes are similar to those currently being introduced in leading sectors of manufacturing industry, through methods of stockless production or 'just-in-time' techniques. These methods facilitate the decentralisation of production, a development which also has consequences for union strategy.

The construction industry in the Federal Republic of West Germany has lost more than 600,000 jobs since 1973.[1] This amounts to about 40 per cent of total employment in this sector. However, in 1988 construction investment in constant prices was only 7 per cent below the level of 1972, the peak of all post-war years.[2] Therefore only a small extent of the decrease in employment can be accounted for by a reduction or shift in demand for construction goods. While employment in the construction industry in 1988 was at the same

Table 5.1 Building investments and employment in main construction trades

	Investments (bn DM)[a]	Employees	Percentage change in investments[b]	Percentage change in employees
1950	54.8	960,900		
1964	168.3	1,716,900	+206.6	+78.8
1972	213.6	1,579,600	+26.9	−8.0
1980	208.5	1,281,200	−2.4	−18.9
1988	198.5	975,000[c]	−4.8	−23.9

(a) 1980 prices.
(b) Compared to the year shown before.
(c) Estimate.
Source: see note 3.

level as in 1950, construction investment was 3.6 times greater.

This decrease in employment was not a consequence of a reduction in investment in new buildings and losses of employment in construction have not been balanced out by gains in other sectors such as repair and maintenance (Syben 1987: 674). Rather, the evidence suggests that rationalisation has taken place and that there has been a continuous increase in productivity. The emphasis in this paper is laid on the changing organisation of work, to which a large part of the increase of labour productivity can obviously be attributed.

Technical Development, Productivity and Labour Substitution

In the following pages technical development is regarded as a process which 'successively removes the necessity of human intervention in the production process by increasing the "self-acting capacity" (Eigenfähigkeit) of the technical apparatus itself' (Kern and Schumann 1970, vol. 1: 55). The economic objective of this process is to increase the productivity of labour by the substitution of human labour by technical tools. For this reason I differentiate here between 'technical' and 'technological' modifications. Technical modifications occur where three conditions are met: firstly, a new item of machinery is used, for example, a crane instead of a conveyor belt; secondly, no new technological principles are involved; thirdly, if the degree of substitution of labour remains constant, in qualitative terms. In other words, the level of qualification and the extent to which labour power contributes to the finished product remains the same. In contrast, technological modification involves a qualitative increase in the degree of substitution of human labour power by the application of new technical principles.[4]

Though the relations of production, technique, work and economy are the oldest subjects of sociological research in Germany, there is no systematic empirical analysis of these relationships in the construction industry (Spannhake 1986). The exception was a study conducted in Dortmund focusing mainly on reinforced concrete work and prefabrication (Richter 1981; Janssen and Richter 1983). The following consideration of essential operations on building sites is based on a qualitative interpretation derived from industrial sociology of the development of the use of equipment and qualification in building production in the Federal Republic since 1963 (Syben 1987). An investigation of tools used on building sites which examined their 'self-acting capacity', shows that differences in the degree of mechanisation can be attributed to the type of industrial work process to which the operation is attached (Altman, Bechtle and Lutz 1978).[5] So in different aspects of production processes there are varying forms and possibilities for increasing labour productivity.

Operations of the Transporting Type

In the 1950s and 1960s, processes of horizontal and vertical transportation on building sites which had been carried out by traditional tools such as shovels and wheelbarrows and forms of work organisation such as the 'human chain' were replaced by equipment; conveyer belts, elevators, hoists and cranes. In this way simple work actions like shovelling, lifting, and carrying were replaced by machinery, but the tools introduced were far from having 'self-acting capacity'. Increases of productivity were obtained by the mid 1960s by a simple quantitative enlargement of equipment on the same technological basis. That is to say, the number and size of cranes increased but the basic technological principles did not change. The 'self-acting capacity' of the equipment was not altered nor was the substitution of labour qualitatively modified.

The post-war boom ended in the mid 1960s and this marked the beginning of normal trade cycles in the West German economy. The construction industry boom came to an end with the first crisis in 1967, and simple means of transportation were increasingly displaced by tower cranes. Increased productivity in transportation processes represented technical progress in so far as technical efficiency was raised by the specific form of mechanisation achieved by using cranes. The range and the load capacity of the cranes were higher than those of other means of transportation; the operating radius was three-dimensional instead of one-dimensional, and increased mobility made it possible in principle to reach every point of the building site without altering the crane's position. The wide range of applications of this lifting capacity made it possible to transport nearly every material used on the building site with just one means of transport.

In spite of the crane's greater efficiency and the complexity of operations it can perform, the control of it and the positioning of the material transported remain in human hands. The importance of human control to the work process is not reduced by the greater range of applications of cranes as opposed to earlier and more simple methods of transportation. The crane does not involve the use of new technological principles nor a qualitative enlargement of the substitution of human labour by technique. To that extent it is defined as a technical modification within a constant technological base.

Operations of the Material-changing Type

Mixing mortar and concrete can be described as a material-changing process. Material-changing processes can more easily be mechanised because mechanisation requires relatively little technological investment. So the 'self-acting capacity' of the apparatus on building sites has been greater from the outset in mixing operations than in other operations. Whilst the work of measuring the proportion of materials in the mixture was performed manually, the mixing operation was automated in the rotating cylinder. This step in mechanisation only replaced simple, manual operations such as mixing mortar or concrete with a shovel. In contrast to the forms of mechanisation in transportation, the rotating cylinder produces a useful product without any further human intervention. This is the reason why this type of machinery has a higher level of 'self-acting capacity' than machinery linked to transporting operations.

Until the mid 1960s productivity was also increased in mixing processes by a simple increase in the quantity and size of equipment. A revolutionary development led to a displacement of concrete production from the building site to an off-site concrete factory but was not dependent on a change in technological principle. The principle of automation of the mixing procedure by rotation remained the same. The conclusive modification lay in the fact that the size of the equipment for concrete production was no longer bound by technical characteristics nor by work organisation to the size of the construction site, as is the case for other construction equipment. So the economic objective of increasing productivity is achieved for this operation by work organisation based on the principles of industrial mass production. That is to say, it is the concentration of the production process at one point of production which leads to the eventual establishment of the off-site concrete factory. In addition, a qualitative change in the division of labour leads to the disappearance of existing work functions and skills, and the establishment of new ones. It leads to more efficient work organisation by tying operations more closely to the rhythm and pace of the mechanical operation.

This not only affects the organisation of labour in the concrete factory but also the organisation of concrete work on the building site. The timing of concrete work has to be fixed some days before it is due to be undertaken and it must be precise because the concrete is only usable for a limited period after mixing. That is why the necessary equipment for using it (a concrete pump, or a crane and transport bowl, a vibrator to condense the concrete) as well as the labour force have to be available on the building site at a specified time for the duration of the work. Whereas formerly there were sufficient workers deployed on site to do the concrete work because they were occupied in other operations, now their availability becomes a problem of planning. Not only does the production process at the building site have to be planned more exactly, but firms may have to plan operations for several building sites at the same time. A single firm is not normally able to solve this problem by keeping labour and equipment in stock. Obviously this has nothing to do with technological progress because the technological basis of the technique used for making concrete has not changed fundamentally by the fact of moving its production from the building site. On the other hand modified techniques can be

95

observed, for example in the presence of mixing towers at building sites. The fact of being able to adjust and control the proportion of mixture automatically (Stefaniak 1981: 172) is irrelevant to this point because this can be found at the building site as well as in the concrete factory.

Operations of the Assembly Type

Operations for combining materials (bricks, formwork or reinforced steel, to mention the most important ones) have remained human labour in the process of building production. Mechanisation of these assembly operations at building sites has not occurred in the Federal Republic. There have been repeated experiments, for example to mechanise the procedure of bricklaying, but equipment has not yet been developed that would be economic on building sites. Experiments such as those in Japan to automate formwork and reinforcing (Bennett, Flanagan and Norman 1987: 58–62) have not been reported in the Federal Republic. The production of pillars and walls has not been rationalised by the mechanisation of bricklaying, which is an assembly-type operation. Rather the increase in productivity is achieved by the transfer to another type of production, reinforced concrete construction. This is based on a material-changing type of process which is easier to mechanise. On the other hand, new processes have developed of the assembly-type (form work, steel erection) and these have not been mechanised so far.

More Extensive Rationalisation without New Technologies

This short review shows that in spite of all the differences in mechanisation of the operations of different types of construction process there are certain connections between them. Up until the mid 1960s the mechanisation of building production led to an increase in productivity. This was because simple manual operations, which are only based on the use of physical strength for which a long training period is not necessary, were replaced increasingly by mechanical aids and produced better results. The technical development which increased labour productivity in the period since the mid 1960s essentially resulted from an increase in the quantity and the size of the equipment used. It was not the outcome of a change in technological principle on which the existing technique was based. Even where technique has changed (for example, where a crane is used rather than a more simple means of transportation), there has not been a qualitative increase in the substitution of labour. Where labour substitution has been extensive, as in concreting, this cannot be directly attributed to technical measures but to changes in work organisation.

Technical progress in building production occurs through technical modifications using a similar technological basis, rather than in the use of new technologies. This tendency has not changed since the second crisis in construction in 1974/5. With the decline in building demand, a reduction in the number of nearly all types of equipment has occurred except in the use of mobile cranes, very big tower cranes and the construction lifts which are used in reconstruction work. This reduction in the amount of plant relates to changes in the organisation of production. Firms tend not to own their plant but to hire it, resulting in more intensive use of equipment. The displacement of operations to other firms which do not belong to the main building trades (e.g. transportation of concrete by firms in the transport sector) makes some construction equipment appear in the statistics of other sectors. Equipment based on the use of fundamentally new technological principles, for example micro-electronics, the linking of semi- or fully-automatic machines to installation systems and sensor techniques for positioning material and tools, has not appeared. The technical means of production used in construction today have been used widely in the 1960s and were partly introduced in the 1950s.

To date, the mechanisation of building production has not eliminated the need for human intervention in the production process. In fact, the introduction of the tower crane and the use of ready-mixed concrete are important steps towards rationalisation in building production which have led to considerable increases of productivity. However, these developments are not based on new technological principles which increase the qualitative substitution of labour. Although there is a connection between the use of ready-mixed concrete and a massive modification of working operations on site, this is not the result of the application of new technology. Rather, it demonstrates the potential for achieving productivity gains using an existing technology by organising work more effectively. An exception to this is the modification of formwork. The shift to system frames involves the application of a new technological principle. In this case, the process of qualitative substitution of labour, of which workers on site are not always

Table 5.2 Structure of qualification in construction and civil
engineering[a]

	Site management, technical and supervisory staff (%)	Skilled workers (%)	Semi-skilled workers and labourers (%)	Total
1960	12	44	37	1,242,000
1963	10	43	38	1,457,000
1973	14	48	27	1,324,000
1987	17	48	19	783,000

(a) Owners, unpaid family workers, clerical staff and industrial apprentices are not
shown.
Source: see note 3.

aware, is accelerated and intensified.

An additional argument for this interpretation is the development
of the structure of qualification in construction. Until the 1960s,
there was major quantitative substitution of labour by mechanisation, but more recently there has been a qualitative change in the
skill structure of the industry. With the exception of Stefaniak's
work (1981) there are no empirical analyses of skill requirements.
Table 5.2 shows that the proportion of skilled workers rose between
1960 and 1973 and remained constant through the 1980s whilst the
proportion of semi-skilled workers and labourers has reduced considerably over the same period.

Development of Labour Productivity

The absence of technological progress in building production does
not appear to interfere with a steady increase of labour productivity.
In fact the available data indicate that labour productivity in construction has grown constantly, though different data sources are
not exactly comparable because they use different definitions and
measures. For every employee in the main building trades in the
Federal Republic it is possible to calculate an average yearly increase
in gross value added of 3.1 per cent between 1960 and 1983. The
increase of the gross value added per working hour was even higher,
with an increase of generally 4.6 per cent for the period between
1960 and 1979, reaching 5.5 per cent in the 1970s (Schneider,

Thoenes and Trageser 1982: 182–3). These rates do not differ essentially from increases of productivity in other production industries (Schneider, Thoenes and Trageser 1982: 180; Janssen and Richter 1983: 71).

These average rates probably conceal important differences between subsectors of construction and between firms of different sizes. The annual result for building performance for every employee in construction and civil engineering has grown in firms with 20–49 employees by about 43 per cent between 1964 and 1984, and by about 61 per cent in firms with more than 500 employees. In the larger firms the levels of performance per worker were higher in 1964 than they were in smaller firms in 1984.

Limitations in Extending Mechanisation

The increase in labour productivity in building production has been obtained though two important work functions that have not yet been mechanised: assembly processes and the control of construction equipment. The accuracy of assembly operations, which are mechanised and partly automated in many parts of industry, cannot be guaranteed under the conditions of building site production with existing technologies. The mechanisation of the control of the most important item of transport equipment, the crane, is impossible given the complexity of procedures on a building site. The different procedures which have to be performed by the crane include the determination of movements and its relationship to the total production process on the building site. These are complex to organise and are also contingent on conditions which cannot be foreseen. Therefore elements of these operations cannot be planned precisely in advance: this is true of the timing of an operation, its duration, spacing and sequence. With all these elements, modifications may be necessary which require human intervention. Control cannot be transferred to a 'self-acting apparatus' because the operation which has to be based in principle on a programmed set of procedures, cannot be in practice.

The limitations of mechanisation can be attributed to characteristics of building production as opposed to fixed production processes. This is due to the constraint of site position and the character of client-bound, one-off production (Angermaier 1981). In other industries the product is produced by fixed production capacities and is afterwards transported to the place where it will be used. In construction the production capacities are transportable and the product is fixed. Nearly every object of construction is an individual item because of the characteristics of the product or circumstances of production. As a result it is technically difficult to automate production as well as economically risky. In addition, mechanisation of construction is restricted to rough and simple works, whereas the use of skilled labour is an economically more convenient solution for more complex operations, timings, and in securing flexibility of work organisation. These conditions can be understood as a statement about limits to rationalisation. They also raise questions about the kinds of strategies that are needed to overcome them. Two types can be distinguished; technological strategies and organisational strategies.

Technological Strategies to Increase Productivity

Technological strategies can be identified where technical solutions are developed for assembly-type operations despite economic and technological barriers. Within this there are three starting points: (1) planning and design, (2) construction equipment and (3) the use of prefabricated parts.

1   In the planning and design phase attempts can be made to standardise components and to design buildings in such a way that they do not require more expensive production processes. There are two obstacles to achieving this; designers may oppose changes which undermine their conception of professional standards, and clients, as owners of buildings, have individual requirements. These obstacles are significant if buildings made from prefabricated components do not produce profits. In the Federal Republic prefabricated units are only popular in industrial construction where they amount to 35 per cent of construction investment.

In contrast, in housing construction, which amounts to about half of construction volume, single components, such as staircases, pillars or lintels, are used as prefabricated units. The average batch size of production in prefabricated units was of between four and six units in the mid 1970s and there is no evidence that it has increased since then (Schneider, Thoenes and Trageser 1981: 210). The firms producing them or working only with prefabricated units accounted for less than 5 per cent of annual construction performance in 1985. This does not amount to the full share of prefabrication in total construction volume, but it is a conclusive indicator.

2 Technical solutions would have to involve the development of machines which equal or excel human abilities in a number of aspects. These include chronological and spatial coordination in directing material and tools; the ability to change direction and enlarge motions; the ability to control the radius of operation; precision and reliability. Speed of work and ability to react to environmental conditions are also important characteristics. Machinery must also continue to operate, regardless of variations in temperature, vibration, dust and humidity. I suggest that the development of robots which are usable in this way under the conditions of building sites face special problems which are not comparable to those in the fixed production processes found inside factories.

3 In the absence of the development of 'self-acting machinery' of this kind, efforts will be pursued to transform the building process into an assembly process, with an increasing number of parts prefabricated off-site to be assembled on the building site. Apart from prefabricated units, formwork is the main starting-point of this development. The use of formwork systems allows some operations to be simplified so that they remain (crane-supported) manual procedures, but they become much simpler and faster to perform (Stefaniak 1981: 152–64; Janssen and Richter 1983: 72).

Organisational Strategies to Increase Productivity

The technological strategies outlined above are not expected to make a breakthrough to a new technological basis, which would lead to a further increase of labour productivity in construction. A research report of the Institute of the North Rhine–Westphalia Construction Industry notes 'the rate of mechanisation in the individual construction sectors has now obviously reached a threshold which does not make similar increases of production possible (as in recent years) by increasing mechanisation at the present level of technique (BWI 1984: 8). Other writers have concluded from the stagnation of the ratio of capital intensity in the building industry, that 'the rate of mechanisation of building production has come to a stop in the second half of the seventies'

(Schneider, Thoenes and Trageser 1982: 194).

The construction industry has for some time sought work organisation strategies which attempt to circumvent the technologial barriers of rationalisation. In construction a major constraint lies in the recognition that the flexible elements are the production facilities, which have to be organised around a fixed product. So rationalisation is achieved through restructuring, for example, by reducing ownership of fixed plant and hiring it when it is needed on site. If parts of production processes have been technically removed from the building site (for example, concrete production, steel fixing, formwork), they are now economically relocated from the company as well through subcontracting (for example, groundwork, formwork and transportation, reinforcing, concreting, brickwork) (Schneider, Thoenes and Trageser 1982: 215–16; Janssen and Richter 1983: 72). Individual parts of the production process are no longer made by the company which is engaged by the client as contractor, but by legally independent subcontractors, which are sometimes set up as independent, affiliated companies.

In fact it has been often observed in the Federal Republic that construction companies mix strategies of relocation with another strategy which leaves the control of the central production operation to them, through their control of the building of the superstructure. Concrete work is performed by the company's labour force, which allows them to guarantee completion dates and quality to the client. This is not only important in terms of possible recovery claims for faults in quality, but, in particular, for the long-term stability of business relations. Contractors retain the production facilities and labour necessary to complete the superstructure. They buy in capacity from subcontractors for specialist operations. These single operations can then be arranged and timed to fit in with the production process as a whole. In this way 'conditions of sale' can be controlled if the work is done by a number of legally independent companies. This requires more precise planning of production and constitutes another method of controlling production.

The Modernity of Building Production Rationalisation

From this perspective, the rationalisation strategies pursued in construction appear to be comparable with strategies observed in other sectors of industry. This contradicts the common observation that construction is a backward industry because of the technologies employed. Manufacturing industries are also undergoing rationalisation of industrial processes, to the extent that writers have commented on new concepts of production (Kern and Schumann 1984), a new type of rationalisation (Altmann, Deiß, Döhl and Sauer 1986) or rationalisation of systems (Baethge and Oberbeck 1986). It has been argued that the old Taylorist division of labour and organisation of operational procedures is being replaced by a new paradigm of 'flexible specialisation' (Piore and Sabel 1985). This includes the view that improvements to subprocesses and reductions in labour costs are unlikely to result in further productivity gains.

In contrast, attempts are being made to link and integrate subprocesses within the factory and between factories (in relation to suppliers). Technique therefore becomes the flexible element in production, and capital costs are reduced as well. A central concept of this developing organisation of production, as mentioned earlier, is that of 'stockless production' or 'just-in-time' production (Wittemann and Wittke 1987).

In a certain way building production has always been a form of stockless production (Janssen 1981). Strategies to increase productivity through the reorganisation of production extend existing methods for keeping the costs of production facilities as low as possible. The reasons for this are, firstly, that there are spatial limitations to storing components on the building site and they become more limited as the building progresses. In addition, it is technically difficult to utilise different production facilities fully at every stage in a sequential assembly process. Bricklayers cannot erect walls before the excavation works are completed; it is absurd to mix concrete or to fix steel before a building is planned; ceilings cannot be produced and stored while the forms for the pillars are still being used at another building site.

In manufacturing industries the new type of rationalisation is a means of producing more individualised products. There are certain similarities between these new forms of rationalisation and those found in construction, though there are three features which are specific to the technical characteristics of building production.

Firstly, unlike factory-based production processes, improvements in the use of fixed capital and an increased speed in turnover of capital cannot be achieved by improving the organisation of the flow of materials through different fixed productive units. In construction the objective is to improve the flow of the productive units around the fixed product. Consequently the question of whether to produce or to buy in production facilities tends to be resolved in favour of buying in. Therefore the costs of holding fixed stock do not arise at all.

Secondly, the problem lies in the fact that the objective of rationalisation of the whole production process must be translated into developments in its constituent subprocesses (Wittemann and Wittke 1987: 71). This problem has traditionally been solved in building production by a double strategy. The most convenient form of organisation of production on the building site has never been the 'workshop' but the 'line'. Improvement in one part of the production process is of course always economically convenient, but for production management it is convenient only if the results of rationalisation can be transmitted to the system as a whole. This is why specialised subsystems in building production have only been formed where a flexible response to the needs of the system as a whole has not been impeded. Where this principle is not met, construction firms have sought to externalise these subsystems of production. Where relatively inflexible, specialist skills are required, or where specialised production capacity must be used according to its own criteria to be economic, building firms have reacted either by removing these production processes from the site or by removing specialist functions from the enterprise.

Thirdly, in construction, rationalisation attempts to substitute labour. At the same time, labour remains a flexible element in the production process and, in this respect, has not been substituted by technique. If technique in construction contributes to the flexibility of the production process, it remains at a stage of development which continues to require human intervention. In contrast, some applications of data processing do not require it. On site, flexibility of gangs is dependent on the skills of foremen and skilled workers whilst the site manager is responsible for the integration and control of the gangs' work. Electronic data processing is available as a technique for organising and controlling the production process, but it is only used sporadically and to a limited extend. Therefore, in building production in the Federal Republic, strategies of rationalisation show elements of the model of flexible specialisation and, to a lesser extent, elements of traditional strategies of mechanisation and automation (Table 5.3).

Organisational Rationalisation and Workers' Representation

With the new strategies of rationalisation, new problems are appearing for construction workers and for the representation of their interests in firms. The same is true for the trade unions in construction (Altmann, Deiß, Döhl and Sauer 1986: 202). Two features in particular are significant in building production. Firstly, the splitting up of different production functions through rationalisation strategies into legally independent firms has the effect of dislocating workers from the firms where these strategies are developed and implemented. They are therefore unable to bargain over the consequences of rationalisation and to defend their interests. This problem can be overcome by representing workers' interests not only in the firm but at industry level as well. Secondly, the strategic points at which decisions are made about job design and the relation between wages and work load are shifted from the workplace on site to up- and down-stream phases of the labour process. Regulations protecting workers from the effects of processes of rationalisation and specialisation are unlikely to be effective unless these developments are taken into consideration. Therefore union policies protecting workers from rationalisation will have not only to focus on protecting workers from the effects of rationalisation, but also to direct strategy towards the real seats of decision-making, the point at which process of rationalisation is initiated.

Conclusion

Considered in detail, the construction industry appears to be a fairly modern industry, despite stagnation specifically in the development of technology. The organisation of production has similar elements and comparable outcomes with regard to the valorisation of capital as in most advanced industries. The growth of labour productivity has been achieved by reducing unproductive time, during which labour is not occupied on site, as well as externalising costs by hiring plant and subcontracting labour. Enterprises in the Federal Republic of Germany are forced to use a mixed strategy because technical standards, quality of work and completion dates can only be guaranteed by the direct employment of skilled labour. These strategies create organising problems for workers and their unions, which may lead to a shift in representation of workers' interests to the sectoral rather than the company or site level.

Table 5.3 Strategies of rationalisation of production in industry

Traditional automation	Flexible specialisation	Building site production
Type of production		
Market-oriented mass-production with large batches and a low variety of types.	Market-oriented mass-production with large batches and a large variety of types.	Client-oriented individual production with great variety of types.
Form of automation		
Single-purpose machine, inflexible mechanical control, high expense of resetting. Technique as inflexible, labour as flexible element of production.	Multiple-purpose machine, controlled by micro-processor, relatively low expense of resetting. Labour and technique as flexible elements of production.	Multiple-purpose and general machines, control by human labour, nearly no expense of resetting. Labour and technique as flexible elements of production.
Philosophy of the company.		
Labour as a source of interference and cost factor in production.	Labour as guarantee of production (mainly fault clearance).	Labour as guarantee of production.

Pattern of rationalisation		
Decrease in labour costs by transfer of a technological maximum of work functions to machines. Optimisation of partial processes in the firm.	Decrease in labour costs by transfer of economic and technological optimum of work functions to machines. Decrease of fixed capital costs by optimisation of the production process as a whole; optimisation of the flow of material through the production units (stockless production, just-in-time production).	Decrease in labour costs by transfer of simple work functions to machines. Decrease of fixed capital costs by optimisation of the production process as a whole; optimisation of the flow of production units around the product (hiring of plant and labour by subcontracting).
Division of labour		
High degree of division of labour, total dislocation of knowledge out of the workshop.	Partial redrawing of division of labour, partial relocation of knowledge of production into the workshop.	Low degree of division of labour, knowledge of production mostly on site; higher degree of division of labour by dislocation of production processes from site.

Gerd Syben

Notes

1. In the Federal Republic the building sector includes all trades which deal with the production, interior work, restoration and demolition of buildings. Steel construction firms and architects' and engineers' offices are not included. The building sector is differentiated into the main building trades and the finishing trades. In addition to construction and civil engineering companies, the following belong to the main building trades: carpenters, roofers and some smaller trade branches like chimney builders, and demolition firms. Painters and decorators and firms in the plumbing, heating and ventilating trades belong to the finishing trades.

2. The rate of building investment is normally used in the Federal Republic to show the state of the building trade cycle. Building investments represent expenditure on new civilian buildings. Other building expenditure such as military buildings, restoration, modernisation or architectural works are added together with these building investments to form the so called 'building volume' which is regularly calculated by the Deutsches Institut für Wirtschaftsforschung (German Institute for Economic Research), Berlin.

3. All data of economic cycles and employment are notified by Fachserie 4, Reihe 5.1, 5.2 and S 7 and 8, as well as by the publication *Wirtschaft und Statistik* of the Statistisches Bundesamt and by my own calculations based on data from these sources.

4. A quantitative increase in the substitution of labour occurs where more of the same work function is substituted. A qualitative substitution in labour occurs where more functions are substituted by technique, for example, where lifting is replaced by lifting and moving.

5. This typology of processes of production was developed in the Institut für Sozialwissenschaftliche Forschung in Munich in the late 1960s as a method of classifying work functions in empirical studies of industry. In the most common version, it consists of seven categories of process: the material-producing type, the material-preparing type, the material-changing type, the material-shaping type, the assembly type, the transportation type and the packing type.

Bibliography

Altmann, N., G. Bechtle and B. Lutz (1978), *Betrieb – Technik – Arbeit*, Campus, Frankfurt/New York

Altmann, N., M. Deiß, V. Döhl and D. Sauer (1986), 'Ein "Neuer Rationalisierungstyp" – neue Anforderungen an die Industriesoziologie', *Soziale Welt*, 37, 2/3, 191–207

Angermaier, M. (1981), 'Einige Aspekte der Rationalisierung am Bau', in Richter (1981), 69–81

Baethge, M. and H. Oberbeck (1986), *Zukunft der Angestellten*, Campus, Frankfurt/New York

Bennett, J., R. Flanagan and G. Norman (1987), *Capital and Counties Report: Japanese Construction Industry*, Centre for Strategic Studies in Construction, Reading University

BWI (1984), 'Personalstrukturveränderungen im Baugewerbe', Research Report Betriebswirtschaftliches Institut der Westdeutschen Bauindustrie, Düsseldorf

Janssen, J. (1981), 'Das Baugewerbe – ein rückständiger Wirtschaftszweig?', in Richter (1981), 27–61

Janssen, J. and W. Richter (1983), *Arbeitsbedingungen der Bauarbeiter*, Campus, Frankfurt/New York

Kern, H. and M. Schumann (1970), *Industriearbeit und Arbeiterbewußtsein*, 2 vols, Europäische Verlags- Anstalt, Frankfurt

—— (1984), *Ende der Arbeitsteilung?*, Beck, Munich

Piore, M. J. and C. Sabel (1985), *Das Ende der Massenproduktion*, Wagenbach, Berlin

Richter, W. (1981) (ed.), *Bauarbeit in der Bundesrepublik*, Pahl-Rugenstein, Cologne

Schneider, A., H. J. Thoenes and A. Trageser (1982), 'Die Deutsche Bauwirtschaft', HWWA Institut für Wirtschaftsforschung, Hamburge

Spannhake, B. (1986), 'Arbeitsbedingungen und Humanisierung in der Bauwirtschaft – Forschungsdokumentation', Research Report Düsseldorf

Stefaniak, R. (1981), 'Qualifikationsanforderungen am Bau', in Richter (1981), 138–83

Syben, G. (1987), 'Alte Probleme und neue Rationalisierungsstrategien in der Bauproduktion', *WSI-Mitteilungen*, 40, 11, 672–80

Wittemann, K. P. and V. Wittke (1987), 'Rationalisierungsstrategien im Umbruch?', *Mitteilungen des Soziologischen Forschungsinstituts* Göttingen, 14, 47–86

6

New Management Strategies and the Fast-track Phenomenon in Britain

David Gann

Introduction

This chapter addresses the implications of restructuring for management in the construction industry. The principal issues discussed are the increased use of alternative forms of contracting and the new roles of the various actors in the building process.

Fast-track techniques have been widely adopted in the construction of large office developments. The implications of fast-track for technical change, employment, skills and training are examined. There is controversy about the extent to which such techniques are more generally applicable for organising construction work, and this issue is also considered. The examples discussed here are drawn from the British construction industry, but increasing internationalisation means that the analysis is likely to have some relevance to other countries.

Background

The construction industry is undergoing a process of restructuring, arising from changes in the market, and from new competitive pressures. Prior to the recession of 1979–82, construction activity in Britain was split evenly between the public and private sectors. The rapid decline of public sector work combined with a drop in international orders and increasing international competition forced firms to look at new ways of sustaining their workloads and profitability. One outcome was the shedding of directly employed labour to reduce overheads. This led to the increased use of sub-contractors and self-employed labour, accompanied by reduction in training.

In the mid 1980s, private sector demand began to grow rapidly, particularly for commercial developments in London. This growth provided the stimulus for innovation by construction companies.

A number of conditions have provided the stimulus for changes in the techniques used to manage engineering and construction projects. Clients began to demand buildings of increasing complexity.[1] The widespread diffusion of Information Technologies (IT), and the need for greater environmental control has led to increased sophistication in building services (Gann 1989). Spiralling prices and poor project completion rates in the 1970s led in the 1980s to private-sector clients imposing more stringent contract conditions, and demanding better performance.

Contracts which impose large penalties for failing to complete projects on time are creating a highly competitive environment: profit margins are often small. Increased project complexity and fragmentation due to the rise of subcontracting, together with increasing technical sophistication, have led to growth in the number of specialist trades (Bennett and Ferry 1988). The sourcing of building materials, components and equipment from a growing international market has added to the complexity of managing many large projects.

There are two interrelated ways in which construction firms have adapted their competitive strategies to respond to these conditions. First, they have sought to extend their markets by offering different services – of particular interest here is the shift into Professional Construction Management. Second, they have attempted to reduce their costs. There are four principal mechanisms by which cost reduction can be achieved. They are:

1 To adjust labour inputs through organisational changes.
2 To adopt new materials and components.
3 To shift production off site by the use of prefabrication.
4 To utilise more capital equipment.

The move away from traditional methods of contracting has had profound impacts on skills and employment, but leading-edge firms have also attempted to innovate through the use of new technologies. We shall explore the links between organisational changes and technical changes later.

New methods of contracting include management contracting, management fee, construction management, project management, design/build contract,[2] and two-stage tender. This proliferation of new forms is an indicator of the industry's state of flux. Fast-tracking is a management technique as opposed to a contractual form. It is, however, often used in management contracting in attempts to link and overlap design and construction.

Types of Construction Firm and Management Techniques

There are two basic forms of construction organisation which apply to new build work.[3] Firms either act as speculative builders, or they act as contractors to clients. In the case of speculative building, the role of building firms is relatively simple. Without any specific purchasers in view, they buy land, and construct buildings for sale: this is often done in the house building sector. The speculative builder may employ labour directly, such as bricklayers and carpenters, or subcontract work to specialist building contractors, such as building services firms. These subcontractors then operate in a similar way to those discussed below. Speculative building does not only occur in house building but is also found in larger projects including office developments. In this case, the key role of initiating the project is usually played by a developer. The building firm then operates as a contractor to the developer.

In Britain, speculative office development often takes the form of 'core and shell' construction. The developer designs a building for occupancy by unknown tenants, and provides the basic structure and amenities, but leaves the internal finishings, or 'fitting-out', to the tenant when the building is let or sold. The tenants are responsible for fitting the building with air-conditioning, telecommunications and whatever else is required to meet their needs. Much building work is carried out directly under contract for clients, but clients can vary enormously. Some clients have considerable experience of the building process, as in the case of speculative developers, public bodies such as the Property Services Agency, and large private companies such as supermarket chains. In contrast, many clients have little knowledge of the building process. Even a client for a very large and expensive building may only employ the services of the construction industry very infrequently.

Traditional Contracting

The most common way to organise building work is in accordance with the traditional Standard Form of Contract in which a client approaches an architect to design a building.

This traditional method of contracting originates from the shift from feudal forms of organisation to capitalist forms (see Ball 1988: chapters 4 and 5). In feudal times, building work was carried out by a number of building guilds, representing each craft, and supervised by the architect. Capitalist building firms emerged when master craftsmen began to coordinate and organise the entire building process in the eighteenth and early nineteenth centuries. These firms then entered relations with clients, architects and other building professionals, as contractors. The architect coordinates and manages the design phase. Even though the professionals in the design process are usually managed by the architect, their contract is usually with the client.

After the design is completed, the architect prepares an invitation to tender which is submitted to a number of contractors. The architect may specify the use of particular subcontractors and suppliers for certain parts of the work. These appear in the tender document as nominated subcontractors or suppliers. The architect oversees building work during construction, but the day-to-day coordination of the project is in the hands of the main contractor – often the firm tendering the lowest bid. Figure 6.1 illustrates the typical organisation of this traditional method of contracting. The main contractor has a contract with the client, and the subcontractors have contracts with the main contractor.

In the Standard Form of building contract, specialist contractors are either chosen by the architect (on the advice of the consultant services engineer) and then act as nominated subcontractors, or they are selected by the main contractor through a competitive tender process. The architect may request the use of nominated specialist contractors or suppliers to undertake particular tasks for which they have a known reputation.

Ball argues that there are two problems inherent in the traditional form of contract: the division into separate contracts makes it impossible to have continuity of work across projects for a unified

Figure 6.1 Traditional contracting

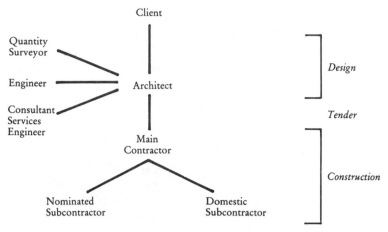

Source: Adapted from CIOB (1982).

team of management, workers and equipment; and the division between contractual obligations does not necessarily permit blame for mistakes to be apportioned fairly (1988: 80).

The most distinctive point to note about the traditional form of contract is the division between the design stage and construction. This separation often leads to long project times and has been a major factor in the shift to alternative forms of contracting. It may also lead to the design of unbuildable details, a problem that often hinders the construction process, but is more acute when the contractor and methods of construction are unknown at the design stage. Alternative forms of contract are no sure guarantee against bad design, but earlier involvement of the contractor can often forestall some of these problems.

The problems inherent in traditional contracting have sometimes led to extensive project delays, prolonged and extensive litigation and problems with quality control. This has occurred most frequently in relation to large, complex, engineering-type projects. In consequence, clients, contractors, and others involved in the building process have developed alternative forms of contract. These have attempted to clarify the allocation of decision-making responsibility between clients, designers, main contractors and subcontractors, and thereby ensure that complex projects are more manageable, are performed on time, and that blame can be easily apportioned.

A number of alternative forms of contract are now in use including management contract, management fee, construction management, two-stage tender, project management and design/build (Building EDC 1987: 57–8). These have been adopted by innovative firms at the 'leading edge' of change in the industry. Each involves the contractor in a slightly different role in relation to planning, pricing and managing the project. Each type of contract relies upon subcontracting large parts of the work. Work packages are either subcontracted to a general subcontractor who then sub-subcontracts to specialists, or they may be let directly to specialist firms. In most cases, this results in a pyramidal form of subcontracting.

Some forms, in particular project management, were originated by American firms in the early 1970s to manage and reduce costs on large complex projects such as the construction of petro-chemical plant and oil installations in the Middle East.

Below, we provide in outline some examples of these different forms, indicating the relationship between design and construction, and the role of the specialist contractor and subcontractors.

Project Management

In project management forms of contracting, a client approaches a project manager, or project management team, and requires them to coordinate and manage the complete process from design through construction to hand-over of the finished building. The project management team may be an established firm which handles various projects: or it may be set up specifically to construct an individual large building. The team, or project management firm, may possess in-house design capabilities or, alternatively, it may commission design work.

Project teams include managers who are responsible for coordinating construction. Such project managers perform similar roles to the main contractor in traditional contracting, but usually buy in all the resources required. This results in a pyramid of subcontractors. A building contractor may act as one of the subcontractors, and then sub-subcontract other work. In this case the contractor is behaving as a general subcontractor: this often occurs with building services. Figure 6.2 illustrates the project management arrangement of contracting.

Project management allows construction work to be planned and to begin before all the design work is completed, thus offering the

Figure 6.2   Project management

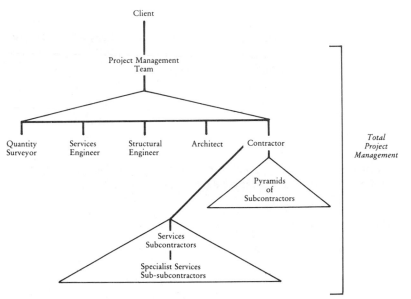

Source: Adapted from CIOB (1982).

potential for faster project times than in traditional contracting. Responsibility for the whole project is placed with one management team which often works full time on a major project. This may be an advantage if the project is particularly complex, or if the client is unfamiliar with the building process. However its success depends heavily on the management skills of each member of the project team. If the team is highly skilled, the project is likely to be run well: but if skills are inadequate, there can be disruption within a complex of mutually dependent parallel operations, and there are no effective mechanisms through which other professionals can step in and sort out the ensuing chaos.

In contrast, in traditional contracting, an architect oversees the work and the main contractor has a hierarchical chain of command from the building site back to head office which can provide skills which may be needed to supplement those on the particular project. If something goes wrong in an essentially sequential operation, other people in the management structure may be able to intervene effectively.

117

Design/Build

In some ways project management is similar to design/build forms of contract. In design/build a client approaches a firm which has full in-house expertise to design and construct a building. This leaves total project control in the hands of one firm. This firm may have their own in-house specialist contractor skills, as in the case of some traditional main contractors, or they may subcontract specialist work. In either case, the design/build firm is responsible for installation. Design/build is used mostly for the erection of largely standardised buildings where the firm can be fairly certain of the problems involved: for example agricultural sheds, warehouses or timber-framed housing may be produced in this way.

Management Contracting

Project management and design/build both attempt to speed up the building process by providing better coordination – and reducing the time taken – between design and construction. Another form of contracting, management contracting, similar to management fee, is also aimed at reducing the time of the building process, and providing a more manageable method of organisation.

Management contracting developed out of the traditional form of contracting. Its use became more widespread during the recession between 1979 and 1982, when main contractors shed many of their directly employed workers. Main contractors' function changed from managing their own workforce to managing chains of subcontractors. When workloads increased, main contractors preferred to continue to manage subcontractors rather than bear the risks of employment directly: increased specialisation meant that specialist skilled labour was often only required on site for short periods of time.

Greater coordination of the design phase, and of all the stages between design and construction can be achieved. On large projects, construction can begin before the design is completed through the use of a two-stage tender mechanism. This permits various stages to be carried out simultaneously. The management contractor can be involved in planning construction at the design stage, so reducing the risk of designing unbuildable details. Unlike project management, design responsibility remains separate from construction.

Management contracting also aims to off-load main contractors' risk onto subcontractors, who have to sign contracts which exact

Figure 6.3 Management contracting

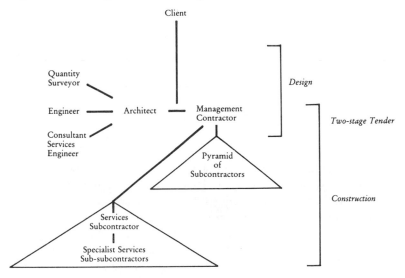

Source: Adapted from CIOB (1982).

high penalties if they fail to perform in accordance with prescribed conditions. The organisational form of management contracting is illustrated in Figure 6.3.

The use of management contracting, particularly the off-loading of risk, has drawn criticism from subcontractors and suppliers, who find themselves operating in an increasingly competitive environment. The cost of building may have also increased due to the use of this form, because each parcel of work is put out to tender. On a large project this can mean that hundreds of contracts are let, and therefore several hundred tenders produced. The costs of unsuccessful tenders are eventually passed on to clients in future projects. When tenders are drawn up for both detailed design and construction, as is increasingly the case in some specialist areas, the cost of tendering can be high.

Relationships between Organisational and Technological Change

Some of the pressures that have led to the adoption of new ways of organising the building process have been discussed, with illustrations of the relationships between the main actors in these different forms of contracts. Forces conducive to the development of new technologies, and the links between technical and organisational changes, will now be considered.

Technical change in construction is a piecemeal process. It is related to the nature of the product, to the organisation of the industry and to firms' strategies for production. The industry is not renowned for rapid technological advance, and contractors have usually only played a small part in the process of technical change.

There are signs, however, that the traditional view of construction as a conservative industry is becoming outdated. The stimulus to change discussed above, the impact of micro-electronics on the industry, and developments in Japan where competition through innovation is practiced widely (Westney 1987; Bennett et al. 1987), all point to the industry becoming more dynamic.

Some modern buildings are highly complex and involve the use of a multitude of diverse components, combined in different ways. Complexity may stultify innovation for a number of reasons. Architects and designers are often reluctant to specify new materials and components unless they have a proven track record. The risk of failure – as experienced in some of the new 'systems' used in high-rise buildings erected in the 1960s in Britain (McCutcheon 1975) – helps to perpetuate conservatism in design. Conservatism is reinforced by designers' need to take public safety into account. For example, 'building sickness syndrome', or legionnaires' disease may result from inappropriate designs adopted by specialist contractors. Such risks are very difficult to assess.

The longevity of many building components places pressure on suppliers to maintain stocks of spares. This may reduce the incentive for manufacturers to change their product ranges. Longevity and the need for durability also create problems in the testing of new materials: it is difficult and expensive to attempt to stimulate the effects of weathering on a material over a sixty-year life span. The costs involved may render the price of new materials prohibitive.

Industrial organisation also affects the process of change. Product innovations emerge mainly from designers and component and systems producers, while builders are responsible for process innovations (Nam and Tatum 1988: 143). This results mainly from fragmentation in the building production process and separation of design from production. Coupled with increased specialisation, this hampers the flow of information in the industry and is often responsible for paralysing many types of technological innovation (Bowley 1960). Professionalisation, codes of practice, standard procedures and building regulations,[4] together with traditional craft demarcation lines upheld by trade unions, create a 'locked system' (Nam and Tatum 1988: 140). When innovation occurs, diffusion is often slow. It takes time to test new component systems, and to establish training programmes to teach construction workers the skills required by new technologies. For these reasons, technological change in construction occurs in a piecemeal fashion: but small incremental changes occur continually, often the result of the tacit skills acquired by site operatives and managers over long periods of time.

Nevertheless, set against the disincentives to technological innovation are very strong pressures for change. These emanate from a number of sources including the manufacturers of materials, components, plant and machinery looking for opportunities to create markets for their products in the construction industry.

Suppliers develop new materials, components, plant and machinery to extend existing markets, or exploit new markets. These firms may already be suppliers to the building industry, or they may enter the construction market from elsewhere (such as the automobile, electronics, telecommunications, or aerospace industries) to introduce materials or components originally developed for other purposes, but with perceived market potential in construction.

Materials and components manufacturers are also instrumental in trying to introduce standardisation in their products, as this permits them to benefit from economies of scale in production. For example, standard pipe lengths and ductwork sizes are now the norm, although the application of computer control to their production processes offers the potential for some manufacturers to meet demand more flexibly.

The role of designers is very important in innovation, because although conservatism in design may retard the rate of change, some designers act as a catalyst for change through the development of state-of-the-art buildings. Changes in design philosophy, such as the adoption of dimensional coordination, have facilitated the use of modularised components. The adoption of computer-aided design (CAD) systems using databanks of standardised components has contributed to these changes.

Clients sometimes play a key role in sponsoring new developments: whether by their patronage of high-tech construction such as the Lloyds building, by responding to economic pressures, or by

stimulating faster construction work. Clients may also have requirements for special buildings, for example to house new office IT
equipment, clean-air rooms, operating theatres and laboratories, or
they may demand that buildings meet stringent energy conservation
standards.

Contractors who are involved in planning and carrying out
construction also have roles in technological change. Contractors
are more likely than speculative builders to initiate process changes.
This is because contractors derive their profits solely from the
construction process, while speculative builders have two sources of
profits – the production process and land development gains.
Speculative builders often reduce their risks by producing standardised buildings. Contractors are under greater pressure to
deploy new cost-cutting techniques in production such as prefabrication and new plant equipment: speculative builders usually adopt
such techniques after they have been tried and tested by contractors
(Ball 1988).

Over the past eighty years there have been many attempts to
industrialise the building process through the use of prefabrication
(White 1965). But the difficulties involved in integrating prefabrication and systems building into such a heterogeneous industry
have stifled many such attempts (McCutcheon 1975; Russell 1981).

It is often large contractors or innovative specialist firms in the
'leading edge' of construction which introduce new technologies
first. Large firms may find opportunities for growing even larger in
the 'Europe without Frontiers' after 1992. Large European markets
may convey advantages to market leaders who could gain significant
cost advantages by standardising components in a wider market,
using this to increase their market share still further.

So far in this chapter we have discussed changes in organisation of
the building process, and the pressures for and against changes in
technology. Construction in Britain has moved into a dynamic
phase typified by the use of alternative forms of contract, rapid
technical change through the diffusion of micro-electronics and
increased use of prefabrication, and growing international competition. We will now examine one example of new methods of
construction in more detail: fast-track.

Fast-track: Principles and Case Studies

Fast-track is a management technique aimed at cutting costs by speeding up the construction process, giving a faster capital turnover time, thus shortening the time that clients' capital is tied up in production. This method of construction is in some respects similar to the Japanese 'just-in-time' methods used to speed up manufacturing output.[5]

Fast-track owes its origin to techniques developed by US project management teams. Fast-tracking in American construction has become a way of thinking about construction, and therefore, a method for instilling performance into the workforce. In Britain fast-track means something more specific. It is a method of overlapping design and construction into concurrent processes. In fast-track, the work is divided into work packages which enables working drawings to be prepared just before they are required, rather than a long time in advance.

Work is usually carried out in phases: phasing permits construction to begin before design is completed, thus reducing total project time. It also permits partial occupation before the whole development is complete, thus providing clients with an earlier return on investment. The potential time saving due to concurrent design and construction is illustrated in Figure 6.4.

In fast-track, the main contractor is usually employed as a management contractor. The management contractor acts as a project manager, and is brought in by the client at an early stage, well before the design is completed. A strong client who understands the construction process and is prepared to enforce punitive measures is a prerequisite for proper operation of the system. The management contractor acts as a 'buyer', purchasing subcontractors' efforts, building materials and components for the client. Subcontractors usually have a direct contractual duty to the client (rather than via a main contractor). Stocks on site are kept to a minimum, and where possible, deliveries of modular components are installed immediately in their final location.

Employment of all site operatives is through subcontractors. But on many large projects, the management team often insists on the use of directly employed labour, and encourages membership of trade unions, in the belief that this helps to maintain quality and site safety. In some cases, site working rule agreements are drawn up between the management contractor and trade unions.

David Gann

Figure 6.4 Potential time saving of fast-track

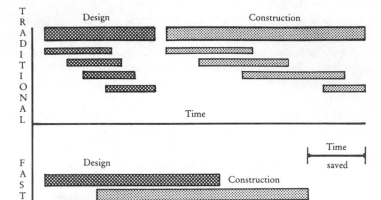

Source: Adapted from Fazio et al. (1988: 196. figure 1).

While fast-track is essentially a management technique, it has been closely linked with changes in technology. Management teams aim to reduce on-site labour to a minimum in order to achieve faster construction times. The recent shortage of skilled labour in London and the South-East has provided added incentives for reducing reliance upon site operatives. This has been achieved through the use of prefabrication wherever possible. A wide variety of prefabricated components are now used, from toilet pods, plant rooms, lifts, and cladding panels, to steel work, ductwork and new pipe joints. This reduces the content of labour on site primarily to tasks of clipping together components.

Broadgate

The Broadgate office development at Liverpool Street Station in London was the biggest site of its kind in Europe. The project began in 1985 and was due to be completed by 1990. The plan was to build 3,250,000 sq. ft of offices to accommodate 30,000 workers. The original cost of the project was estimated at £500m, but this may rise to between £600m and £800m. The size of the project made the client's threat to use competitors from overseas realistic, and so enabled them to put considerable pressure on the construction industry to change its methods.

The management contractors were Bovis-Schal, a consortium of the British firm Bovis, and the American firm Schal. Construction was divided into fourteen phases, and the design brief was for 'core and shell' offices to be fitted out by the tenant. Fast-track construction techniques were used, in so far as detailed design was carried out while the initial construction work was underway, and design for later phases was undertaken while earlier phases were under construction.

The first phase of construction was completed in one year. Six months later, tenants had fitted out and were in occupation. The total design to hand-over time was about twenty-three months. This compared with between thirty-two and thirty-six months for a conventionally built one million sq. ft office development.

Bovis-Schal were instrumental in accelerating the pace of technical change on this project, through their attempts to use as much prefabrication as possible. Initially the construction of the structure and cladding was speeded up: this having been achieved, attention was then turned to increasing the speed of installation of services and fittings. This led to the use of prefabricated cladding panels and curtain walling which included radiators. Toilet pods designed on the lines of the modules used in the North Sea oil industry and used in the Lloyds building were installed. These weighed between 8 and 11 tons, and were floated into place on 'air skates'. Plant rooms and lifts were also prefabricated on a modular basis. Victaulic joints for pipe runs were developed, which permitted connections to be made ten times faster than traditional welded joints. New lifting equipment was used to transport the components, and site managers use CAD systems and IT.

Bovis-Schal attempted to keep self-employed labour off the Broadgate site, because it was difficult to exercise direct control over them. Trade unions were encouraged because they were easier to bargain with than individuals, and they promoted safer working conditions. NEDO and the AEU recommended that the safety standards set on Broadgate should be widely adopted by the construction industry.

Other Examples

In many ways, the Broadgate development was a showcase for management contracting and fast-track construction. The management team was competent and maintained tight control over the project. The redevelopment of Canary Wharf and of King's Cross both dwarf Broadgate in size and fast-track techniques will be utilised on these projects. Many of the management team from Broadgate are involved in managing the Canary Wharf development. Other fast-track sites can be found in many of the large commercial developments in the City of London, and in London Docklands: for example, construction at the Royal Mint, a 21-month, £60m project, managed by John Laing Construction. In this case the architects specified the use of prefabricated techniques wherever possible.

Fast-track is not limited solely to office development. Cascades, a twenty-storey luxury block of flats, was built in London Docklands in just eighteen months. Fully prefabricated bathroom pods were used in this development by Kentish Homes. The project management team had the additional problem of managing heavy construction work over the heads of the first residents. There are indications that fast-tracking techniques are being adopted more widely throughout Britain on large development sites in the Midlands and in South Wales. This phenomenon does not appear to be limited solely to the boom in commercial sector projects in the South-East. There are, however, problems with the technique, but if its use proliferates it will have far-reaching implications for the future of construction. We will explore some of these below.

Implications

Fast-track techniques have some important implications for employment, skills and training. The main effect on employment will be a reduction in the use of on-site labour, compared to that used in more traditional techniques. However, if the technique becomes widely used, some construction workers will be required in prefabrication factories.[6] The length of time spent by workers on a particular project will also be reduced.

On-site skill requirements will shift towards the use of specialists rather than craft workers. Two types of specialist will be required: semi-skilled operatives involved in clipping together standardised components, and highly skilled specialists capable of installing sophisticated systems, such as micro-electronic controls. Direct employment has been sustained in some specialist firms, because the work is more technically demanding, and it permits some degree of technical change based on the skills of the existing workforce. Contract clauses imposed by large clients seem likely to maintain standards and conditions for these workers. It is, however, unclear on what basis semi-skilled specialists will be employed. A higher level of management expertise will be required to plan and coordinate concurrent processes.

The use of semi-skilled operatives means that it is possible to devise special 'limited skills' training. The Training Agency in conjunction with contractors has established an adult training centre, specifically for fast-track skills, at Poplar Baths. This is seen as the only way that local unemployed adults will be able to find work on the Dockland sites. A full craft training would be too long and too expensive for fast-track projects. A six-month to one-year programme is seen as optimal by the contractors.

Fast-track sites may make it more difficult for trade unions to organise labour, because the speed of production is increased, and because the skills involved may not fall immediately into traditional craft areas. Trade unions need to address the new divisions of labour involved and the implications for training. It appears that some project management teams seem keen to maintain unionisation because it offers bargaining machinery, and encourages site safety as well as quality of work.

Problems

Several problems have been identified with fast-track construction techniques. Fazio et al. in their comparative study of fast-track methods found that the technique could result in unexpected additional costs, and it did not always lead to shorter project duration. If the approach was to be successful, particular attention had to be paid to the following: design errors and omissions, design changes, coordination between design and construction, and coordination between work packages (1988: 206). The attempt to implement 'just-in-time' design in construction means that it is difficult to alter design decisions. It is paradoxical that the increased use of pre-fabrication often requires early design so that factories can be geared up for production of components and modules.

Fast-tracking is heavily dependent upon the skills of the management team. Unlike traditional contracting, if something goes wrong, it usually has more severe consequences because decision-making time is compressed, and decisions are often made in parallel with other operations. There are fewer links between the management team and other construction professionals that can be used in times of difficulty.

Some of the suppliers and subcontractors working on fast-track sites find that the technique is being used to squeeze more work out of them. The onus of responsibility for performance is placed on them rather than on the project manager, a situation they may resent. Contracts impose heavy damages for lack of performance. These changes have increased competitive pressures.

It is difficult for project management teams to maintain control over subcontractors, and to ensure that their workforces are appropriately skilled. For example, the work often does not require the use of traditional craft skills. This hampers training of traditional craft workers in the industry because short project times and rapid low-labour schedules make it difficult to place apprentices; and because 'limited skills training' provides people with very specialised skills. The people trained on these 'crash' programmes may find it difficult to find work subsequently in other areas of construction: this problem has not so far appeared to be high on the agenda of the fast-track contractors, nor on that of the Training Agency.

The Future of Fast-track

In this chapter we have examined some alternative management techniques which have been adopted by the British construction industry during the phase of rapid growth in the mid 1980s. We have discussed the pressures for and against technological change in construction, and we have argued that the boom has been accompanied by changes in technology, initiated by leading-edge firms. Fast-track is one technique that involves the use of alternative forms of contract as well as promoting the adoption of new technologies. Its main aim is to speed up construction.

Ironically, the fast-track methods developed in construction have been recommended as techniques for reducing costs in the computing industry. Firms in the more high-tech, dynamic IT industry have been learning that installation times can be reduced by deploying techniques developed in the more traditional construction sector (Price Waterhouse 1988: 6).

While Fazio et al. (1988: 208) are probably correct in their conclusions that few projects lend themselves to the successful application of the fast-track approach, growing internationalisation and more stringent demands from some powerful clients have created competitive pressures that could lead to more widespread use of these techniques.

The spread of fast-track techniques depends upon several conditions, including the attitude of the client, and the nature of the project. But equally important are competitive pressures within the industry, including the demand for labour. Labour-saving technical change in the form of prefabrication is being stimulated by suppliers, in particular by components manufacturers. While labour shortages persist, more clients and project management teams may be prepared to turn to these systems. There are already plans to prefabricate kitchen modules, operating theatres, and laboratory modules: this indicates that firms seeking competitive advantage in faster construction times may already envisage the spread of fast-track techniques into the industrial and domestic sectors.[7]

The prospect of 'Europe without frontiers' after 1992 will tend to increase construction trade within the European Community. Leading British contractors with experience of fast-track methods could be well placed to use this technique on large projects in other parts of Europe in the future.

Notes

1. Clients sometimes play a key role in sponsoring new developments: whether by their patronage of high-tech construction, or through response to economic pressures stimulating faster construction work. Sometimes they need special buildings to house new office IT equipment, or require clean-air rooms, operating theatres and laboratories.

2. It may be, however that the integration of design/build has the potential to provide a greater competitive edge as it could permit more efficient application of CAD/CAM systems: see Winch, chapter 8 below.

3. This chapter is mainly concerned with changes that have occurred in the organisation of new build projects, or of installation work in retrofit. The market for retrofit – the installation of new equipment in existing buildings – has been expanding rapidly in the London area. The potential market is huge (Gann 1989).

4. For example, the regulations covering the specification of copper cylinders for unvented hot-water systems stipulate that the cylinders should be of a certain thickness. British manufacturers claim that it would be uneconomic to produce

cylinders of this thickness because the adoption of unvented systems places them in competition with foreign firms. These foreign firms use different materials, and if British manufacturers are to compete effectively they will have to re-tool their factories. British manufacturers are resisting the change to unvented systems unless the building regulations are relaxed (Pat Bowen, interviews for Doctoral Thesis, Science Policy Research Unit see also *Plumbing*, Autumn 1983: 28).

5. 'Just-in-time' derives from the Japanese system of production management where production is organised so that stocks are kept to a minimum. Finished goods are delivered 'just in time to be sold, subassemblies just in time to be assembled into finished goods, fabricated parts just in time to go into subassemblies, and purchased materials just in time to be transformed into fabricated parts' (Schonberger 1982: 16).

6. Many questions have been raised about the nature of employment and skill requirements in prefabrication factories. At present skilled construction workers are often required, but processes are easier to automate in factory conditions: if the use of prefabrication spreads then the need for high-level factory skills may be reduced.

7. Kitchen modules are similar to those already sold by DIY stores, and used in large housing schemes, and it is possible that the big DIY manufacturers will also move to the production of complete, prefabricated modules.

Bibliography

Ball, M. (1988), *Rebuilding Construction: Economic Changes in the British Construction Industry*, Routledge, London

Bennett, J., R. Flanagan and G. Norman (1987), *Capital and Counties Report: Japanese Construction Industry*, Centre for Strategic Studies in Construction, University of Reading

Bennett, J. and D. Ferry (1988), *Specialist Contractors*, Centre for Strategic Studies in Construction, University of Reading

Bowley, M. (1960), *Innovations in Building Materials*, Gerald Duckworth and Co. Ltd. London

Building EDC (1987), *Achieving Quality on Building Sites*, NEDO, London

CIOB (1982), *Project Management in Building*, Chartered Institute of Building, London

Fazio, P., O. Moselhi, P. Theberge, and S. Revay (1988), 'Design Impact of Construction Fast-Track', *Construction Management and Economics*, 5, 195–208

Gann, D. (1989), *New Technology, Employment and Operative Skills in Building Services*, Science Policy Research Unit, University of Sussex

McCutcheon, R. (1975), 'Technical Change and Social Need: The Case of High Rise Flats', *Research Policy*, 4, 262–89

Nam, C. H. and C. B. Tatum (1988), 'Major Characteristics of Constructed Products and Resulting Limitations of Construction Technology', *Construction Management and Economics*, 6, 133–48

Price Waterhouse (1988), *Information Technology Review 1988/89*, Price

Waterhouse, London

Russell, B. (1981), *Building Systems, Industrialisation, and Architecture*, John Wiley, London

Schonberger, R. J. (1982), *Japanese Manufacturing Techniques*, Free Press, London

Westney, D. E. (1987), 'Managing Innovation in the Information Age: The Case of the Building Industry in Japan', *Managing Innovation in Large Complex Firms*, proceedings of INSEAD Symposium, August–September 1987, Institut Européen d'Administration des Affaires

White, R. B. (1965), *Prefabrication: A History of Its Development in Great Britain*, HMSO, London

7

Computerisation Strategies in Large French Firms and their Effect on Working Conditions

Elisabeth Campagnac

Introduction

During the last few years, faced with increasing market variability, there has been no evidence of any particular technological revolution within the building sector; this is particularly true of the execution phase of production. However, the sector has been affected by the development of information technology (IT) and its application to the conception, organisation and control of the production cycle. Thus, the development of new technologies, centred on computerisation, has primarily affected the rationalisation of the whole production process, from conception to realisation, rather than the strictly defined execution tasks, particularly those that take place on-site.

Nevertheless, some important developments have made their mark on the labour process. However, these would seem to depend more on organisational changes linked to the industrial strategies of firms, especially those of large firms, than on the actual development of techniques to be used on-site. Despite the limited nature of the spread of IT within the construction industry, as compared with other industrial sectors, there can be no doubt that computerisation is at the heart of the major organisational and social developments that have accompanied firms' strategies to adapt to market developments.

Based on the results of our research (Campagnac 1985; Campagnac et al. 1987), the aim of this paper is to identify the place of IT in the strategies of large firms in France, with particular reference to its role in the emergence of new forms of rationalisation, which take place around the search for a more integrated management of the whole production cycle, from conception to construction. The restructuring of the organisational phase of production, dictated by the search for a greater flexibility of production structures, allows the specific constraints of site-based production to be taken into account.

As Veltz has stressed, as far as the manufacturing sector is concerned, information technology is both a component of a wider process of reorganisation 'where the effects of a deep cultural and sociological crisis in labour relations and those of greatly increased economic pressures come into combination', and at the same time a vector of marked socio-organisational transformations (Veltz 1986). Amongst the characteristics he identifies, the marked ability of IT to 'extend its effects from the [local] organisation of labour to the global organisation of the whole labour process' is also in evidence within the building sector.

These characteristics make it clear that the 'social' effects of computerisation cannot be grasped through a straightforward relationship between technological change and transformations of labour relations and qualifications, but must rather be approached through an examination of the global reorganisation made possible by the introduction of IT.

Economic Constraints and Rationalisation of the Production Process

As compared to the manufacturing sector, the construction production process is characterised by three main features:

1 A lengthy production cycle, divided into many distinct stages, each of which is undertaken by different economic actors, each with different and often conflicting interests.
2 A complex system of relationships between the various interventions, which is traditionally organised around a 'vertical' and hierarchical (from planning to construction) set of relationships.
3 A discontinuous production process, which is particularly illustrated by the marked separation between the product conception stage and the realisation stage.

Each of these aspects is currently the object of profound transform-ations: the hierarchical and discontinuous pattern of traditional project management no longer seems adapted to the economic constraints being experienced within the construction sector. Since the beginning of the 1980s there is evidence of actors developing new strategies aimed at ensuring the control of a more integrated management of the production cycle. The actors most heavily implicated in these new strategies are essentially the *maîtres d'ouv-rage* (clients)[1] and the large construction companies.

The clients attempt to exercise control over the final stages of the production cycle in order to guarantee conditions of commercial-isation and maintenance, in a situation where household insolvency, the reduction of public-sector subsidies, increases in interest rates etc. all serve to increase the economic and financial risks attached to the launch of a project. The large firms attempt to exert some control over the preliminary stages of the production process in order to control cost-planning in a situation of extreme market uncertainty.

The first group tends towards the product development stages of production, whilst the second adopts an approach of designing, managing and building the construction product. Both of these approaches necessitate a requestioning of the traditional legal and economic divisions between the various stages of the production process and to the development of new forms of rationalisation, which not only affect the labour process on-site, but also the organisation and management of the whole production process.

Through such approaches, one can identify a single orientation towards a 'systems rationale', which replaces the partial rationalities of the various actors implicated in each of the narrowly defined stages of the production cycle. Once the characteristics of these new approaches have been identified, we shall establish the role played by IT, with the example of CAD (computer-aided design).

The Orientation of the Client towards 'Project-study'[2] Development

The increase in financial risk attached to the launch of property development operations has led the clients to make new demands on the *maîtrise d'œuvre*[3] in order to ensure their own control over the conception–realisation cycle. These demands cover three areas:

1 Product quality control, during both the conception and construction stages of production.
2 Control over completion delays, which has become one of the major imperatives and requires improvements in the quality of preliminary research and construction, so as to avoid wasting time due to dysfunctions or poor workmanship.
3 Control over future costs, which not only covers construction costs, but also the operating and future maintenance costs of the project.

If, during the last few years, clients have equipped themselves with computer software capable of helping them to exert some control over the economic and financial parameters of development projects, it is essentially because they hope to attain greater control over the whole of the production process through a new integration between product conception and construction. From this desire stem new demands that are particularly placed on the *maîtrise d'œuvre*. These include the integration, with the aid of reliable estimates, of the economic and financial repercussions of various technical and architectural choices made at different stages of the project. They also include the systematic development of analysis in terms of 'global cost' (investment cost + operating and maintenance costs) and the optimisation of the economic returns of the project, requiring the ability to stimulate and select technical and architectural variations at the planning stage of production. These new requirements contribute to a redefinition of the responsibilities of the *maîtrise d'œuvre*, who must henceforth be capable of collaborating with the client on questions relating to the analysis of economic risk, the technico-economic optimisation of decisions, cost and quality control. Thus, the *maîtrise d'œuvre* must be able to demonstrate some knowledge of the estimated cost-price of the project and of the elements involved in the constitution of tenders, so that contracts may be negotiated with some degree of 'cost transparency'.

In 1985, a legislative measure concerning public sector construction was introduced in France. This measure serves to stress the importance, as far as the economic impact for the client is concerned, of a transformation of project management, based on a redefinition of the responsibilities of the *maîtrise d'œuvre* (legislation voted 12 July 1985 on 'public sector clients and their relationship with private sector *maîtrise d'œuvre*'). It identifies necessary transformations as lying not in a re-allocation of responsibilities between the various actors, nor in a redefinition of their respective boundaries, but rather in the establishment of permanent relationships between actors, from the launch to the completion of the construction process. In so doing, it attempts to equip the client with the means to increase 'project study' development. However, in practice, different configurations can already be identified.

The 'Design, Manage and Build' Approach of Large Firms

Large construction firms did not wait for such legislative measures before redefining their role and modes of intervention in the organisation and management of the production cycle. The increase in economic pressure, under the two-fold effect of the depth of the recession and of an increase in competition, has led them to look for solutions in the global economic control of the construction process, with the aid of an integrated systems approach. The following four basic elements characterise the evolution of the strategies adopted by large firms:

1 A clear tendency to increase intervention in the early stages of production, to greater direct contact with the client (including the pre-tender stage of the project).
2 The search for a more integrated functioning of the whole production cycle.
3 A greater importance, within the production process, accorded to the conception stage.
4 Increased integration of structural work and finishing trades, through the introduction of new forms of site organisation at the construction stage.

Through these characteristics, the role of large firms is becoming increasingly distant from that of the traditional building contractor responsible for the study and execution of a main contract and the coordination of peripheral tasks. It is becoming closer to that of the 'design, manage and build firm', involved in negotiations concerning product conception and also the organisation and management of the entire project from the outset. This observation is corroborated by the results of a study by the Société pour L'Étude du Développement Économique et Social, which identifies one of the principal developments of the past few years as lying in the passage from the 'traditional building contractor' to what it calls the 'modern building contractor' (SEDES 1985). The latter is characterised by increased intervention in the stages preceding the execution of building work and by more direct participation in all the preliminary stages of construction (negotiations, design of buildings, technical study, cost evaluation, site preparation), as well as the search for greater control over later stages (undertaking of tasks peripheral to structural work, increased control over direct site supervision).

The development of such approaches can be explained by both the commercial and the production factors at stake.

1 Firstly, they relate to the commercial factors at stake: the sharpening of competition and the qualitative evolution of demand have generally led all firms to implement commercial innovations in order to attract increasingly scarce and specific contracts. By offering the client a proposal that covers a wide range of provisions and services, this approach has two main objectives: to enable firms to escape from a competitive system based solely on price, by stressing the advantages, in terms of time and quality control, of an integrated management of the production process; and to enable them to escape also from a competitive system based solely on tenders or auctions to the lowest bidder, so as to benefit from contracts negotiated by mutual consent. Since 1979, the number of negotiated contracts, as a proportion of all construction contracts, has risen steadily. In 1984, for example, they represented 86 per cent of the contracts signed for the construction of state-subsidised housing.

In each case, the aim of large firms is to set themselves apart from competitors, by offering the client diverse services, and to diversify the source of profit returns (through the optimisation of investments and financial management), by negotiating the financial conditions of contracts.

2 Secondly, there are production factors at stake within such approaches, the aim being to achieve a reduction of costs through the economic control of the whole production cycle. The search for economic control serves to redefine the role and the place of conception. From this strategic point of view, intervention in the early stages of the project plays an important role as it is this that enables the firm to exert some control over the parameters of conception and the regulation of construction costs, which are largely determined at the stage of pre-project proposals. Henceforth, the integration of conception and realisation would seem to

represent the main guarantee of the efficiency of the system. This means that new channels of information have to be developed and managed, in order both to ensure a certain coherence between the diverse stages of production and to guarantee a feedback of information from each site.

It is within this context of sectoral transformations and the redefinition of strategies that the development of CAD should be placed.

CAD and Organisational Change

The examination of CAD within the building sector usually takes place within approaches most frequently based on the evolution of the technical characteristics of CAD software, on a study of the potential demand for IT, or on the implications of the introduction of CAD for the professional activities of various actors, the case of architects being the most frequently studied from this last point of view.

In general, these approaches stress distinctions based on size, capacity or cost of various systems and insist on the differences in access to such systems that exist between various actors. In this project, we have attempted rather to study CAD in terms of the factors at stake with its use, with particular reference to the transformations that take place within the conception–production cycle. In order to do this, we were not only concerned with an examination of the inherent functions of CAD software, but also with the ways in which it is 'grafted' onto the strategies of various actors and where, in each case, it is used in conjunction with other types of IT. Three areas for consideration were highlighted by our research.

1 *The wide disparity of CAD within large firms as compared to the systems of other actors.* Within the building sector, there exists a wide range of CAD software. Although the application of IT to conception is still fairly limited here, and is not nearly as widespread as certain writers would have us believe, the 1980s have seen the emergence of 'general systems' of CAD, often developed within a mechanical engineering context before being applied to construction. In conjunction with these general systems of an industrial nature, numerous professionals have developed specific software

that can be used on less expensive and less complex equipment.

At the same time, the theoretical and methodological capacities of CAD have been modified, from a stage where basically it made it possible to obtain a variety of graphic representations, to one where the programmes have integrated performance and cost criteria and serve as an aid to decision-making and finally, to one where, thanks to more complex dialogue interactions and the introduction of logical reasoning through the use of expert systems, it is possible to talk of a true CAD (Zeitoun 1982).

Although on average the CAD systems used in the sector remain essentially a means of obtaining graphic representations and of organising technical and economic data, large firms, with the aid of general CAD systems of an industrial type, have nevertheless undertaken ambitious development programmes with the aim of attaining, in the words of the advertising literature of one of these CAD systems, 'total control over the act of construction, from the purchase of land to maintenance management, covering every stage from conception to realisation'.

Although, in practice, firms have yet to attain these expressed desires, there can be no doubt that large firms can already be distinguished from others not only on the basis of the strength and capacity of their systems, but also on the basis of the functions they include. These cover the preliminary and the later stages of the production process. As far as the preliminary stages are concerned, these systems have a greater capacity than CAD software used by architects, since they also cover the stages and responsibilities that are directly linked to the client. In the conception stage itself, the CAD systems used by large firms aim, with the support of complex systems of data management, to bring technical and economic analysis into association with the graphic function. However, this characteristic does not serve to distinguish large firms from engineering firms who satisfy the same objectives by drawing on different data and experience than that available to large firms. Lastly, in the later stages of the production process, some large firms have ambitions to link in with the site-management phase. There is some development of integration with CAD/CAM (computer-aided design and manufacture) within strategies based on the use of pre-fabricated components.

2 The *two-fold status of CAD in terms of the organisational changes that affect the system of relationships between diverse actors.*

An examination of the characteristics of the CAD systems developed by different actors illustrates the two-fold status of IT as far as changes that take place within the system of relationships are concerned. On the one hand, through its direct effects, the introduction of IT serves to accelerate the questioning of functional divisions between actors and the breakdown of boundaries between the different stages of the production cycle, from computer programming to realisation. With its help, actors are able to appropriate functions that had not hitherto been part of their traditional role. On the other hand, the use that each actor makes of this capacity is largely dictated by their respective interests and strategies. At the end of the day, these interests and strategies are what shapes the nature of the CAD systems.

Thus, to the idyllic image of CAD as 'computerisation to enhance communication' between all actors, one can oppose the reality of new configurations based on privileged relations between just some actors, which in turn implies, if not the elimination, at least the marginalisation of other groups. These new configurations are organised around four patterns that we have defined in the following way:

1 The client–large firm pattern, which in practice signifies the marginalisation of architects and the *maîtrise d'œuvre*. Nowadays, this pattern would seem to dominate contracts undertaken by building contractors and illustrates the will of large firms to obtain total economic control over the whole of the production process.

2 The client–engineering firm or large engineering and design department pattern: this illustrates the clients' desire to obtain the means to reinforce their engineering base, independent of the large firms. This pattern is most in evidence in large public sector and civil engineering contracts and relates to contracts involving several firms.

3 The architect–large engineering and design department pattern, which illustrates the will of certain architects to exert control over conception and to obtain total direction of the project. This pattern essentially concerns small, highly specialised contracts (timber frames or one-off housing projects) and relates to contracts undertaken separately by small firms with insufficient resources to undertake research.

4 The architect–engineering pattern, which illustrates the desire of

the latter to encroach upon markets dominated by large firms, by offering the client the guarantee of similar provisions.

Thus, CAD appears to act as the linchpin and the mainstay of a vast reorganisation taking place in the preconstruction stages of production and as the main means of obtaining the new form of market segmentation that all actors are attempting to bring about in the face of sharpening competition.

3 *The way in which CAD is grafted onto other types of information technology actually to bring these various strategies into practice.* The emergence of the four patterns we have defined above shows just how conception and the integration of the conception and the realisation stages of the production cycle currently represent the essential factors at stake within the sector. The integration of project conception and realisation takes place in the preliminary stages of the production cycle, essentially by the feedback of formalised data which may be put to both technical and economic ends.

Thus, the introduction of CAD has been accompanied by profound transformations of the system of contract management, i.e. the use of software capable of estimating future costs. In each professional body in the whole of the building sector, actors attempt to link CAD to quantitative and estimating functions. Along with traditional methods of price-fixing, new methods of estimating future costs at the preliminary stages of a project have been developed which are capable of calculating, on the basis of ratios, the economic repercussions of the project at each stage of its development. However, significant disparities continue to exist between the positions of different actors.

The methods adopted by large firms are based on interests expressed in terms of the cost of construction, taking the cost-price/sale-price differential into account, and using the firms' particular mode of price determination as a guide; the rapid estimation methods of the client depend to a greater extent on parameters capable of evaluating the consequences of various architectural options; as for the methods adopted by engineering groups and large engineering and design departments, these depend to a greater extent on interests expressed in terms of the cost of specific construction functions and in terms of the actual sale prices in operation in the market place (Bofferty 1985).

The desire to exert some control over cost-fixing from the earliest conception stage of the project leads large firms to invest to a greater extent than was previously the case in obtaining information concerning the constituent elements of costs within finishing trades (through a breakdown in terms of supplies, material and labour costs) and to integrate this information concerning operations and site practices as rapidly as possible into their systems. Thus, CAD is accompanied by the development of the rationalisation of production, essentially in response to the need to identify and to exert some control over realisation costs. Such an approach requires firms to multiply their collection of information direct from the site and to undertake frequent analysis of such data.

But this rationalisation of production is also extended to the later stages of the production cycle, to the study of the site timetable, schedule and methods. The aim here is to concentrate production combinations, taking the specific characteristics of each site into account and to identify the most appropriate forms of organisation in order to obtain some control over, or even a reduction of, costs and delay, in a situation of variability. It is here that the forms of rationalisation adopted in the preconstruction stages are carried over, through other forms of rationalisation, to the later stages of the production cycle.

The Flexibility of Productive Structures

Economic control over the entire production cycle, from conception to execution, requires a redefinition of the conditions and factors of productivity in a highly variable market situation. In this sense, the strategies of large firms have undergone important transformations and the solutions adopted have important implications for working conditions.

With the advent of the recession, the problem of adapting to generally increasing market fluctuations and variability had to be faced by the whole of the construction sector. This problem was particularly important for large firms involved in large sites and receiving huge orders based on repetitive operations. It was these same firms that had taken investment in industrialisation and labour rationalisation inspired by Taylorist principles the furthest. Faced with market evolution they had come up against excessive rigidity within the organisation of production and had experienced technico-economic dysfunctions in efficiency levels. It thus became necessary for them to adopt less rigid, more flexible forms of production, in order to adapt to the increasing fragmentation of demand, the reduction in the size of projects, the variability of products, without however jeopardising the benefits of large-scale production in terms of productivity.

However, in the course of this orientation towards more flexible production processes, large firms have had to face a certain number of specific constraints.

The first of these constraints is related to the specific character-istics of site-based production. As Campinos-Dubernet (1984a) has stressed, this type of production can be distinguished from others not only in terms of the unitary character of production, but also, to a greater extent, by the two-fold constraints of variability to which it is subject. These concern external and internal variability. *External variability* is linked to the heterogeneous nature of products (qualitative variability) and to the variability in the size of oper-ations (quantitative variability). In contrast, *internal variability*, is linked to the variation in the quantity of labour required at different stages in the production process, which implies specific constraints as far as the overlap of tasks and the distribution of the workload over the duration of the project are concerned. So, to use Campinos-Dubernet's expression, the site represents the 'nodal point of varia-bility' within the production cycle.

To this general constraint is added another that is particularly specific to large firms and which relates to the *labour factor of production*: in the face of market evolution, large firms have had to deal with the mismatch between these new requirements and the level of qualification of their labour force. This labour force is basically trained on site to carry out repetitive or highly specialised tasks. Large firms have also been confronted by the loss of auton-omy of site management and the crisis in the transmission of traditional trade skills. Thus they now bear the brunt of the specific forms of labour-force management inherited from their labour rationalisation policies implemented during the 1970s (Campinos-Dubernet 1984b). To this is added the problem of the ageing of the labour force: one of the effects of the recession has been to reduce the mobility of workers aged over twenty-five. Combined with the departure of the immigrant labour force, the low levels of recruit-ment of young workers, and especially the problems experienced in retaining them within the sector, this phenomenon has led to an increase in the average age of the manual labour force: in the first half of the 1980s the average age of manual workers in large firms was over forty.

The specific constraints of site-based production and the crucial question of labour helps to explain why large firms have developed specific, but also diverse, forms of adapting to the increase in market variability. Even over and above employment flexibility, which of course has been developed, adopting new forms (Tallard and Oeconomo 1983), within the building sector, large firms have attempted to develop forms of organisation that are capable of combining a more integrated management of construction, of structural work and finishing and a greater flexibility of productive structures. We have attempted to construct a typology of the strategies adopted by large firms, based on a distinction between the potential channels of flexibility within the building sector (Campagnac 1984) and on the modes of the management of variability to which they relate (Campagnac et al. 1985). This typology is organised around the following three dimensions.

The Industrialisation Option: the Strategy of Reduction of Variability

This option is based on the completion of fabrication before the site stage of production and basically aims to obtain greater adaptability through the use of techniques and prefabricated components, within the framework of an 'open' industrialisation. The main evolution within this option during the 1980s has been its extension to finishing trades, particularly to the technical professions (electricity, plumbing, sanitary fittings, pipe-cladding, etc.). This option is accompanied by a new form of site organisation: because the use of prefabricated components makes it possible to combine certain tasks, it involves replacing the traditional succession of interventions based on trade specialities with a division of the process according to broad 'functions' (e.g. foundations, superstructure, first fix, fitting-out and services). In theory, a single multi-skilled team which fits components and carries out associated tasks is responsible for each of these sequences.

This option relates to a *strategy of reduction of variability* that is both external (the search for the standardisation of subgroups of products) and internal (the autonomous organisation of each 'sequence' serves to reduce the problems associated with an overlap of tasks between trades and simplifies the process of reducing the number of hand-overs). The firms that develop this option usually employ their own teams of workers for the initial construction stage, i.e. they take on part of the tasks associated with the structural construction stage.

This is the strategy that introduces the most pronounced break from traditional trade qualifications and is accompanied by the appearance of a new actor: the multi-skilled builder–fitter. Here the notion of multi-skilling refers to the broadening of interventions to associated simplified tasks. The competence required centres on knowledge relating to the fitting of components and to a sufficient level of autonomy to manage the internal overlaps within each sequence.

This option is not generally associated with any particularly innovative social strategies. Although its success depends on a certain degree of stability within the labour force, the difficulties that contractors experience in finding adequately qualified teams of workers for each sequence often leads to a cascade of subcontracting, or even to the use of piece-work.

The Engineering Firm Option: the Strategy of Transfer of Variability

In this case, it is extensive investment in preliminary research and preparation, undertaken, in theory, after discussions with those responsible for execution, within an industrial 'partnership' framework, that is expected to offer a source of flexibility. The aim of such investment is to identify the technical and organisational solutions best suited to each project and to avoid dysfunctions, in order to obtain perfectly planned site progress 'without any surprises'. The large firms that adopt this option withdraw simultaneously from the execution stage of production and confide these tasks preferably to small firms or craftsmen. Thus, in order to make the most of the multiple technical and organisational options, they externalise production and reserve responsibility for its definition, optimisation and coordination. This approach is close to the 'general contractor' model.

This option can be defined as a *strategy of transferring variability onto other agents*. It is characterised both by the acceptance of a high level of external variability and by the refusal to suffer the consequences of it as far as the direct management of internal variability is concerned. It is thus this internal variability that is transferred onto other agents. This transfer onto other agents (generally of a small size) often implies a worsening of working conditions within regressive social strategies (e.g. unsatisfactory conditions of health and safety, disorderly subcontracting which sometimes leads, in practice, to the employment of pseudo-craftsmen, etc.). However, this approach has no particular consequences for levels of qualification. The small firms on which the others rely (if they do not in turn subcontract) often represent pools of qualified labour.

The Labour-force Training Option: the Strategy of Integration of Variability

This remains a minority option amongst large firms and is found in particular in those firms that had taken the labour rationalisation process furthest. It is often associated with a policy of recruiting young workers, with the aim of guaranteeing the replacement of an ageing site management, often with inadequate levels of qualification. Thus, it may be defined essentially as the implementation of policies to motivate and manage the labour force. However, in order to meet these training and qualification objectives, it is often accompanied by innovative forms of labour organisation: thus, for example, the firm takes responsibility for the whole of the production stage, from structural work to finishing and fitting-out, with the exception of highly technical tasks, and uses the same homogeneous team of workers from start to finish. The firm organises the passage of each worker through each of the tasks, whilst offering theoretical and practical training to each worker, within the standard constraints of time and cost.

This option is usually adopted on small sites. In this case, an increase in flexibility is expected to come from the combination of a new form of work organisation and the training qualifications of the labour force. The training given not only aims to give workers practical knowledge, but also to give them an insight into the technical aspects of the whole production process. At the same time, the technical knowledge taught does not relate to a single field, and even less to a 'trade'. It covers a much wider field and offers a vision of the building profession as a whole.

This option depends on a certain degree of professional qualification. It relates to a *strategy of integration of variability*. Whilst accepting the principle of external variability, firms do not attempt to reduce the consequences of this for site management, but rather attempt to adapt the site to the instability of products and processes. This option is accompanied by innovative social strategies. It is here that stress is most heavily placed on encouraging workers' motivation, responsibility and identification with the interests of the firm. This option also demands rigorous economic management of each site.

Each of these options may be simultaneously defined in terms of production interests (flexibility and reduction of site duration), in terms of work organisation, management of the labour-force or of qualifications. It would therefore seem to be within the various models of site organisation that one can identify the most significant criterion for distinguishing between various flexibility options. In the majority of cases, large firms attempt to get around constraints, either by reducing variability or by transferring it onto other groups.

Information Technology and the Restructuring of Production

The objectives which characterise the strategies of large firms, those of circumventing site production, or restructuring it under the labour force option, can only be attained by a unitary approach to organisation. The search for greater flexibility within the productive structures thus leads to the emergence of distinctive organisational models, relating to each of the strategies. Thus one can distinguish flexible organisation through integrated structures (the strategy of integration of variability), through fragmented structures (the strategy of transfer of variability), or through an intermediate situation (the strategy of reduction of variability). This distinction is not simply based on the differences between firms as far as the integration or externalisation of production is concerned. It also takes the nature of the relationships established between the firm and other productive units into account (either integration of workers into the large firm itself or into external units of production, small firms or craftsmen). The manner in which the systems of information and control are structured according to the different organisational models adopted represents a vast field of investigation and is the subject of a research project currently being undertaken (Campagnac et al. 1990).

One of the important questions relates, in particular, to the role that IT plays, under the domination of large firms, in combining an integrated management of the production cycle and flexible structures. One can hypothesise that computer techniques play a two-fold role: on the one hand, they facilitate the feedback of information from the productive structures to the large firm, thus enabling the latter to increase its awareness of the constituent elements of realisation costs (e.g. within large firms adopting an organisational flexibility approach, one can identify investment in a more sophisticated organisation of data relating to the costs of the finishing trades and in a more detailed breakdown of their constituent elements – covering supplies, materials and labour).

On the other hand, they act as a vehicle for the transmission of the rationality of large firms to small and medium-sized firms or craftsmen. The study of an experimental project relating to the use of CAD/CAM software (within a strategy of reduction of variability and transfer onto other agents) can be used to illustrate this point, whilst underlining the distance that separates the potential of IT and the way in which the unit of production or the partnership approach really works in practice (Caro 1988). Another piece of research exposes the methods of 'co-operation' that exist between large firms and the small and medium-sized firms they attempt to bring into some form of association (Bobroff and Caro 1987).

This restructuring of the organisation of production is also accompanied by a profound evolution in attitudes towards productivity. The search for improvements in levels of productivity is no longer limited to the narrowly defined execution stage of production, but rather covers the whole of the construction process. This has two consequences. Firstly, large firms look for improvements in productivity within the finishing stages of production, in which they have become increasingly involved, productivity gains are expected to come both from technical developments, in particular from the use of prefabricated components, and from the rationalisation of interventions based on a more detailed prescription of tasks and procedures. Secondly, increased stress is placed on the management of the time taken up between interventions: this preoccupation confers increased importance to the functions of planning and coordination.

Each of these flexibility options is accompanied by innovations based on new forms of site organisation, of which the objective is to reduce the duration of site execution, as far as both the structural and the finishing stages of production are concerned. However, this reduction in site duration is not expected to come from the contraction of a specific phase of execution, but rather from a revision of the organisation of the entire process. In each of the options studied, attention is primarily paid to the constraints associated with the relationship between various tasks and to better management of task overlap. Productivity gains are not expected to come from the reduction of time spent on individual operations, but rather from a reduction of time linked to the articulation of various tasks.

Although each of these strategies identifies new sources of productivity within the site stage of production, these gains are defined less directly in terms of technical innovations than in terms of organisation and of the development of new capacities within the labour force. Along with the development of various forms of multi-skilling, a significant proportion of the productivity gains are expected to come from the individual and collective 'motivation', 'autonomy' and 'responsibility' of the manual labour force. The development of these capacities aims to reduce the unplanned non-productive slack periods, linked to the regulation of production, i.e. the 'connected time' (Dutertre 1988), either through an improvement in the management of the sequence of tasks or through a reduction of poor workmanship, based on a quality controlled productivity.

Conclusion

The evolution of qualifications, of types of employment and of working conditions would therefore seem to be more directly determined by the organisational strategies of large firms and by their management of variability than directly by the introduction of IT. However, the latter represents a necessary condition for the whole of these organisational transformations. In fact, the changes made possible by its introduction are not limited to the internal sphere of the firm. Through its capacity to break down the functional divisions within the production cycle and to affect the entire production process, the introduction of IT would seem to act as a positive factor in the extension of the interests of large firms over and above the strict legal limits of the firm.

Also, it would seem that the orientation of large firms towards a 'systems rationale', has been accompanied, within the building sector, as in industry, by the destabilisation of types of management based on the normalisation of duration and a procedural definition of tasks. Does this mean that the specific types of work rationalisation that had been developed within the building sector until now, based on the principles of time-saving, are likely to be called into question (Campinos-Dubernet 1984a)? There does not seem to be a single, straightforward answer to this question.

On the one hand, it is true that the very instability of the market has made the application of a prescriptive approach and of control of tasks and basic costs increasingly difficult. In the face of such limitations, the notion of a 'function', of a goal to be reached, has now replaced the notion of a strictly prescribed task. The control of site duration is less a question of the management of a stable succession of stable sequences of labour than of the management of unforeseeable circumstances within periods of more or less diffuse control. This would explain, in particular, the search for more participative approaches to workforce management in order to compensate for the inherent limitations of a normative approach. On the other hand, it is impossible to ignore the fact that, far from being abandoned, the control of tasks and basic costs is being increased and has tended to be extended to cover the whole of the production process.

It would therefore seem that the neo-Taylorist types of labour rationalisation that Campinos-Dubernet has identified within the building sector, are currently still being implemented, but are simply used in interaction with new groupings of tasks and new types of compromise between autonomy and control.

Notes

1. The term *'maître d'ouvrage'* has no exact equivalent in English. It refers to the body or person who decides to commission the building, choses the proposed solutions and guarantees, or arranges the guarantee, of its financing. This term has been translated as 'the client' in the text.

2. The French term *'ingénerie renforcée'* refers to the technical, economic and sometimes also the financial studies made in the planning phase of production.

3. The *'maîtrise d'œuvre'* is the person to whom the *maître d'ouvrage* entrusts the conception, study and management of the works, and eventually the coordination of specialised technicians. Since there is no equivalent in Britain, the term *'maîtrise d'œuvre'* has been retained in the text to refer to this function.

Bibliography

Bobroff, J. and C. Caro (1987), *Démarches ensemblières; quels modes de coopération avec les petites et moyennes entreprises?*, École Nationale des Ponts et Chaussées/Ministère de l'Equipement Paris

Bofferty, A. (1985), *Méthodes informatisées d'estimation des prix et des coûts du bâtiment*, École Nationale des Ponts et Chaussées Paris

Campagnac, E. (1984), *Construction et architecture: métiers en mutation?*, Édition l'Équerre Paris

—— (1985), *Le marché du petit collectif: les nouvelles stratégies des acteurs de la construction*, École Nationale des Ponts et Chaussées/Éditions du Plan-Construction. Paris

Campagnac, E., M. Campinos-Dubernet and M. Tallard (1985), 'L'intervention des salariés dans le Bâtiment et les Travaux Publics: un enjeu dans les stratégies économiques?', *Critique de l'Économie Politique*, 32, p. 114–56

Campagnac, E., A. Picon and P. Veltz (1987), *La Conception Assistée par Ordinateur dans le Bâtiment: enjeux et stratégies des acteurs*, École Nationale des Ponts et Chaussées Research Report Plan-Construction. Paris

Campagnac, E., J. Bobroff and C. Caro (1990) '*Approches de la productivité et système de gestion dans les grandes entreprises de construction*', Éditions du Plan Construction, Paris

Campinos-Dubernet, M. (1984a), 'La rationalisation du travail dans le BTP: des avatars du taylorisme orthodoxe au néo-taylorisme', in M. Pastre and O. de Montmolin, *Le Taylorisme*, Éditions Maspéro, Paris

—— (1984b), *Emploi et gestion de la main-d'œuvre dans le BTP: mutations de l'après-guerre à la crise*, Dossier du Centre d'Études et de Recherche sur l'Emploi et les Qualifications n° 34, La Documentation Française, Paris

Caro, C. (1988), *Mise en place d'une démarche de partenariat à partir d'une procédure informatisée*, École Nationale des Ponts et Chaussées/Ministère de l'Équipement. Paris

Dutertre, C. (1988), *Flexibilité organisationnelle et productivité dans le Bâtiment*, Éditions du Plan-Construction Paris

SEDES (1985), *Étude sur les modes d'exécution des travaux de bâtiment collectif dans les grands groupes de BTP*, Ministère de l'Équipement. Paris

Tallard, M. and H. Oeconomo (1983), *Travail précaire et politiques de gestion de la main-d'œuvre dans le BTP*, Centre de Recherches, d'Études et de Documentation sur la Consommation Ministère de l'Équipement. Paris

Veltz, P. (1986), 'Informatisation, organisation et gestion de la production industrielle', unpublished article

Zeitoun, J. (1982), 'La variété des approches de la Conception Assistée par Ordinateur en Architecture: problèmes actuels', in *Informatique et cybernétique*, Mimeo Centre Scientifique et Technique du Bâtiment. Paris

Part III

Technological Change and its Consequences for Work

8

Computer-aided Design and Project Management in the British Construction Industry

Graham Winch

Introduction

CAD/CAM (computer-aided design and manufacture) technology is now becoming widely diffused in the production industries. The design and manufacture of micro-electronic circuits would be impossible without it, but even in the traditional batch metalworking industries, it is an established feature in many large companies, and central to their technology strategies. The definition of the various elements of this technology will be discussed later in this paper. The analogous technologies to CAD/CAM within the construction industry are CAD and Project Planning Systems (PPS); again, their precise definition will be discussed later.

The diffusion of CAD and PPS in the construction industry has not been as rapid as CAD/CAM in metalworking. A recent survey of medium to large firms in the industry found that 62 per cent of architectural practices and 71 per cent of civil/structural engineering practices were using some form of CAD software, but that the use of PPS was a lot less common, apart from amongst civil engineering contractors (CICA 1987). A survey coordinated by Leeds College of Building (1986) found that 19 per cent of medium and large building firms contacted (employing more than 40 people) used some form of PPS. Most importantly, in terms of the comparison with the metalworking industries, there have been very few attempts to link design and draughting systems with either quantity surveying or project management software to form a fully fledged

CAD/CAM type system. Day et al. (1986) found no cases of data exchange amongst their case studies. A survey by the Building Services Research and Information Association found that 27 per cent of their sample of design practices had exchanged data between systems, but that the bulk of these exchanges were not interactive, and involved architects accessing land survey data (Wix and McLelland 1986), a function not central to the construction information flow.

A number of reasons for this relatively poor diffusion may be proposed. The organisation of design firms on a partnership rather than a limited liability basis probably inhibits capital expenditure due to difficulties of access to capital markets. The recent trend for design practices to become incorporated has been partly encouraged by the necessity to raise relatively large amounts of capital to purchase CAD systems. Secondly, contractors tend to favour maximising their flexibility rather than reducing production costs in their operating strategies (Ball 1988: ch. 5). They are therefore reluctant to make the fixed capital investments which would tend to restrict their freedom of manoeuvre but increase their productivity. Thirdly, most construction firms are relatively small. So, CAD and PPS can represent a relatively large fixed capital investment in relation to total turnover in a sector used to low fixed overheads. It therefore presents a significant risk should it go wrong. However, the recent advent of cheap personal-computer based CAD and PPS software is rapidly reducing this problem. This paper will present a further factor which, it will be suggested, inhibits the diffusion of CAD and PPS technology – the organisation of the industry into a contracting system characterised by the market allocation of resources to the construction project.

The paper will first outline the features of CAD/CAM technology which characterise it as an integrating technology. Then it will briefly discuss the organisational implications that this characteristic has had in the batch metalworking industries, before the structure of the construction industry is assessed in terms of its inhibition of the organisational forms which have favoured CAD/CAM implementation in batch metalworking. Thus it is assumed that the same potential for an integrated CAD/PPS system exists in construction as has been proven for CAD/CAM in metalworking. The conceptual framework for this analysis will be drawn from Williamson's transaction cost analysis (see Williamson 1975; also Eccles 1981 and Winch 1989 for applications to construction).

Figure 8.1   The production information flow

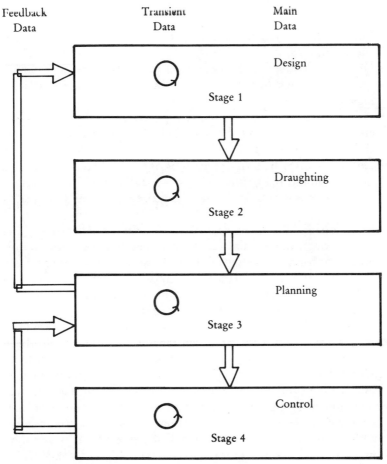

Source: Winch (1988).

CAD/CAM: an Integrating Technology

The production of any goods (as opposed to services) necessitates a flow of both information and materials, starting with the original conception of the product right through to its sale. The information flow can be divided into four distinct stages, as shown in Figure 8.1. This model of the production information flow is discussed in

157

greater detail in Winch (1988). At each stage, the characteristics of the product are specified at increasingly greater levels of detail thus:

1 Design – the overall conception of the product has to be outlined and clarified, and then put into a communicable form.
2 Draughting – the detailed characteristics of the product must be specified in order to eliminate ambiguities once material processing starts.
3 Planning – the sequence of material processing must be specified, costings calculated and the availability of raw materials, labour and plant established.
4 Control – once material processing is under way, its progress must be monitored against the criteria laid down in the previous three stages in terms of specification, programme and budget.

Traditionally, the main data flow of product information has passed through these four stages by verbal and paper communication in the form of meetings, informal discussions, drawings, bills, and schedules. Transient data flows (Wix 1986) are those flows of information which do not enter the main flow between stages – only their output does. For example, design analysis routines and stock control procedures do not enter the flow as such, but are restricted to stages 1 and 4 respectively. Traditionally, the flow has also been linear in that it moved sequentially through the stages without any feedback loops – it was restricted to the main and transient data flows – and information generated in the downstream stages such as production planning data was not incorporated in upstream decisions such as design. In terms of Thompson's (1967) typology the 'interdependence' between the stages of the product information flow traditionally took the form of 'sequential interdependence'.

Computers have become increasingly used at various points in the information flow to 'mechanise' the process since the 1960s, starting in the micro-electronics and aerospace industries (Arnold 1983). The earlier use of computers was in transient data flows within each section such as finite element analysis in stage 1, and part programming in stage 3. During the 1970s, the possibility of links between the stages began to develop, and by the beginning of the 1980s, CAD/CAM had emerged as a distinct technology. There is now a significant diffusion of computers into the production information flow in both the metalworking and construction industries, a diffusion made more significant by its concentration amongst the more competitive firms in each sector.

The nomenclature of this new technology is inconsistent: for instance Boaden and Dale (1986) discuss the wide variety of definitions of the term computer-integrated manufacture (CIM). For the purposes of this paper, the following terms will be used. Computer-aided design, or computer-aided engineering, or computer-aided architecture (CAE/A) involves the use of computers in the first stage for design analysis and simulation. Stress analysis software in structural engineering, heat loss calculation packages in services engineering, and wire-frame 'walk throughs' in architecture are examples of construction use here. The most familiar application in construction is to stage 2 – computer-aided draughting (CAD) for the detailing of floorplans, pipe-runs and so on. An example of this application is described in detail in Buchanan and Boddy (1983: ch. 9).

Downstream, the computerisation of the production information flow can be divided into computer-aided production planning (CAPP), and computer-aided production control (CAPC). Computer-aided manufacture (CAM) usually refers to a subset of CAPP concerning process planning procedures such as part programming, the preparation of bills of materials, and tool design. When integrated with a CAD system on a network basis it forms a CAD/CAM system. Resource planning systems such as MRP 2 are usually implemented on separate systems. The integration of resource planning and CAPC is usually called computer-aided production management (CAPM). In construction, PPS can be used for various stage 3 functions, in particular, network analysis with packages such as Hornet and the preparation of bills of quantities.[1]

A considerable variety of benefits for management have been cited for CAD/CAM implementation – productivity gains, product lead-time reductions, the ability to design ever more complex products, and improved design quality, for instance. However, the essence of these benefits is the creation of a design data base at stage 1, which can then be accessed and developed at subsequent stages. Most of the direct productivity improvements reported for CAD/CAM come from the elimination of redrawing and ease of access to design standards. ACARD (1980) also report a number of other benefits which essentially constitute the advantages of a uniform set of data from which everyone can work, and the fact that work output is stored and ready for others to access.

The development of a common data base means that those who access it downstream have an interest in the way in which it is generated upstream. As Atkin and Gill point out, 'the way in which designs are created largely determines how other computer-based systems interpret designers' intentions' (1986: 562). This means that the information flows are no longer sequential, but contain significant feedback loops from the later stages to the earlier ones. These are shown on Figure 8.1 as 'feedback data'. Thompson (1967) has described these sorts of linkages as 'reciprocal interdependence', in which coordination is achieved through mutual adjustment between the different elements of the organisation. It is in this sense that we can call CAD/CAM an integrating technology, for its effective implementation profoundly alters the way in which information flows around the production organisation, and hence affects the relationships between the various functions within the structure of the organisation.

Organisation Design and CAD/CAM: the Case of Batch Metalworking

Some firms in the metalworking industries have made considerable progress in integrating the computer systems used in stages 2 and 3 into single CAD/CAM systems; stage 1 activities are now often included as well. A perennial question of organisation design is whether to organise by function or product. Functional organisation, it is argued, allows maximum utilisation of resources, such as expensive machinery and scarce skills. Product organisation, on the other hand, greatly eases coordination between the various elements of information and materials processing, and encourages more flexible and responsive organisations. Functional organisation makes coordination difficult, and product organisation threatens resource utilisation (Mintzberg 1979: ch. 7). In practice, batch metalworking firms have faced both ways in their response to this dilemma. The engineering side covering stages 1 and 2 has tended to be organised by product, thereby easing customer liaison and aiding responsiveness to market pressures, while the manufacturing side covering stages 3 and 4 has tended to be functionally oriented in order to achieve economies of scale. Such firms have only been able to face both ways in this manner because the sequential interdependence in the information flow has allowed the two halves of the organisation to remain largely uncoupled (see Winch 1983 for a more detailed discussion).

The problem posed by CAD/CAM implementation for such organisations is that it integrates across the engineering/manufacturing divide. Now that the information flow is reciprocally interdependent, the two halves of the conventional batch metalworking firm can come into conflict due to their mutually incompatible organisation structures. Various organisational linkage mechanisms have been developed to cope with this problem (see Ettlie and Reifeis 1986), and the solution adopted in some batch metalworking firms has been that of the matrix organisation in which product managers within the manufacturing function also report to the product divisions within the engineering function.

Organisation Design in Construction

Presenting the initial results of a comparative study of the organisation of construction sites in the Federal Republic of Germany, France, Italy, and the United Kingdom, Campinos-Dubernet distinguished between two models of contractor operating strategy.[2] She identified the *internalisation of variability* ('acceptation de la variabilité') strategy as being prevalent in France and Germany, where the construction company tends to own the plant and employ directly the workforce required for the project. The *externalisation of variability* ('extériorisation de la variabilité') strategy, she identified as being prevalent in Italy and Britain, where construction companies tend to hire the plant and casualise the workforce. She also identified the distinctive duplication of project control management in Britain through the main/management contractor for programme and process control, and the quantity surveyor for cost control which leads to comparatively high levels of project management overhead.

The strategy that Campinos-Dubernet has identified is a part of the recent development of what Bowley (1966: sect. 4) called 'the system' of contracting in the British construction industry. Traditionally, this contracting system is characterised by the commissioning of an architect by the client on a non-competitive basis, who then recommends the appointment of services and structural engineers and other specialist consultants. A quantity surveyor is also appointed separately to advise the designers on cost, and prepare contract documents for tendering and valuation purposes. This hierarchy of professions dominated by the architect is what

Bowley called 'the establishment'. The construction firm – the main contractor – is then selected by competitive tender, usually on the basis of the information provided by the quantity surveyor. The main contractor then either selects specialist subcontractors, again usually on the basis of competitive tenders, or chooses to carry out the work internally using direct employees or labour only subcontractors. With the exception of the specialist subcontractors all the firms involved usually have separate contracts with the client.

The model we now have of the traditional organisation of the British construction industry is of a set of projects initiated and capitalised by the client to which firms allocate resources according to the terms of their own individual contracts with the client or the contractor. Each firm has a portfolio of projects in which it is engaged, and each project is a coalition of firms. Within this 'project coalition' (Winch 1987) each firm is trying to meet both individually its own goals as an independent organisation and jointly the goals of the client as the customer for the project. This pattern of interdependent firms and projects is illustrated in Figure 8.2. Clearly, there is no necessary reason why the individual and joint goals within the project coalition should be compatible. The project, then, consists of a series of market transactions as each firm allocates resources of plant, labour and materials to the project in accordance with the terms of its contract.

Within this contracting system, each of the firms tends to be organised on a basis of pooled interdependence (Thompson 1967), where each project group does little more than share overheads with its colleagues. Thus, the architectural practice will be organised into a group for each project, while the contractor will be organised into a set of contract/project managers, each supported by a dedicated site management team. In the traditional contractors, there were some functionally organised elements such as the joinery workshop and the plant department shared between projects, but the increasing extent of specialist subcontracting has significantly reduced this influence. In contrast, specialist subcontractors, particularly those committed to task-specific plant and expertise, may tend towards a functional structure.

More recently, traditional contracting has tended to be replaced by management contracting (CIRIA 1983). Here, the management contractor is appointed on a fee basis similar to the architect and consultants with a direct contract with the client. The programme of works is then divided up into packages which are let on a competi-

Figure 8.2 Projects and firms in construction

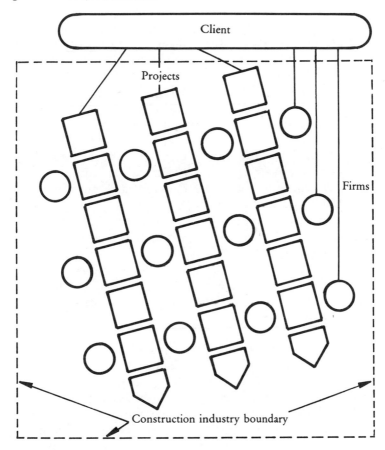

Source: Fellows et al. (1983).

tive tender basis to works contractors. Their contract may be with either the client or the management contractor. Most management contracting firms are divisions of existing large construction firms whose construction divisions often act as works contractors to competing management contractors. Thus the large construction firms in Britain are becoming increasingly intertwined in market relations of contract and subcontract as well as competition. This modern version of the contracting system seems to predominate on large new build projects.

Graham Winch

Organisational Integration in Construction

The traditional production process in the British construction industry broadly follows the Royal Institution of British Architects' *Plan of Work,* and is a classic case of sequential interdependence in terms of the flow of design information. Morris (1973) provides a model of this information flow which is notable for the absence of feedback loops within the flow. Most construction projects in Britain are still organised with information flows on this model. Over the last twenty years a variety of alternative models has been developed, all of which attempt to use organisational linkage mechanisms – most notably project management techniques – to introduce an element of feedback into the sequential information flow. The most sophisticated of these on the very large projects implement matrix type project organisation structures (see Morris 1983), and these are also the type of project which may be able to bear the overhead cost of integrated CAD and PPS and the associated dedicated electronic data transfer technology. However, the vast majority of project organisations cannot hope to achieve the level of integration offered by the type of matrix organisation which has been found to be beneficial in batch metalworking due to their temporary, short-term nature.

Within this information flow, the various functions of the process are organised into economically distinct firms which relate to each other through transactions governed by contractual relations in a market. This is in strong distinction to the usual model in metalworking where the transactions within the main data flow are almost entirely under the ambit of a single economic unit, or firm, and transactions are governed by hierarchical relations. Thus while the same distinction between design and production exists as in metalworking, the links between the architects and associated consultants on the one hand performing stages 1 and 2, and the contractor and subcontractors on the other performing stages 3 and 4 are of a market rather than organisational nature.

This picture is made more complex in the British contracting system by the quantity surveyor performing a contractually independent role at stages 2, 3 and 4 directly on behalf of the client. The quantity surveyor, respectively, advises on project cost, prepares bills of quantities, values variations and settles the final account. Further, within stages 1 and 2 there is additional fragmentation because design practices are rarely multifunctional, and so engineering design is usually carried out by contractually independent consultants. Similarly, within stages 3 and 4, the actual construction is normally let to specialist subcontractors. Attempts to create organisational linkage functions within this maze of market relations has encouraged yet another firm type to appear – the management contractor.

CAD and PPS in the Construction Process

The problem posed by this network of market transactions within the production information flow in construction is that the development of reciprocal relations of interdependence is extremely difficult. If we turn again to Figure 8.1, we can see that, in construction, the key data flow from stages 1 and 2 to 3 and 4 is through a market transaction between the architect and contractor, rather than the hierarchical transactions normal in batch metalworking. Secondly, the fragmentation within stages 1 and 2 generates a further set of market transactions which would normally be governed by hierarchy in a metalworking firm. The fragmentation in stages 3 and 4 between the main contractor and subcontractors, or the management contractor and the works contractors, also creates problems. In particular, the process expertise required for the effective development of network modules is located with the individual sub/works contractors, rather than with the organisation responsible for overall planning – the main/management contractor. This can make the development of comprehensive project network analyses very time-consuming and inefficient. Similarly, the cost data which is required for design decisions which facilitate the effective use of resources is possessed by the sub/works contractors and is only available to the quantity surveyor as price data which inevitably contains distortions.

This pattern of interdependent transactions within the project's production information flow governed by the market poses severe problems in making the organisational adjustments required for the effective implementation of CAD and PPS.[3] In particular, problems arise at five points.

1   The technical problem of achieving compatibility when each member of the project coalition will have made its investment decisions in CAD and PPS technology independent of the other

members. This problem is now starting to be tackled by the industry which has set up working parties on interface standards. It is not, in principle, insurmountable, but the process of negotiation of industry standards is much longer and more difficult than the merely administrative one whereby a single firm ensures that all its in-house systems are compatible. Wix and McLelland (1986) provide a very useful discussion of these issues.

2   Standard forms of contract for governing the market relations between the members of the project coalition contain strict routines for the documentation of the progress of the project. Electronic data transfers do not necessarily meet these requirements. The temptation, and indeed legal necessity, will be therefore to replicate the electronic flow of information with a traditional paper one, thereby reducing the cost and time benefits of CAD and PPS. Again this is not insurmountable, but can be predicted to take a long time to resolve, and any new standard arrangement can still be overriden by the common law of contract,[4] which cannot be the topic, as such, of negotiation between the parties. Here the implementation of CAD becomes linked with the vexed issues of design liability and the ownership of data bases.

3   Firms in the industry tend to justify capital investment on the basis of a single project, rather than their overall cost structure. The uncertain and lengthy return period for CAD and PPS technology means that it can only be justified on this basis on the largest of projects. However, until the interface problem identified above in section 1 is resolved, this is the only way that the downstream integration benefits can enter the justification. In the absence of downstream benefits, CAD can usually only be justified on drawing productivity; if it is justified on that basis it will tend to be used on that basis, and other benefits lost.

4   Each of the members of the project coalition processes the information it requires about the project in idiosyncratic ways. Walker has argued that

> information produced during the construction process at present relates to the specific needs of the information generator rather than being useful to the process as a whole. . . . What is needed is an information system in which the data are transposable between contributors rather than needing to be translated. This would require a fundamental rethink of the way in which information is classified, structured, co-ordinated and prepared. (1984: 93)

In particular, Atkin and Gill (1986) propose that designs should be created as collections of components to allow the best to be gained from an integrated CAD and PPS system.

5   The issue which is perhaps at the root of these previous four is that there is no agency which can push through the type of organisational changes which have been so important in the effective implementation of CAD/CAM in metalworking and other industries. In particular, it is difficult to see where the organisational drive to implement the kind of reciprocal linkage mechanisms described earlier can come from, and the imposition of such linkages upon the existing informal project matrix would probably generate a contractual nightmare. While management contracting is an important attempt to implement organisational linkage techniques across market relationships (see Winch 1987), it can do little to resolve the problems already identified in sections 1 and 2 above. Moreover, the second aspect of management contracting, that of dividing the actual construction up into packages and seeking competitive tenders on that basis further fragments the construction process and, arguably, would undermine any advantage that might be gained through the management contractor's linkage function.

Organisational Alternatives in Construction

The previous discussion has shown the way in which the traditional contracting system, even in its contemporary management contracting form, inhibits the implementation of integrated CAD and PPS systems. However, at least two other distinctive forms of organisation exist in the construction industry – speculative housebuilding firms, and design and build firms. From the perspective of the arguments presented in this chapter, they both have one significant advantage over the contracting system – many of the main transactions within the production information flow are brought within hierarchical rather than market governance.

Speculative housebuilding firms take responsibility for all stages of the production information flow from design conception to the programming and control of site activities. However, there does not appear to be any evidence that such firms have made any greater progress with integrated CAD and PPS systems than firms within the contracting system. This may be due to the relatively low design content of their product, and their traditional lack of concern for construction efficiency. The main source of housebuilders' profits lies in the development of land, rather than construction itself, and this reduces the competitive pressure for technological innovation (Ball 1983: ch. 6). In any case, this is clearly a specialist type of firm, and the model cannot be applied more generally.

Design and build firms have been increasing market share during the 1980s. Such firms, at least in their integrated forms, again have the advantage of bringing the main transactions along the production information flow under hierarchical governance. Also known as 'package dealing', design and build was strongly advocated by Bowley (1966: ch. 16) as a way of circumventing many of the weaknessess of the traditional contracting system. Whatever their benefits in general terms, such firms do seem to have made greater progress with integrated CAD and PPS implementation than the rest of the industry. It can plausibly be suggested that as integrated design and build firms move up the learning curve of integrated CAD and PPS, they will gain competitive advantage over firms operating within the contracting system in both its traditional and modern forms.

Many of the arguments made here for design and build firms also apply to multidisciplinary design practices. However, while such practices can achieve hierarchical transaction governance within stages 1 and 2, the retention of a separate quantity surveyor and of the practice of competitive tendering for selection of the contractor means that there is no additional integration between stages 1 and 2 and 3 and 4. Perhaps when such practices start to include project managers amongst their disciplines greater progress can be made.

Conclusions

It has been the contention of this paper that the present organisation of the British construction industry into a contracting system will greatly inhibit the implementation of integrated CAD and PPS systems. The traditional contracting system in the British construction industry has nearly two centuries of history and vested interest behind it. From the point of view of the implementation of CAD and PPS systems, and especially their integration, this system is characterised by a fragmentation into market transactions within the production information flow. Over the last twenty years a modern form has evolved around the growth of management contracting, but this has done little to remove these barriers. Indeed, there is, if anything, greater fragmentation and reliance upon market governance of transactions within the production information flow in the modern system than in the traditional contracting system. While heroic efforts will doubtless be made, it is unlikely that significant benefits from the implementation of CAD and PPS will be realised except on the largest projects which can absorb the entire cost of the system and the associated dedicated electronic data transfer technology. The key contention here is that the barriers to implementation are more organisational than technical. An illustration of this point is given by Day et al. (1986: 21) when they cite the case that integrated draughting and quantity surveying software is not being used, despite full technical compatibility, due to the architect's concern not to enter the professional preserve of the quantity surveyor in order to safeguard both good interprofessional relations and the terms of professional liability insurance.

It can be reasonably concluded from this analysis that in order to achieve the promised benefits of integrated CAD and PPS in terms of improved project quality and performance, 'drastic innovations in the structure of inter-organisational and professional relationships will be necessary' (Day et al. 1986: 30). The analysis has used Williamson's transaction cost framework to show the organisational roots of the problem and to facilitate comparison with the metalworking industry which is organised on a different basis. This comparison has shown the importance of the hierarchical, as opposed to market, governance of transactions for the relatively successful implementation of CAD/CAM in metalworking. Even there, hierarchical governance only creates the conditions for the development of the stronger forms of organisational linkage mechanism which facilitate CAD/CAM implementation. Many metalworking firms are having to make significant adjustments to their operating structures and patterns of work organisation to accommodate CAD/CAM technology.

The example of the metalworking industries gives a clue as to one possible way forward for the construction industry. Arguably, the diffusion of the technology through the main bulk of the industry will depend on a restructuring of the industry towards the 'design and build' type of organisation. Even here, though, much of contemporary design and build practice takes more the form of a reordering of project coalition relationships than a genuine organisational integration. In this context, it is interesting to note

Campagnac and Caro's (1987) observation that in France, contractors are using CAD/CAM as a weapon in their strategy of vertically integrating up the information flow into the design process.

Notes

1. Computers are also rapidly diffusing onto construction sites run by management contractors in data base, spreadsheet and word-processing applications.
2. 'Des rigidités de la flexibilité: le BTP dans quatre pays européens', presented at the Colloque Europe et Chantiers, Paris, September 1988. See also Campinos-Dubernet and Grando (1988).
3. The Implementation of CAD/CAM Project at Warwick University, which started in January 1988, is undertaking a series of case studies of large construction projects in an attempt to establish the extent to which market-based contract relationships are barriers to CAD and PPS implementation, as well as address the issues of implementation strategies, organisation design and work organisation. Access has been negotiated with 10 organisations, who will be interviewed regarding the implementation of their CAD or PPS systems. They have also promised to introduce the research team to the other members of the project coalition so that a full picture of the flow of production information and the role of computers within it can be gathered.
4. This point is, of course, specific to those countries with Anglo-Saxon legal systems.

Bibliography

ACARD (Advisory Council for Applied Research and Development) (1980), *Computer Aided Design and Manufacture*, HMSO, London

Arnold, E. (1983), 'Information Technology as a Technological Fix: Computer Aided Design in the United Kingdom', in G. M. Winch (ed.), *Information Technology in Manufacturing Processes*, Rossendale, London

Atkin, B. L. and E. M. Gill (1986), 'CAD and Management of Construction Projects', *Journal of Construction Engineering*, 112

Ball, M. (1983), *Housing Policy and Economic Power*, Methuen, London

—— (1988), *Rebuilding Construction*, Routledge, London

Boaden, R. J. and B. G. Dale (1986), 'What Is Computer-Integrated Manufacturing?', *International Journal of Operations and Production Management*, 6

Bowley, M. (1966), *The British Building Industry*, Cambridge University Press London

Buchanan, D. A. and D. Boddy (1983), *Organizations in the Computer Age*, Gower, Aldershot

Campagnac, E. and C. Caro (1987), 'CAD/CAM For New Strategies In Construction', paper presented at CAD/CAM In Construction, Karlslunde, Denmark

Campinos-Dubernet, M. and J.-M. Grando (1988), 'Formation professionelle ouvrière: trois modèles européens', *Formation/Emploi*, 22

CICA (1987), *Building On I.T.*, Construction Industry Computing Association, Cambridge

CIRIA (1983), *Management Contracting*, Construction Industry Research and Information Association, London

Day, A., A. Faulkner and E. Happold (1986), *Communications and Computers in the Building Industry*, Construction Industry Computing Association, Cambridge

Eccles, R. G. (1981), 'The Quasi-Firm in Construction', *Journal of Economic Behavior and Organization*, 2

Ettlie, J. E. and S. A. Reifeis (1986), 'The Integration of Design and Manufacturing for Deployment of Advanced Manufacturing Technology', paper presented at TIMS/ORSA Joint National Meeting, Los Angeles, California

Fellows, R., D. Langford, R. Newcombe and S. Urry (1983), *Construction Management in Practice*, Construction Press, London

Leeds College of Building (1986), *Survey of the Use of Information Technology in the Construction Industry*, mimeo, Leeds College of Building

Mintzberg, H. (1979), *The Structuring of Organizations*, Prentice-Hall, Englewood Cliffs

Morris, P. W. G. (1973), 'An Organisational Analysis of Project Management in the Building Industry', *Build International*, 6

—— (1983), 'Project Management Organization', *Construction Papers*, 2

Thompson, J. D. (1967), *Organizations in Action*. McGraw-Hill, New York

Walker, A. (1984), *Project Management in Construction*, Collins, London

Williamson, O. E. (1975), *Markets and Hierarchies*, Free Press, New York

Winch, G. M. (1983), 'Organisation Design for CAD/CAM', in G. M. Winch (ed.), *Information Technology in Manufacturing Processes*, Rossendale, London

—— (1987), 'The Construction Firm and the Construction Process: The Allocation of Resources to the Construction Project', in Lansley, P. R. and P. A. Harlow, (eds.) *Managing Construction Worldwide*, Vol. 2, F. and F. N. Spon, London

—— (1988), *The Implementation of CAD/CAM; Concepts and Propositions*, Working Paper in Management No. 24, University of Warwick

—— (1989), 'The Construction Firm and the Construction Project: A Transaction Cost Approach', *Construction Management and Economics*, 7

Wix, J. (1986), *Information Flow in Building Services*, Building Services Research and Information Association, Bracknell

Wix, J. and C. McLelland (1986), *Data Exchange Between Computer Systems in the Construction Industry*, Building Services Research and Information Association, Bracknell.

9

New Technology in the West German Construction Industry and Trade Union Policy

Joachim Reus and Gerd Syben

Introduction

'Nearly all medium and large-sized construction enterprises are using electronic data processing (EDP) today. But even in more than half of the small construction firms the use of data processing is routine, and this tendency is increasing' (Zentralverband des Deutschen Baugewerbes 1987: 1). If this statement in a report of one of the two West German employers' associations in the construction industry is correct, the hypothesis can no longer be maintained that the industry in the Federal Republic is backward with regard to using new technology. This would revise a common prejudice, so it seems helpful to provide some information about the literature on the application of new technology in this sector at the present time. We shall concentrate on electronic data processing and its use in the construction industry as this has been researched most extensively.

EDP in the Construction Industry in the Federal Republic

The assumption of technological backwardness in the construction industry is the result of the nature of the production process on site. This is true especially for processes of horizontal and vertical transport and assembly operations, which are still mechanised at only a very low technological level, compared to the type of automation mainly based on micro-electronic control which is used in other industries. However, there are two reasons why it is inadequate to speak of backwardness. The first is that the absence of micro-electronic control in the production process on site does not indicate lack of rationalisation and effective means of improving productivity levels (see Syben in this volume). The second reason is that when commercial, organisational and design processes are considered, which are situated up and downstream as well as alongside the production process on site itself, it becomes obvious that EDP in construction firms is no less widespread than in comparable firms in industry in the Federal Republic.

A survey conducted in 1985/6 showed that, for example, in banks and insurance companies 59 per cent of employees work for all or part of their time with computers or computer-controlled machinery. This compared to 25 per cent of employees in the public sector and 21 per cent and 20 per cent in the production industries and commerce, respectively. The rate for the construction industry was only 9 out of 100 (Institut für Arbeitsmarkt- und Berufsforschung and Bundesinstitut für Berufsbildung 1987: 36). However, if it is considered that the application of EDP in the construction industry is limited to work of commercial and technical staff then, in fact, about 50 per cent of these employees work with computers – far above the average. A similar result is given by a union survey of Betriebsräte[1] in 84 firms, which were mainly construction, architectural, civil engineering and building material firms. In this survey it was shown that in engineering firms that have been using EDP for a long time and for many purposes there are, on average, 134 employees per 10 screens in use per firm. Nearly exactly the same rate is reported from enterprises in the construction and civil engineering industries. Other enterprises in this sector (civil engineering and architectural firms, the building material industry) had rates of between 90 and 170 employees per 10 screens in use. Only those firms whose activities are restricted to construction work on a very low technological level, with a low level of capitalisation and which normally do not employ any technical or commercial staff, were far behind this rate with 580 employees per 10 screens in use (Industriegewerkschaft Bau-Steine-Erden 1985: 15–16).

Strategies of establishing systems and their grade of integration can be observed in large enterprises in other industries (Baethge and Oberbeck 1986), but have not been reported for the construction industry. The use of EDP for commercial work such as invoicing, accounting or payroll administration is a matter of course today even for many smaller firms in this sector, especially since hardware costs have decreased rapidly and personal computers have become more efficient. A characteristic of the construction industry seems to be that EDP encircles the production process on site in the planning and design stages in the organisation of work, especially in tendering, cost accounting and cost control. Software producers offer special programmes for the construction industry for practically all tasks from tendering to settlements of account for a completed site (Zentralverband des Deutschen Baugewerbes 1988). To date, EDP in the construction industry has served as an organising tool (Müller, Richter and Steinfelder 1989).

The Application of EDP in the Construction Industry

A few studies have recently been published reporting the quantitative diffusion of EDP in the construction industry in the Federal Republic (Industriegwerkschaft Bau-Steine-Erden 1985; Krämer 1986; Zentralverband des Deutschen Baugewerbes 1987). The employers' association, Zentralverband des Deutschen Baugewerbes, conducted a survey of its members in 1986 on the use of EDP. On the basis of their findings, from 3,159 firms, they estimated that about 45 per cent of all construction and civil engineering firms used EDP in one way or another (1987: 17). Nearly all firms with 200 and more employees used it. Firms with 50 to 199 employees had a user-rate of over 90 per cent whilst one in four very small firms (less than 10 employees) used EDP (1987: 24).

Despite some differences in the frame of reference and in approach, these levels can be confirmed by a regional study conducted in 1987 in the Bremen area.[2] In this study firms which worked in either construction or civil engineering were included. It examined only those fields of activity usually performed by civil engineers. Trades such as roofing, plastering or carpentry were not included, nor were commercial and office work. In this study 39 per cent of the 92 firms answering the survey used EDP (see Table 9.1).

These two studies show that variations in findings on the extent to which small firms use EDP can be explained by differences in the survey questions. The study of the Zentralverband asked for all uses of EDP, whilst the Bremen study asked questions on its use for technical, planning and organisational purposes. The Bremen study omitted the use of EDP for commercial work, which in smaller

Joachim Reus and Gerd Syben

Table 9.1 Application of EDP in construction firms in the Federal Republic by size of firm

Size of firms (employees)	Percentage with EDP	
	ZDB study	Bremen study
1–9	26	13
10–19	64	37
20–49	77	74
50–99	94	93
100–199	96	*
200+	99	*

* no percentages are provided here because of the low number of firms surveyed

Table 9.2 Application of EDP in construction firms in the Federal Republic by field of action

Field of action	Usage of EDP (per cent)
Calculation of wages	57
Accounting	60
Word processing	13
Estimates	21
Technical calculation	5
Project management	3
Computer-aided Design and Manufacturing (CAD/CAM)	1
Others	5

Source: Zentralverband des Deutschen Baugewerbes 1987; 45.

firms is probably often the only field in which EDP is used. The ZDB study shows clearly that EDP is mainly used for commercial and office work in the construction industry (see Table 9.2).

It must be pointed out that in Table 9.2 the rate for using EDP in technical calculation probably does not correspond to the real extent of its application since EDP is used especially for this purpose. This work is not conducted in construction firms but in engineering firms which statistically do not belong to the construction industry and so were not included in this inquiry. The table does justify the conclusion that construction firms only use EDP in

Table 9.3 Application of EDP in technical and organisational fields of action in the construction industry in the Bremen area

Field of action	Usage of EDP (per cent)
Estimating, working on tenders etc.	36
Making draughts, lists, computation of quantities etc.	23
Stress analysis	20
Daily management accounts on site	10
Project management	7
Others	5

Source: From a survey of 92 firms.

commercial work and that the technical process of construction has not been affected by EDP.

The Bremen study, which examined only organisational, planning and technical work, shows three main applications of EDP: estimating; stress analysis and draughting; and making lists of building materials, computation of quantities, and surveying of earthwork. This suggests that the study by the Zentralverband may have underestimated the extent of application of EDP for these purposes (see Table 9.3). Tables 9.2 and 9.3 indicate the relative weight of the categories of EDP usage, but not how they relate to the workload of the firms, which would actually provide more information.

Table 9.3 shows that only a very low rate of application of EDP was found in project management. In Bremen, project and site managers, when asked about this, commented that they did not use, did not need and did not like EDP-assistance for managing a site. Sometimes they pointed to computers standing unused in a corner of the site manager's office. If one thinks, however, of the many advantages that managing a site by EDP has for the enterprise (and it has some for the site manager too), it is possible to envisage that in a few years' time it will be an ordinary working instrument on sites. This is because some 'windows of opportunity' such as, for example, daily management accounts or project network techniques, already exist. So although EDP was not an ordinary working instrument on sites when this survey was conducted, it is possible that this will change in the not too distant future. Apart from this, the inquiry amongst Betriebsräte mentioned above shows that in the

Table 9.4 Development of application of EDP in construction in the
Federal Republic, 1974–1986

Size of firms	Percentage of firms using EDP	
(employees)	1974	1986
1–9	8	26
10–19	15	64
20–49	35	77
50–99	40	94
100–199	57	96
200+	88	99

Source: Zentralverband des Deutschen Baugewerbes 1987: 24.

construction industry (and probably in industry in general) EDP is used for other purposes such as the registration and measurement of working time, control of access to certain buildings or using data links and information networks (Industriegwerkscraft Bau-Steine-Erden 1985: 18).

The study by the Zentralverband makes it possible to compare results with those of a similar inquiry conducted in 1974 and to analyse the development of the application of EDP in the construction industry over this period. In 1974, 18 per cent of all construction firms used EDP. Table 9.4 shows that the increase up to 1986 was the greatest amongst small and medium-sized firms (Zentralverband des Deutschen Baugewerbes 1987: 24).

The conclusion of the study of the Zentralverband is that firms first use EDP for payroll functions, using an external accountant, then they apply it to their accounts using a computer agency, before finally buying their own computer (Zentralverband des Deutschen Baugewerbes 1987: 26). Firms obviously first experiment in using EDP for commercial work, before they start to use it for organisational and technical purposes.

In the Bremen study, it was found that firms employing civil engineers are more likely to use EDP than those which do not employ them. That this is not a trivial effect of firm size can be shown by examining the distribution of both elements in small firms (with less than twenty employees) where EDP and employment of civil engineers are normally least likely to be found (Table 9.5).

Looking at these results it is possible to put forward a hypothesis about the conditions which may be responsible for the application

Table 9.5   Application of EDP and employment of civil engineers in construction firms with less than twenty employees in the Bremen area

	Percentage of firms employing civil engineers	Percentage of firms not employing civil engineers
Firms using EDP	26	14
Firms not using EDP	74	86

of EDP in construction. It is known that most construction firms are very small and owners are often craftworkers rather than managers or technicians. It is now common for construction firms to employ civil engineers, both amongst small and large firms. However, the causal relationship between the employment of engineers and the use of EDP is difficult to determine. Does EDP require an engineer to use it or does the engineer seek EDP as a tool? This question needs further research.

Consequences of the Application of EDP

Until recently there has been no systematic study or representative survey of the consequences of the application of EDP in the construction industry. In contrast to other industries there is little empirical knowledge concerning how EDP affects the employment, skills and working conditions of employees in construction. There is also little empirical knowledge about how it changes the content and organisation of work performed in the process of designing and planning a building and organising and controlling its construction.

The only information available comes from a survey by the West German construction union Industriegewerkschaft Bau-Steine-Erden (IG BSE)[3] of its white-collar members, including technicians, clerical staff, typists and others (Industriegewerkschaft Bau-Steine-Erden 1987). The survey examined the consequences of the application of EDP for employees. Of the 70,000 questionnaires sent out, 6,300 responses were received. Consequently, the answers are not representative, although a great amount of material is provided.

The findings of this inquiry show that EDP has contradictory outcomes for employees (Table 9.6). Respondents were asked about

Table 9.6 Consequences of application of EDP for employees in construction firms

Aspects of work	Percentages of sample		
	Reporting positive changes	Reporting negative changes	Reporting no change
Responsibility	41	5	54
Demand for professional qualification	44	9	47
Interest in the job	30	11	59
Payment	4	6	90
Working time	5	10	85
Autonomy	10	17	73
Advancement	5	14	81
Security of the job	8	28	64
Communications with colleagues	7	28	65
Stress	5	36	59
Rivalry	3	33	64
Monitoring performance	3	36	61
Pressure to be productive	4	59	37

Source: Industriegewerkschaft Bau-Steine-Erden 1987: 14.

all aspects of work recorded here and could indicate positive, negative or no change. Negative effects were more commonly reported than positive ones with respect to aspects of work such as the monitoring of performance, pressure to be productive, stress, communication, rivalry between colleagues and job security. However, the number of positive changes was far greater with respect to aspects of work such as level of responsibility and demand for professional qualifications.

One hypothesis which could be put forward is that positive and negative changes were reported by different groups of employees who have different jobs, different levels of skills and different positions within firms. This hypothesis is strengthened by the finding that women and older employees reported negative experiences more frequently than others (Industriegewerkschaft Bau-Steine-Erden 1987: 17–20). It is these groups that commonly have the least skilled and lowest paid jobs and are most likely to experience negative effects.

In the Bremen study, in addition to the construction firms, twenty-five civil engineering firms were included in the survey. EDP has been used in civil engineering firms for a longer time, to a greater extent and for more purposes than in construction firms in general. In interviews with the owners or other representatives of these firms, it was possible to obtain further information about the consequences of the application of EDP in the building sector as a whole. Although these answers may not be representative, they are reported here, because they may lead to hypotheses for further research work. Four points are noteworthy: firstly those interviewed said that no redundancies had been caused by the application of EDP. Of course, an increase in productivity and output with a stable workforce does represent a saving of labour and, in fact, an indirect loss of jobs. In many cases employers are using EDP not as a means of substituting labour but to improve the level of its utilisation.

Secondly, EDP no longer provides competitive advantage for the firms which use it but firms which do not use it are at a disadvantage. For example it is now possible using EDP to increase the number of tenders submitted. However, this improves the chances of winning a contract only so long as few firms have this advantage. If all firms use EDP for preparing tender documents then it only increases the workload inside a firm, not the number of orders.

Thirdly, a consequence and frequently an explicit goal of using EDP is for employers to obtain greater knowledge of working processes and better control of employees. This is especially the case with working processes such as estimation, stress analysis or architectural work, which until now have not been susceptible to such controls.

Finally there seems to be agreement amongst those who use EDP that it is unlikely to reduce the demand for qualifications, but will in fact increase it. Really efficient use of EDP, it is argued, is only guaranteed if, in general, employees understand the functions for which they use it.

In the Bremen study five intensive interviews were conducted with estimators about the way their work had changed since they started to use EDP. In Table 9.3, estimating was shown to be the area in which EDP is most used apart from commercial work. The interviewees considered that estimating may be a window of opportunity for EDP to enter the construction firm. This is because estimating is the first point inside the construction firm where data about the planned building is generated, and this may compel its use for integrating processes which are currently separated. This compulsion may become greater if CAD is used in the design stage as well.

In the Bremen study a comparative analysis was undertaken of the estimating function with and without the application of EDP. It showed that the skills of the estimator (who in the West German construction firms is mostly an older engineer with considerable experience) are still needed at those points of the working process where decisions of strategic relevance for successful tendering have to be made. These decisions depend in principle on the policy of the firm and therefore cannot be controlled by technical norms. The demand for flexibility is very high and it is not possible to substitute this flexibility by the knowledge embodied in computer programmes. The latter concern the choice of parameters used in the estimating process, the valuation of cost–performance relations and the adaption of parameters of estimating to the conditions of a given building project. However, EDP obviously does release employees from routine work such as calculation, searching for data of all kinds, comparing estimated and real values, and word processing. If this results in the labour substitution, it seems most likely to affect groups of employees such as typists, because their work will then be done by the estimator in dialogue with the machine programme.

EDP in Construction and Trade Union Policy in the Federal Republic

Although an increasing number of commercial and technical staff are employed in the West German construction industry (Syben 1988) the trade union for this industry, the IG BSE, mainly organises manual workers. Whilst in 1988 about 17 per cent of all employees in the construction industry were salaried staff, this group forms only about 7 per cent of union members. When the IG BSE increased its policy emphasis on the application of EDP in firms, there were two main objectives. EDP changes work content and threatens the jobs, skills, earnings and employment of all employees in the construction industry. Initially it directly affects only the commercial and technical staff, because these employees are working with computers. So on the one hand, a focus on the problems relating to the introduction of EDP may provide the IG BSE with an approach for uniting all employees in a company and in the industry in general. On the other hand, this work may demonstrate the benefits of union membership to clerical workers, technicians and engineers and this may improve their access to the union as well as improve the union's access to them.

Whilst the defence of working conditions is a goal of all union policy, the central aim of the IG BSE in pursuing this strategy is to develop policies which are compatible with workers' interests. This position is based on the conviction that opposition to the introduction of EDP is not reasonable, because it can help to replace many of those work functions which are boring, tiring and have little demand for higher levels of qualification. The aim of union policy in this field is defending jobs and earnings, maintaining and expanding the demand for qualifications, improving working conditions including aspects of health and safety, and safeguarding against the misuse of personal data.

The most important means of achieving the IG BSE objectives is through the West German system of codetermination in industry. This gives employees and unions certain rights to participate in decisions in firms. In the firm, Betriebsräte have a right to be informed about the introduction of new technologies at an early stage of the process and to take part in decisions relating to the social consequences of introducing them. In companies which are organised as joint-stock companies or which are of a certain size, information about long-term plans of investment must be given to employees' delegates on the board of trustees or to the economic commission of the firm. These delegates are mainly union members or union officials.

In order to provide better advice to members confronted with EDP and other new technologies, the IG BSE has appointed an officer with responsibility for new technologies, whose duties involve giving advice and information, organising seminars and producing written material. The union has initiated research programmes to improve knowledge of the issues and to contribute to the development of policy.

Early experience shows that employees in the construction industry do discuss the problems of new technologies and seek advice from their union, but they often only give consideration to the technical aspects of the problem. Organisational means of rationalisation which can be facilitated through the use of the EDP, for example, the division of corporations into several firms or the increased use of subcontractors, are often neglected or their significance is underestimated.

In 1987 Betriebsräte of one of the biggest companies of the construction industry reached a formal agreement on EDP with the help of the IG BSE which may become a model for the sector. The planning, introduction and operation of EDP in the company are now governed by the agreement. Emphasis is laid on saving jobs and maintaining and improving the skills of employees, and consideration is given to job design and content. There are safeguards against the monitoring of performance and behaviour through data collection. Since reaching this agreement workplace representatives in many companies have begun to bargain for similar agreements and in some cases have obtained successful results.

A company agreement is an achievement for the employees of one firm, but its application is limited. Now the IG BSE is trying to reach a collective agreement at national level concerning rationalisation. Whether this will be achieved and how comprehensive it will be has yet to be seen. However, there can be no doubt that the most difficult task by far for Betriebsräte and employees is to implement these agreements in everyday working life inside the company.

Notes

1. The German term Betriebsrat cannot be translated into English. Betrietsräte are the members of the Betriebsrat, an institution of codetermination in the firm, and are also workplace representatives. The Betriebsrat is elected by all employees of a firm and these elections and workers' rights to representation are determined by law. In medium-sized and larger firms to be a Betriebsrat can be a full-time job. Betriebsräte do not have to be members of a union, but most of them are union representatives.

2. A report on this inquiry is given in an unpublished manuscript by Gerd Syben (in German).

3. See the note on the IG BSE to chap. 14 of this volume.

Bibliography

Baethge, M. and H. Oberbeck (1986), *Zukunft der Angestellten*, Campus, Frankfurt/New York
Industriegewerkschaft Bau-Steine-Erden (1985), *Bestandsaufnahme zur*

Einführung und Anwendung neuer Technologien im Organisationsbereich der IG Bau-Steine-Erden, Frankfurt.

Industriegewerkschaft Bau-Steine-Erden (1987), *Angestellte und Interessenvertretung im Organisationsbereich der IG Bau-Steine-Erden*, Frankfurt

Institut für Arbeitsmarkt- und Berufsforschung and Bundesinstitut für Berufsbildung (1987), *Neue Technologien. Verbreitungsgrad, Qualifikation und Arbeitsbedingungen*, Nuremberg

Krämer, K. (1986), 'Mehr Verbandsberatung und Erfahrungsaustausch ist gefragt', *Bauwirtschaftliche Informationen*, 19, 54–5

Müller, C., W. Richter and J. Steinfelder (1989), *Computereinsatz und Neue Technologien in der Bauwirtschaft und ihre Folgen für die Baustellenarbeit*, Research Report, Fachhochschule, Dortmund

Syben, G. (1988), 'Mit der Bedeutung wachsen auch die Probleme', *Fundamente, Zeitschrift der IG Bau-Steine-Erden für Angestellte*, 1, 34–9

Zentralverband des Deutschen Baugewerbes (1987), *EDV-Einsatz und EDV-Planung im Baugewerbe*, Bonn

——(1988), *Softwareinformation Bauwirtschaft*, Bonn

10

Computers, Control and Working Conditions on Site in the Danish Construction Industry

Sten Bonke and
Elsebet Frydendal Pedersen

Introduction

This paper has been written on the basis of a research project concerning use of computers in the Danish construction industry. The particular aim of this project, which is part of a national technology programme, is to examine the prospects for and consequences of an increased computer use on site. Furthermore it has been crucial to identify and apply research methods, which could lead to an optimisation of user participation in technology investments and thus improve the efficiency of the future use of information technology.[1]

Although the major purpose of this is indeed connected to the rationalisation perspective of the Danish official technology policy, the intention of the project and of this article is also to demonstrate the degrees of freedom inherent in any technological development. The question is how to match the demand for higher productivity with democratisation, autonomy and good working conditions on site. Background problems and the major findings of the research project are discussed in the following paper section.

Building Technology and Post-war State Intervention

The construction industry makes significant contributions to the

187

economic and social life of a developed nation. For example, in Denmark, construction activities account for approximately 10 per cent of the Gross National Product and 7 per cent of employment, to which should be added significant derived effects in other industrial as well as service sectors.

Building products, in particular dwellings, also represent an additional influence on the political level of the society. Since the Second World War, building policy has formed a fundamental part of the establishment of the social-democratic welfare states in Scandinavia. In the late 1980s, subsidised public dwellings still amounted to 75 per cent of the Danish construction industry's annual output in new housing.

In the postwar period heavy ideological and financial state engagement in Danish building policy involved very early state intervention in the development of technology in the construction industry. In the late 1950s a radical building technology programme was launched, having as its object the reduction of building costs and an increase in productivity. The policy was partly realised during the 1960s and 1970s, primarily by means of the diffusion of subsidised and standardised prefabricated systems, combined with a compulsory reduction in the ratio of skilled workers compared to traditional building projects. The annual average increase in labour productivity on site consequently attained 7 per cent in these decades (Bonke and Jensen 1983). The success of the technology policy, however, did not quite lead to the expected reduction of building costs!

Thus, by the end of the 1970s, when the construction market – and the economy as a whole – suffered a heavy crisis, the government launched a new technocratic concept as the main feature of its industrial policy.

Technology Policy of the 1980s

Under the designation 'Programme of Technology Development' this concept aimed at a rapid introduction of advanced technologies, such as, for instance, computers as a means of solving the profitability problems of the industrial sectors. The programme was financed with 1.5 billion Danish kroner (about £125 million) (Arvedsen 1989).

In construction a number of research and development projects were supported in order to facilitate the use of computers both in consulting and contracting firms. By far the major part of these projects had their basis in the handling of information in the design and planning process and focused on computers as a necessary new tool for the technicians in the bigger firms of the sector. Incidentally the Danish R&D projects under this programme often implied state investments in big computer systems such as those for computer-aided design (CAD) and networks.

Besides the attempt to intensify technicians' work, this computerisation undoubtedly expressed a tendency towards a more international market orientation of the Danish construction industry. In international building projects the need for fast and homogeneous communication – languages and structures – was magnified and this aspect is becoming even more important, due to the EC's current policy towards the opening of the internal market.

The New Approach to Technology Assessment

However, a minor 1.3 per cent (20 million D.kr.) of the technology programme's financial budget had been set aside for so-called technology assessment (TA) activities, of which this article reports on the findings of the one and only research project within the construction sector.

TA projects, unlike the dominant technology-promoting part of the programme, were supposed to concentrate on the consequences of new technologies in a wider sense, evaluating, for instance, indirect effects of technology on working conditions. Due to the low political and financial priority of this part of the programme, however, projects with such overall considerations have been very sporadic, and it might even be claimed that the most important function of TA lies in its legitimising impact on the general technology policy of the Danish government (Bonke et al 1989).

Nevertheless the positive possibilities inherent in TA should also be underlined. They offer an opportunity to evolve an understanding of the construction process as a communication system of deep complexity. Furthermore, on this basis, they also allow the development of alternative strategies for the implementation and use of the technology. These particular intentions, however, must be qualified by reference to the specific characteristics of the Danish construction process, especially the functions and qualifications of the labour force.

In the following section these characteristics and their relationship to the theory and methods of the TA project will be described.

Sten Bonke and Elsebet Frydendal Pedersen

Computers in the Construction Process

Formal and Informal Communication

Computers are tools meant for the processing and distribution of large quantities of information. As each new execution process in construction requires a considerable stream of information from architects and engineers to the site operators, it is therefore no wonder that great expectations of productivity gains are attached to the introduction of computers in firms. In trying to develop efficient computer-aided communication processes it is crucial to consider the different types of information and their specific functions and also the different communication channels of this information.

It is a striking characteristic of most computerisation projects in the construction industry that they tend to concentrate only on the *formal* types of information, represented by the contract documents, budgets, drawings, plans, descriptions and timetables.

Such information is primarily of formal and legal importance, for instance in connection with the division of jobs and responsibility between firms. Correspondingly this information typically passes through formal channels of communication – from top to bottom – in the project organisation as well as in the firm.

When it comes to the construction process on site, the importance of the formal information diminishes. Site operations are, of course, determined at a higher level by the official project plans, drawings, quantities and timetables. Nevertheless, it is a well-known fact, in Denmark as well as internationally, that this information undergoes a substantial transformation process as it is distributed to the various parts of the site organisation. The effects of this transformation become particularly evident as operations are carried out and the building product materialises, very often resulting in significant changes in schedules and design details.

This phenomenon is reflected for instance in the term 'tegnet som udført' ('as-built drawing'), expressing the reformalisation of information. An important conclusion relating to this phenomenon is that the labour process on site is based to a high degree upon an informal content and structure of communication, made up of the team of site managers, foremen, gang leaders and construction workers.

Informality, Autonomy and Power

In Denmark the informal character of site communication is closely connected to the strong autonomous status of the site staff. The efficiency of the construction process is in fact basically dependent on the ability of the site organisation to act upon unclarified situations, to coordinate work functions, to define *ad hoc* tasks and to adjust and verify the uncertainties of the project documents.

We shall not in this context develop in detail the background of autonomy in the building labour process, apart from referring to the many analytical contributions on this topic (for instance, BISS 1984) which have emphasised the special production and market conditions in construction. However it seems important to underline especially the strong dependence on the local and uneven nature of given circumstances, which, together with several other peculiarities, cause a basic lack of concentration and standardisation of the labour process as well as construction products.

One-off production means a rather changeable labour process which varies from place to place, again implying high demands on the flexibility of the workforce. The mechanisation of construction sites reflects this situation as well, a very predominant trend being the development of movable machinery and hand-tools which are often adaptable to the functions of correcting and adjusting.

Given this background, it is obvious that the strategy of the construction industry for rationalising the production process had to utilise alternative methods, compared to the straightforward development of the industrial production in general. Due to the unpredictable conditions of construction work, the combination and proportion of the factors of production simply cannot be determined in precise project planning. Consequently this planning is, to a large extent, substituted by rough estimates or even totally left to the building workers on site. This is then typically combined with so-called 'indirect forms of control' such as piece-work or bonus wage systems and casual employment.

Returning now to the question of forms of information and communication on site, it is striking that the preconditions of site activities described above cause a dual information structure, constituted by, on one the hand, the formal project information which is communicated at the firm/management level, and, on the other hand, informal communication on site which is the main basis of daily operations of the construction workers.

In Denmark this twofold determination of site activities represents an important basis for understanding of social relations on site. Although the development of modern industrialised construction technology, as in other European countries, has aimed at and implied an extension of management control, it is certainly still possible to consider *autonomy* a fundamental characteristic of working conditions on site. Investigations in relation to our research project, which we shall later refer to, provide current evidence on the workers' notion of this autonomy.

However, the fact that the Danish building trade unions have historically reinforced the autonomous status of the construction workers must be taken into consideration. For instance one important element in the policy of the unions in relation to their members consists in providing educational and practical consultative back-up for the construction gangs' own daily production management and wage negotiations.

Thus with a level of unionisation close to 100 per cent and a correspondingly highly qualified skilled and semi-skilled labour force, the building trade unions have been able to exploit quite successfully the autonomy of work as a power base in relation to the employers. The construction firms are indeed very dependent on effective self-management of the gangs, and the construction workers in fact earn the highest salaries amongst labourers, which are often even higher than those of the site engineers.

Another effect of this autonomy/power mechanism has been a built-in motivation for the use of productivity-increasing methods. In this respect a negative consequence has been the acceptance of a reduction of the numbers of workers employed in the Danish construction sector and a weakening of social networks on site (for instance in 1980 the same output of new construction in square metres was produced by half as many workers as in 1970). Closely linked to the motivation of autonomy are in fact some negative aspects of working conditions such as time pressure and stress, which are nowadays considered a serious problem on Danish construction sites.

Computerisation and the Authority of Information

As mentioned above, the Danish 'Programme of Technology Development' represents a huge effort by the state in order to achieve a rather narrow goal: the introduction of more computers in industry. However, considering the actual progress of the computerisation of construction firms throughout the 1980s, it is quite evident that the complexity of the communication structure and the forms of information constitute an impediment to the rapid and smooth introduction of computers, which other sectors of industry have experienced in this period.

In order to overcome this problem, the computerisation policy of the construction firms has gradually changed from large mainframe 'head office based' systems, towards a more decentralised and sporadic use of personal computers. The latest step in this line of development might be seen in the present efforts of the bigger firms to recentralise information structures by means of networks and work routines which link the units together in a more disciplined way.

No matter what the level of computer use in the individual firm it has become a common understanding for all parties of the construction projects that the possession and treatment of information is crucial to the technical and economic efficiency of the production process (see also Burn 1989). This awareness has made computer technology an important strategic resource, not only to firm managements in their efforts to improve productivity and performance and to gain competitive advantages, but also the Danish building trade unions. Some unions more than others have been raising their profile in their attitude towards computer technologies since the mid 1980s. Some started developing at a very early stage very expensive, centralised computer-based services for their members. But lately – and this is more interesting – unions have shown an understanding of the new technology as a means to maintain and improve the working conditions of their members.

The last point of view reflects the above-mentioned role of informal information on site and the relative autonomy of the construction workers, which may eventually be threatened by the computerisation policy of the firms. Consequently the unions speak for the democratisation of computer use and the development of a new training policy, which can provide their members with adequate qualifications for the new information tools and communication structures of the construction process.

The TA project offers an opportunity to support this strategy on the premises of efficiency criteria. The crucial question, however, has been whether this process could be rooted in fundamental interests of the building workers, and thus more generally include improvements of working conditions on site.

193

Sten Bonke and Elsebet Frydendal Pedersen

Computerisation and a Proactive Strategy for Better Working Conditions on Site

Methodology and Findings

As indicated in the former sections, the basic assumptions of this TA project focus on the interrelationship between new computerised information systems and (the efficiency of) the labour process on construction sites. During the first, exploratory stage of the project the critical issue gradually narrowed around the role of the construction workers as the end-users of information. This recognition, however, was not of immediate value, considering the present absence of computers on most Danish building sites, not to mention the workers' ignorance of and reluctance to use the technology.

Nevertheless, as mentioned above, the trade unions expressed their interest in a further elaboration of the question. Even the employers' representatives in the management committee of the project supported this point of view. Partly, we believe, they were forced by the poor results so far with their own computer management and a growing acceptance of the fact that the motivation of site staff was the basic precondition for successful investment in computers (on the motivation factor, see for instance McFillen 1989).

As this situation of superficial consensus became clear on the basis of a rather tentative and speculative *assessment*, the project had to include an element of *verification* before a final *plan of action* could be defined and experimentally carried out.

In order not to let these stages of the project be determined by the computer technology (or its proposers) itself, the focus of the verification efforts was placed more generally on the content of the working conditions in the construction labour process. With this purpose data was collected by means of interviews on Danish building sites, covering all groups of staff and all trades. The main findings of these investigations are described below (see Pedersen 1989).

Positive and Negative Aspects of Work

1 *Freedom in work*: construction workers clearly experience some range of autonomy within the work. These include having influence of planning, management, organisation and execution. There are, however, variations from gang to gang and trade to trade.
2 *Variations in space and pace/working outdoors* were characterised

as positive aspects and linked to *independence from stationary machinery*.

3 *Making on-the-spot solutions* brings variation to the work and puts demands on qualifications. Consequently construction workers feel satisfied on seeing the raising and completion of the building *as a result of their own effort*.

4 *A close social network* is a highly estimated quality of the work, in relation to the specific gang and trade as well as to the site.

5 *The increasing time pressure* is found to have negative influence on all aspects of work, for instance the quality of workmanship, and jeopardises interpersonal relations and causes accidents.

6 *Low influence on working conditions* is experienced as a result of bad management and poor information, for instance outdated blueprints, missing materials, etc.

7 *Increased specialisation* is described primarily as a threat to qualifications, secondly as affecting social relations due to new divisions of labour.

8 *Outdoor work in cold and damp weather* is considered a problem of growing importance because of the introduction of all-season building techniques combined with shorter execution periods.

9 *Unpleasant or dangerous new materials*: lack of knowledge about the specifications of such materials together with difficulties of choosing alternatives is experienced as a growing problem by the construction workers.

These examples of major work issues, as they are expressed by Danish construction workers today, in principle represent a set of key preconditions to the assessment and introduction of any new technology, the one and only reasonable objective always being the preservation of the good aspects and the reduction of the negative aspects of work.

The element of autonomy proved to be of substantial importance to the workers, and the next sequence in the research process was therefore to select a technique in order to make the computerisation adaptable to the demands and possibilities of the site environment.

The Proactive Approach

The development of an operational plan of action for new technology must be based on a strategy and technique, which integrate the findings of the assessment analysis. In this project a *proactive* strategy as opposed to *reactive* strategy indicated a research approach which had as its primary goal the piloting and stimulation of a future development process rather than the explanation of historical phenomena.

The technology problem was unmistakably clear: as the available computer-based systems did *not* depend on and embody the underlying functions of the real production system that they attempted to model and control, the efficiency of the computers turned out to be poor. Furthermore the potential negative consequences on the working conditions on site would be more or less out of the range of control of construction workers, because they were only *indirect* users of the computer.

Hence the ultimate task of the project consisted in the developing and testing of a technique, which could reverse the determinants of the technology implementation process by incorporating elements of norms, rules and culture from the basic organisation of workers on site.

An Educational Experiment

On this basis the specific experiment, which was carried out in the final stage of the project, combined the profile of construction work described above with Oskar Negt's experience-based education philosophy (Olesen 1985).

A thirty-lesson course, entitled 'The Future Construction Site – Electronic Data Processing – Education', was developed, supported financially and ideologically by the construction trade unions. The course was launched as a *critical* technology course, sensitive to and of current interest to the everyday life of construction workers.

Three courses were given, for concrete workers, carpenters and for plumbers. The electricians were also initially involved but withdrew, possibly due to the union's diverging point of view on computer strategy.

A total of forty-nine construction workers participated in the three courses, guided by four persons from the Technical University of Denmark. On each course lessons were given one day a week over a four-week period, leaving room for anchoring the input in the daily working life on site.

On the *first day* computer technology was put into an overall frame of reference. The participants worked with the historical aspects of changes in their trade in the post-war period. Most of them had extremely relevant experiences in relation to technological development and changes of work routines.

The *second day*, one week later, introduced the computer itself. This 'hands-on' day was related to the computer policy of the respective trade union, testing the utility of hardware and software available within the unions as well as outside.

On the *third day* the starting point was the future prospects for working conditions on site, leading to a discussion on the question: if you want to exert influence on computer technology on site, how do you obtain this influence?

The *fourth day* concentrated on the need for education in order to reach a situation of desirable working conditions. The participants were engaged in the production of a 'message', which they believed important to pass on to their colleagues on sites, their unions, politicians, family or others.

Evaluation

All three groups responded very positively to the idea of the course and expressed a wide support for the philosophy of the educational experiment. They generally felt demystified in relation to computer technology and defined themselves as future users, privately as well as professionally.

There was a common understanding for the increasing need of interdisciplinary trade relations as a precondition to the exploitation of the positive possibilities of computers.

The experiment confirmed the hypothesis of the project that the key issue in relation to computer implementation is the concept of autonomy, and that computers – in principle at least – can become important means in maintaining and developing this autonomy.

The unions involved, as well as other parties, have lately made inquiries on further developments on this type of course. Apparently the experiment has revealed a need for a clearer definition of computer policy in the unions as well as in the construction process. It looks as though a great potential is at hand when involving the construction workers actively in technology assessment.

Note

1. The research project, entitled 'Proactive Technology Assessment of CAD/CAM in Construction – Consequences upon the Working Conditions On Site', was carried out in the period October 1985 to March 1989. The project was financed primarily by The Board of Technology under the Danish Ministry of Industry, secondarily by building trade unions and The Technical University. The project team included technicians as well as social scientists.

A description of the early theoretical and empirical project work has been published in Bonke, Pedersen and Jensen (1987). That paper also gives additional general information about the Danish construction industry.

Bibliography

Arvedsen, L. (1989), *Teknologipolitik og statslig folkeoplysning* (Technology Policy and the General Education of The State), Roskilde University Centre, Roskilde

BISS (1984), *Production of the Built Environment. Proceedings of the 5th Bartlett International Summer School*, University of London

Bonke, S. and P. A. Jensen (1983), *Teknologisk udvikling og beskæftigelse i b&a sektoren* (Technological Development and Employment in the Construction Industry), The Technical University of Denmark, Copenhagen

Bonke, S., E. F. Pedersen and N. A. Jensen, (1987), 'Consequences for the Working Conditions On Site with Increased Use of CAD/CAM in Construction', *Production of the Built Environment* 8, Proceedings of the 8th Bartlett International Summer School, University of London, 142–50

Bonke, S., E. F. Pedersen, F. Münster and N. A. Jensen (1989), 'Science and Technology for Improved Quality of Labour?', paper presented at the Conference on Labour, Technology and Skills, University of Warwick

Burn, J. M. (1989), 'The Impact of Information Technology on Organisational Structures', in *Information & Management*, 1–10

McFillen, J. M. and W. F. Maloney, (1988), 'New Answers and New Questions in Construction Worker Motivation', *Construction Management and Economics*, 6, 35–48

Olesen, H. S. (1985), *Voksenundervisning – hverdagsliv og erfaring*, (Adult Education – Everyday Life and Experience), Copenhagen

Pedersen, E. F. (1989), 'Computers and Control in Construction', paper presented at the Conference on Labour, Employment and Qualifications in the European Construction Industry, Bremen

Part IV

Skill Requirements and Training Policies

11

Labour Force Fragmentation and Skills Supply in the British Construction Industry

Helen Rainbird

Introduction

Widespread skill shortages have been reported in the British construction industry (House of Commons Select Committee on Employment 1987; *Construction Board News* April 1987: 3). Surveys conducted by the Building Employers' Confederation (BEC) and the Federation of Master Builders (FMB) have noted a significant increase in skill shortages between 1986 and 1988, particularly amongst bricklayers, carpenters and plasterers. They are most acute in London and the South-East of England, the areas most affected by the construction 'boom', but are not unknown in the Midlands and Yorkshire where the industry is now also coming out of the recession. Though it is difficult to produce a precise definition of a skill shortage and to measure its extent, the BEC survey shows that 11 per cent of all firms considered that their inability to obtain sufficient labour was contributing to contract delays (Briscoe 1990).

Two main explanations are generally put forward for this phenomenon. The first of these is that the volume of training is linked to the level of workload, as BEC argued in its evidence to the Select Committee on Employment. When levels of craft training in the economy as a whole are examined, it is clear that the volume of training does tend to fluctuate according to the economic cycle. This is because, in Britain, the primary responsibility for training lies with the firm and the numbers of apprentices undergoing training normally correspond to levels of recruitment. When recruitment is cut back in a recession, investment in training is normally reduced unless countercyclical measures introduced by the state maintain volumes. As a result, skill shortages soon emerge once labour demand recovers after a recession. However, a second argument has been put forward in recent years which is that the decline in training in *construction* is also linked to the replacement of direct employment by labour-only subcontracting and self-employment. Because this is based on a piece-work system of payment it effectively reduces the availability of training places on site. Dereck Gaulter, Chairman of the Construction Industry Training Board,[1] stated:

> The board is highly concerned at the reduction labour-only is bringing about in the number of places available for trainees to learn their trade on site. Most labour-only subcontractors are not in a position to devote time to guiding the work of a trainee. The implications are frightening. Within a few years, if apprentices and trainees cannot find a workplace in which to practice their skills in a proper job situation, the inevitable result will be that there will be very few of them about. And, then, where will the industry get a proper supply of skilled men and women when the present day "subbie" retires or moves out of the contracting industry?' (*Construction Board News*, July 1986, 1)

In addition, relatively high payments paid to self-employed workers compared to negotiated pay rates result in trainees receiving little incentive to complete their apprenticeships. It is now recognised that the growth of self-employment and labour-only subcontracting has contributed to both the quantitative and qualitative decline of training (*Construction Board News*, April 1987, 3; Federation of Master Builders 1982).

In a recent comparative study of the construction industry in four European countries, Campinos-Dubernet and Grando contrasted the 'market model' of the British training system with the French and West German 'educative models' in which training is seen as having an educational purpose. Here, volumes are maintained even in a recession either because training is provided within the education system as in France or through the highly institutionalised involvement of the social partners in sectoral level training bodies as in West Germany. They argue that the current shortages in Britain do not represent a 'crisis' in the training system, but rather the normal functioning of a market model in which the offer of training places is dependent on employers' demand (Campinos-Dubernet and Grando 1988: 25). Despite this, it is difficult to substantiate a direct relationship between levels of trainee intake and workload in the construction industry, as the BEC argument outlined above suggests (Rainbird and Clarke 1988: 14). Rather, when numbers of trainees are compared with the level of employment in the industry, it is clear that training volumes have fluctuated in relation to the decline in direct employment rather than employment as a whole (Rainbird and Clarke 1988: 13). Therefore, whilst employers' control of training intake clearly has contributed to fluctuations in trainee numbers and in particular to the 40 per cent decline in apprenticeships since the onset of the recession of the mid 1970s, this has been exacerbated by rising levels of self-employment.

The aim of this paper is to examine the effect of labour force fragmentation through labour-only subcontracting on skills supply in the construction industry. It will do this through a consideration of the organisation of production in the industry and the effect of recent trends on employment and training. The former requires an examination of the 'contracting system' (Bowley 1966) in the British construction industry alongside what Campinos-Dubernet calls the strategy of 'externalisation of variability' pursued by British employers whereby risks relating to the variability of the production process are shifted from the contractor onto subcontractors and self-employed labour (1988). In contrast to the strategy of 'internalisation of variability' which some French firms are pursuing, producing an increased demand for training (see next chapter in this volume), the externalisation of labour force constraints results in firms abnegating responsibility for operative training. This chapter will examine the growth in self-employment since the 1970s, the decline in training over the same period and the way in which programmes aimed at unemployed youth have affected apprenticeship training. This should be seen alongside broader attempts to deregulate the labour market outlined in Evans's contribution to this volume. The chapter will then proceed to analyse in more detail the class relations between self-employed labour and capital and to evaluate critically the notion that the growth of small firms and self-employment which have characterised the British industry in recent years represents a growth in the relative power of small capital. Finally, through the examination of the findings of a recent in-depth study of the self-employed,[2] it will test the hypothesis that the growth of self-employment reduces training opportunities and is likely to result in a decline in the quality of training. It will use this as a basis to consider the underlying patterns of labour usage in the industry and what measures might contribute to establishing a reliable supply of high-quality skills in the industry.

The Contracting System: Implications for Labour

The organisation of the construction process around a contracting system has been widely documented and analysed (Ball 1988; Bowley 1966; Hillebrandt 1984). In its traditional form, independent design professionals intervene in the building process between the client who commissions the building and the contractor who carries out production on site. The essential feature of this which distinguishes construction from manufacturing industry is the separation of the design phase of the process from production on site. Except in speculative housebuilding, contractors do not control the whole cycle of production. Rather, they compete for the main contract, the specification of which has been drawn up by independent architects and engineers, and then sublet specialist areas of work to subcontractors. This process of fragmentation has a direct impact on employment. 'The division into separate contracts inherent in the form makes continuity of work across projects for a unified "team" of management, workers and equipment impossible. Thus the inherent physical discontinuity of building work is reproduced and heightened in this form of contract' (Ball 1988: 80). In combination with the absence of direct state intervention in the construction process and the relative weakness of the construction unions, construction capital has developed what Ball calls a 'producer–merchant role'. The significance of the merchanting function lies in the fact that '[it] encourages them to keep their productive capital in the most liquid form possible whilst engaged in building production; new methods are only adopted by firms when they enable that liquidity to be sustained' (1988: 76). The merchanting role involves dealing in construction inputs, such as labour and materials, and outputs, namely buildings. In a recession, construction capitals retain profit levels by reducing the costs of inputs and reducing overheads. In Britain this has led to a fragmentation of production demonstrated in the growth of the relative share of specialist subcontractors in construction output, the proliferation of very small firms and growth in self-employment. This has been exacerbated by the development of management fee contracting (see Ball 1988; Massoud 1988), whereby the main contractor which is normally engaged in production is replaced by the management contractor, a team of design and planning professionals, which makes a series of contracts with different subcontractors.

The Extent of Self-employment

A number of broad trends can be distinguished in construction occupations; the relative growth of non-manual occupations, the relative decline of skilled operative trades and the absolute and relative growth of self-employment. In a recent analysis of occupational trends, Briscoe notes the changing composition of operatives directly employed in skilled manual trades. He pinpoints a decline in traditional groups such as bricklayers, carpenters and painters since the mid 1970s, alongside relative increases in electricians, heating and ventilating engineers, roofers, glaziers and scaffolders (1989). A comparison of estimates based on the Labour Force Survey and CITB statistics suggests

> that the percentage of self-employed to direct employees for bricklayers is of the order of 120 per cent, for carpenters 115 per cent, for plumbers 210 per cent, for plant operators 14 per cent, for labourers 20 per cent, whilst for professional staff, it is 150 per cent and for technicians and draughtsmen it is 35 per cent.

From this he concludes that 'traditional skilled trades such as bricklaying, carpentry, and almost certainly, painting and decorating, have relatively high proportions of self-employed workers, whereas skills where the firm needs to provide higher levels of capital equipment, such as mechanical plant operators and technicians, have much lower proportions. The comparatively smaller percentage of self-employment amongst the unskilled labouring group confirms that self-employment is most attractive to those with a recognised skill qualification' (1989: 217).

However, a major problem in analysing self-employment is the unreliability of data and estimates vary according to source. Since the introduction of the Finance Act in 1971 which formalised self-employment, it has grown enormously (see Table 11.1). In 1970 approximately 25 per cent of the private sector work force was self-employed, but by 1986 this had risen to 48.5 per cent. By June

Table 11.1 Self-employed and directly employed operatives in private
sector construction, in thousands

	Self-employed	Directly employed	All employed	Self-employed as a percentage of employed
1970	300	912	1212	24.7
1971	328	856	1184	27.7
1972	367	861	1168	31.4
1973	428	902	1330	32.1
1974	427	874	1301	32.8
1975	375	820	1195	31.4
1976	341	788	1129	30.2
1977	325	756	1081	30.1
1978	365	750	1115	32.7
1979	395	770	1165	33.9
1980	375	760	1135	33.0
1981	388	678	1066	36.4
1982	400	619	1019	39.2
1983	409	600	1009	40.5
1984	464	585	1049	44.2
1985	470	556	1026	45.8
1986	487	530	1017	47.9

Source: Housing and Construction Statistics (HMSO). Taken from Rainbird and
Clarke, 1988.

1987, 410,193 self-employed workers held individual 714 (tax
exemption) certificates (Incomes Data Service 1987: 9) but this does
not include those self-employed workers who have tax deducted at
source under the '25 per cent off' system. Because of the opportunities provided for employment on a cash in hand basis, these
figures tend to understate the extent of self-employment. It is now
recognised that case study methods provide the most fruitful means
of researching self-employment (Hakim 1988).

Recent Trends in Training

Construction is a relatively skill-intensive industry and historically
apprenticeship has constituted the major means for training skilled
labour. Although the number of apprentices in training has been
falling since the 1960s, this has been greatly accelerated since the

Table 11.2 Percentage of CITB trainees in the main apprentice trades, all CITB trainees, and local authority building department apprentices

	Main trainee trades*	All CITB trainees	Local authority building department apprentices
1975	69.9	79.3	8.3
1976	64.5	74.1	7.7
1977	53.1	62.9	6.5
1978	54.3	65.1	6.6
1979	54.5	65.3	7.0
1980	56.2	69.0	7.1
1981	50.8	60.7	6.7
1982	46.8	55.0	6.6
1983	41.8	49.8	5.4
1984**	41.5	49.6	4.4
1985**	39.9	47.5	6.7
1986**	40.4	47.8	5.3
Decrease	(42.2)	(39.7)	(35.9)

* Carpenters/joiners, bricklayers, painters, plasterers, plumbers/gas fitters, heating and ventilating engineers.
** As at April.
Taken from Rainbird and Clarke (1988).
Source: Housing and Construction Statistics (HMSO and CITB).

slump of the 1970s (see Table 11.2) The decline in the private sector, of 42 per cent between 1975 and 1986, is even more acute than in the public sector, where it was 36 per cent. This decline has not abated since the introduction of the Youth Training Scheme in 1983, which subsidises employers to train young people and provides a trainee allowance which in the construction industry was well below negotiated pay rates. Perhaps more significant than the level of the trainee allowance was the fact that *trainee status* broke the link between *training and employment*. Because the YTS scheme originally only lasted one year and since 1986 two years, the employers' associations and the trade unions felt that there was no guarantee that training would continue into the second and third years of apprenticeship. It was likely that this would result in partly trained youngsters working in the industry, diluting training standards and the quality of work. As a result of this, agreements were reached in the sub-sectoral bargaining machinery of the industry on the issuing of contracts of employment to trainees and pay rates (see Rainbird 1988 and 1990 for a full account).

The size of government subsidy to construction industry training through the Construction Industry Training Board is enormous. In 1986–7, of a total income of £93 million, £38.5 million came from YTS and a further £1.5 million from other training schemes. Employers' contributions through the levy amounted to £47 million or half of the total budget (CITB 1988). But, as argued above, this subsidy has not increased the numbers of apprentices in training. In other words, the problem of training in the construction industry is not primarily one of funding, it is a *structural* problem. There are good grounds for arguing that YTS, in cutting the link between employment and training, further contributed to the casualisation of the industry because despite national agreements, it is extremely difficult to monitor the implementation of training schemes at site level.

In summary, the basic problems affecting training are: in the private sector, the decline of direct employment, the lack of on-site training places due to the practice of labour-only subcontracting and the operation of payment-by-results systems. This is compounded by the system of raising the training levy on companies in-scope to CITB on the basis of a payroll tax under conditions of declining direct employment. In the public sector, which falls outside the scope of the CITB's Industrial Training Order, public expenditure cuts have reduced new work and there are limitations on training carried out primarily on repair and maintenance. Legislation requiring public sector building work to be put out to competitive tendering with the private sector also means that private firms which do not train can undercut the costs of the public sector Direct Labour Departments which do train.

Self-employment and Capital Accumulation

At a superficial level, a self-employed worker appears as the owner of an independent business due to the requirement to register as a business for tax purposes. Some of the self-employed work directly for clients, particularly in domestic repair work and house improvements, whilst others work for contractors. They may work for a number of different contractors or work for the same one more or less continuously for long periods. Where the self-employed work for a contractor or subcontractor, there is no employment contract, rather they are engaged under a contract for services. Formally the worker does not receive a wage, nor any of the benefits of the social wage. The self-employed may provide labour only, or may work on a supply and fix basis, providing materials as well. The contention of this paper is that both are forms of casual labour. This is obvious in the case of workers providing only their labour power. It is less obvious in the case of those providing materials as well, since it could be argued that they contribute capital to the production process. However, this begs a more fundamental theoretical question: what is the defining feature of wage labour? If the defining feature of wage labour is the payment of a wage, then providers of materials clearly do not constitute wage labour. But this is simplistic and formalistic. If instead wage labour is defined as the way in which labour, however constituted, contributes to the generation of surplus value and its appropriation – that is to say, if the underlying dynamics of the process of capital accumulation are examined – then it is clear that the self-employed who contribute materials to the production process may also be considered as a form of wage labour.[3] Self-employment represents what Marx has called 'the pygmy capital of the many' and is based on the self-exploitation of self-employed workers and their families rather than the extraction of surplus value from other workers (Rainbird forthcoming). Though in the short term they may obtain a higher income than through direct employment, continuity of work is a major problem and considerable time and effort has to be invested in developing and maintaining social contacts which may lead to work. This and supportive family labour is generally not costed when a job is priced. Moreover, the social wage is lower (for example, pension contributions, sickness benefit) and becomes of increasing significance as the self-employed age. In this respect, a switch from direct employment to self-employment has parallels with the employer who increases hours of work and/or reduces pay; it is a form of increasing the generation of absolute surplus value (that is to say, it is a form of increasing direct exploitation). Because self-employed workers may not experience the direct work discipline of the wage relationship, it may appear and they may also feel, that they are independent. However, the fact of piece-work payment imposes its own discipline and self-employed workers must discipline themselves in order to earn their living. The relative autonomy of the craft worker over the labour process should not be confused with independence from the process of generation of surplus value, the primary beneficiaries of which are larger contractors. This is because the development of self-employment allows them (1) to buy labour in discrete quantities, (2) to avoid paying cumulative benefits and (3) to pass the onus of finding work onto the self-employed themselves who must seek out customers for their labour in order to secure continuity of income. Contractors themselves recognise this. Evans and Lewis (1989) note that contractors quoted typical savings of between 20 and 30 per cent by using subcontractors' tender prices over those based on their own direct labour. Therefore self-employment increases productivity through increasing absolute surplus value (and absolute exploitation of labour) at the same time that investment in technology which makes labour more productive increases relative surplus value (and relative exploitation of labour).[4]

Findings from a Study of the Self-employed

A major problem in analysing self-employment is the fact that official statistics are unreliable. Because of the small scale and informality of individual operations, it is also extremely difficult to conduct survey work. In this section I shall refer to some recent research I have conducted on the self-employed, based on qualitative research methods. Built into the design of the research project was the condition that all those interviewed would be approached through personal contacts, and that an informal, open-ended interview would be conducted. Although this is the best method to conduct research on a group of people who may be operating in part in the informal economy, it is not perfect and there are areas which cannot be probed too deeply. The project is not concerned mainly with the construction industry, though I have detailed information on 12 self-employed tradesmen; they included 5 plumbers, 2 heating engineers, 1 carpenter, 1 electrical contractor, and 2 general builders. The main focus of the study was on their relations of production, how they organised their workload, and their conditions of employment. A subsidiary interest was in how they obtained and developed their skills and whether they were training or would consider training themselves.

The findings are in no way representative in statistical terms of a wider group of the self-employed because of the small number of interviews conducted. The sample is biased due to the way in which contacts were established towards the self-employed who supply materials as well as labour, though some of them also work on a 'labour-only' basis on occasions. However, in so far as all self-employed operatives work on a piece-work system of payment, there are similarities in its implications for training. Only one (No. 1) worked just in small domestic repairs and improvements. For the majority, work fell into a combination of domestic work negotiated directly with customers and work for one or more larger contractors. In one instance (No. 9) 90 per cent of all work was for one large company, a supplier of kitchen units, and significantly the company was considering replacing some of its self-employed labour force by direct employees. The sample includes people who had been self-employed for 20 years as well as those who had only recently become so, including people who had been on the Enterprise Allowance Scheme, a subsidy introduced by the Government in 1983 to encourage unemployed people to set themselves up in business. A summary of the findings is set out in Table 11.3. From this it can be seen that nine of the 12 had undergone formal apprenticeship training and that a further two had undertaken courses under the government-sponsored Training Opportunities Scheme, followed by a period of employment in the Direct Labour Organisation of the Local Authority. The apprenticeship training undergone varied from two years in a Central European country to four- and five-year apprenticeships in firms of varying sizes or in nationalised industry, followed by a number of additional years training in related skills in a number of instances. Only in one instance (No. 5) was training carried out by a self-employed tradesman, but this was an electrical contractor training his own son. No. 14, though not undertaking a formal apprenticeship, learnt his trade from his father and grandfather working at home in India. Therefore, except in these two cases where training was undertaken by fathers of sons, all those currently self-employed had been trained through employment as an apprentice in small, medium or large organisations or through government-sponsored programmes.

However, when we examine what training the self-employed are currently undertaking, we find that long hours of work, safety considerations and unpredictability of workload militate against taking on an apprentice. Six would not consider training at all. This was expressed in terms of 'I'm not training and wouldn't consider it. The insurance is a problem', 'I've never had time to train' and the fact that they felt subcontracting was generally more satisfactory

Table 11.3 Work history and work relations of a self-employed

No.	Years self-employed	Work Relations	Customers	Training of self	Training of others
1	15	Self, occasionally calls in a plasterer.	Entirely domestic. General building.	5-year apprenticeship with plumbing & heating oil distributors.	Not training and wouldn't consider it. Insurance a problem.
2	4	Subcontracts on irregular basis when load heavy. Nephews sometimes help at weekends.	Plumbing, general building. Domestic + commercial. Some grant work subcontracted to him.	4-year apprenticeship with Coal Board. Started B.Sc.	Can't afford to train because of the insurance. People have asked him to take their children on without payment but can't because of potential accidents.
3	7	Sometimes takes on a labourer on irregular basis. Mother answers phone.	Plumbing, bathroom conversions, heating. Domestic.	4-year apprenticeship with medium-sized local building firm.	Registered with CITB but can't afford an apprentice though he could do with the help. Work might not be there to keep apprentice.
5	20	Father (now retired) Mother + wife help 'we don't employ	Electrical contracting + general building. Domestic, but	5-year apprenticeship with father, a self-employed	Has never had time to train. Advantages of subcontracting over

		anybody'. Sometimes subcontracts but requires 715 certificate (on irregular basis).	subcontracted from Gas Board + Central Heating firms. Occasionally industrial or new build.	electrical contractor.	employment relation.
6	7	Has a lad on CITB scheme. Works with a partner. Subcontracts electrical work. Have 2/3 plasterers they call on on a irregular basis.	Other self-employed + businesses (eg. merchants) subcontract to them. Domestic. Partner (a tiler) does more commercial + local authority work.	TOPS followed by 2 years training at Council.	YTS trainee on CITB scheme.
7	3	3 plumbers. Wife answers phone + runs the office. Won't subcontract because they get recommended instead of you.	Waiting for 715 certificate so can tender for work with property developers. Domestic (locally) and domestic for larger companies in London.	Apprenticeship in steam heating. Four and half years + night school.	Has a 'boy' who has done his basic training, now doing advanced plumbing (City & Guilds) but pays for himself. Day release over three years. 'I can't see why it takes so long, he's not stupid.'
8	13	Sometimes employs	Domestic +	2-year apprenticeship	Not able to train. Too

continued on p. 214

Table 11.3 continued

No.	Years self-employed	Work Relations	Customers	Training of self	Training of others
		casually on a part-time basis or subcontracts when busy. Lodging house. Used to employ someone before 1984 (introduction of VAT). Has a partner.	commercial + refurbishments. Some large contracts in London. Has tendered for council work but thinks it takes too much time.	and exam in plumbing + carpentry in Central Europe.	expensive + regulations on safety a problem.
9	4	Doesn't employ anyone. Has two chaps working with him who are subcontracted to him, who run their own companies (i.e. self-employed). 'One is full-time, the other ones we call in when we want them. There are 30 or so of us, and we call each other in when we need to.' Wife does the books.	90% of work from one large company, fitting kitchen units.	5-year apprenticeship in wood machining (City & Guilds) then 2-year course in plumbing on day release, and 16-week basic electrical course with building company which involved factory + site work.	Not training at the moment but 'we've been thinking about it.'

10	14	Doesn't employ anybody. Subcontracts on an irregular basis plumbing + electrical work. Occasionally family or friends help out 'one day, two days, not much'. Doesn't accept subcontracts, 'I do all my own work'. Wife doesn't work, children help with paperwork.	Building work + some grant work from council	Learnt trade from father and grandfather in India.	'I'm not training. My children are mechanics. One – youngest – is at college. They are not in my trade.'
11	4	Partner is self-employed. Keep individual companies to stay below VAT level. Don't subcontract to others. Wife does paperwork other relations on a casual basis when out of work.	Plumbing & heating. About 40% work for large contractors, sometimes supply + fix, sometimes labour only. Sometimes subcontract for Council grant work, housing associations.	TOPs after army. Worked with an in-law who was a plumber whilst on leave. Worked for a contractor for the Gas Board for 8–9 weeks then with Council.	YTS trainee 'he's got no aptitude'. 'Not at Tech college, he should really but that's up to him'. 'We keep him on because we are sorry for him.'
12	7/8	No employees, not even on an irregular	2 or 3 builders small local firms but have	6 years of training. Apprenticeships +	YTS trainee (CITB?) 'I'm not sure.'

continued on p. 216

Table 11.3 *continued*

No.	Years self-employed	Work Relations	Customers	Training of self	Training of others
		basis, had one on a YOP scheme. If I run into difficulty, I call in this self-employed chap. He calls in as well. Sister does the typing. Wife sometimes answers the phone.	just started working for a large company. New build at Univ. + Exhib. Centre in Birmingham.	Advanced City & Guilds in plumbing, heating + ventilation. Indentured with large local firm (heating + ventilation specialists) Also started, but didn't complete a course in gas + arc welding.	(College?) 'No, he works with us. If we take him on a firmer thing, the Government pays half and we pay half the wages. So we can have him for another six months if we want him. Otherwise we get another YTS lad for 2 years.'
13	10 (6 years a proper business)	Employ 2 people + have one subcontractor on a regular basis. All heating engineers/gas fitters. Tiling in bathrooms – subcontracted on an irregular basis. She does the admin.,	Domestic installation – central heating. A larger contractor sometimes calls them in.	He did a 4-year apprenticeship at the Gas Board as a gas fitter/heating engineer. Updating of knowledge through membership of CORGI She worked in a bank. Taught herself to type.	Tried to get a youngster on a CITB scheme. Courses are only available in heating and ventilating which are no good for domestic central heating. Concerned that Gas Board has stopped training this

records etc. Sister or friend helps when on holiday. Teaching brother to do quotes.

year – 'they do the best basic training. Soon there'll be no heating engineers, they'll just be cowboys.'

than taking on an employee. Two were considering taking on trainees, one currently had a trainee on a CITB scheme and another had a 'boy' who had completed basic training and was studying advanced plumbing. However, he was paying his own course fees and his employer clearly resented the amount of time his day release was taking out of productive work, commenting 'It takes three years. I can't see why it takes so long, he's not stupid.' Nos. 11 and 12, who are actually 'partners', have a single YTS trainee between them (and not two as it appears in the table!), but the evasive answers suggest the trainee is receiving no formal training at all. When asked if the trainee went to college, one of the partners replied 'he's not at Tech college, he should be really, but that's up to him. He's got no aptitude – we only keep him on because we feel sorry for him.' The other claimed to be uncertain whether the trainee was on a CITB scheme or not and when asked if he went to college, replied 'No, he works with us.' This suggests that although it may be possible for the self-employed to undertake some training themselves, their conditions of work and particularly discontinuities in workload, make it difficult to guarantee employment beyond the two years of subsidy through the Youth Training Scheme, with the likelihood that skills will be diluted. Moreover, the competitive strategy of the self-employed *vis-à-vis* larger, often more formal businesses, relies on working very long hours and spending considerable time in developing personal contacts as a source of further employment. Therefore the attractions of having a trainee would appear to be in the amount of productive work performed rather than a long-term perspective of training a skilled employee. This is true for firms of all sizes, but the point is emphasised by the fact that only No. 13 claimed to have formal employees (No. 7 probably has, but was a bit ambiguous) and the remainder have extensive systems of 'calling in', subcontracting and informal partnerships.

Conclusion

The evidence presented here suggests that historically the self-employed have received their training primarily through formal employment during and after their apprenticeship period. Government schemes such as the Training Opportunities Scheme have also contributed to the stock of skills, though in the two instances noted here, both were followed by periods of employment in public sector building departments (which also provide apprenticeship training). However, in the present context, we also have to ask how far the self-employed themselves and those who employ self-employed labour can be expected to train and, indeed, pay for training. The answer to the first part of the question must be that only a limited amount of training can be expected and that it carries the possibility of dilution. The answer to the second part must be that there is no rational reason why the self-employed and labour-only subcontractors should not contribute to the costs of training, though the imposition of the CITB's levy on all firms with a payroll of more than £15,000 per annum penalises people who are essentially workers in the industry. More importantly, the way in which the levy is calculated – as a per capita tax, in the case of firms with direct employees, and 2 per cent of payroll in the case of labour-only subcontractors – means that many of the beneficiaries of labour used in this way make little or no contribution at all to training, because the labour they used is packaged in different subcontracts. Therefore in the interests of equity a tax on turnover is more appropriate.

However, the structural problems of training within the construction industry will not simply be solved by the injection of more cash, as the experience of YTS has shown. There seem to be a number of possible outcomes to the present situation of acute skill shortages. The most obvious one is that new techniques and technology will be introduced in such a way as to reduce the skill requirements of the industry. This may well be the most viable solution, but it stands in stark contrast to the route taken by West German and French employers who are increasing the skill levels of their workforces (see the chapters by Bobroff, and Streeck and Hilbert in this volume). This raises the old question of the international competitiveness of the British industry, especially as these pressures are likely to increase rather than decrease with the completion of the European market in 1992. In contrast, if a consensus could be established that more training is desirable to meet current and possible future skill shortages, then there are a number of fronts on which this objective could be approached. The three main areas would seem to be: (1) the need to avoid sharp fluctuations in workload, which requires consideration of the method of financing of construction projects and, with this, the balance of public and private sector work; (2) the improvement of basic wage rates and conditions of employment to the extent that self-employment is no longer an attractive proposition to construction workers; (3) a strengthening of trade union organisation which is essential both to the improvement of working conditions and to the regulation of apprenticeship. All of these areas require a political solution rather than one that can be generated internally within the institutions of the training system. The suspicion is that neither the employers nor their representative organisations have the political will to effect this whilst the unions do not have the political strength. It seems that direct and active state intervention in the construction industry is the only way to solve current problems of skill supply by actually seeking to reverse the underlying rationale of the system which produces labour force fragmentation. Above all, it is clear that the organisation of the production process and the institutionalisation of self-employment lie at the root of the problem.

Notes

1. The Construction Industry Training Board (CITB) is a tripartite body set up under the provisions of the 1964 Industrial Training Act to oversee training arrangements in the private sector construction industry.

2. The research project 'Unemployment, Self-employment and Small Business Formation' was financed by the Leverhulme Trust.

3. A parallel debate in the Third World concerns share-croppers. Although tenant farmers provide part of the working capital for production under share-cropping arrangements, they do not own the means of production. They mainly provide wage labour whilst the capitalist farmer controls production decisions and passes some of the risks of investment onto the share-cropper. In this context, it has been argued that share-cropping constitutes a transitional form of wage labour, which arises under specific conditions of labour and capital scarcity.

4. Lenin argues 'The development of forms of industry, like that of all social relationships in general, cannot but proceed very gradually among a mass of interlocking, transitional forms and seeming reversions to the past. Thus, the growth of small industries may express (as we have seen) the progress of capitalist manufacture; now we see that the factory, too, may sometimes develop small industries. . . . To give a proper assessment of the significance of such phenomena, we must consider them in conjunction with the whole structure of industry at a given stage of its development and with the main trends of this development' (1972: 536).

Bibliography

Ball, M. (1988), *Rebuilding Construction. Economic Change in the British Construction Industry*, Routledge, London

Bowley, M. (1966), *The British Building Industry*, Macmillan, London

Briscoe, G. (1989), 'Occupational Study. Construction Occupations', in *Review of the Economy and Employment*, vol. 2, *Occupational Studies*, Institute for Employment Research, University of Warwick, 215–39

—— (1990), 'Skill Shortages in the Construction Sector', *International Journal of Manpower*, vol. 11, 2/3, 23–8

Campinos-Dubernet, M. (1988), 'Des rigidités de la flexibilité: le BTP dans quatre pays européens', paper presented to Colloque Europe et Chantiers, Paris, 28–30 September

Campinos-Dubernet, M. and J.-M. Grando (1988), 'Formation professionelle ouvrière: trois modèles européens', *Formation/Emploi*, 22, 5–29

Construction Board News (1986), Construction Industry Training Board, Bircham Newton, July

Construction Board News (1987), Construction Industry Training Board, Bircham Newton, April

CITB (1988), *Cost Effective Training with CITB*, Construction Industry Training Board, Bircham Newton

Evans, S. and R. Lewis (1989), 'Destructuring and Deregulation in the Construction Industry', in S. Tailby and C. Whitston (eds), *Manufacturing Change: Industrial Relations and Industrial Restructuring*, Blackwell, Oxford

Federation of Master Builders (1982), *Training Standards in the Building Industry*, August. Document, Federation of Master Builders, London

Hakim, C. (1988), 'Self-employment in Britain: A Review of Recent Trends and Current Issues', *Work, Employment and Society*, December, 421–50

Hillebrandt, P. (1984), *Analysis of the British Construction Industry*, Macmillan, Basingstoke

House of Commons Select Committee on Employment (1987), *Skill Shortages*, HMSO, London

Incomes Data Services (1987), *Building Workers' Pay*, Study 396

Lenin, V. I. (1972), Vol. 3, Collected Works, *The Development of Capitalism in Russia*, Progress Publishers, Moscow, first published 1899

Massoud, N. (1988), 'New Forms of Control over Production Associated with the Management Fee System of Contracting', *Production of the Built Environment* 9, Proceedings of the 9th Bartlett International Summer School, University of London, 74–9

Rainbird, H. (1988), 'Government Training Policy and Apprenticeship in the British Construction Industry', *Production of the Built Environment* 9, Proceedings of the 9th Bartlett International Summer School, University of London 88–93

—— (1990), *Training Matters. Trade Union Perspectives on Industrial Restructuring and Training*, Blackwell, Oxford

—— (forthcoming), 'Self-employment or Disguised Wage Labour?', in A. Pollert (ed.), *Questions of Restructuring Work and Employment*, Blackwell, Oxford

Rainbird, H. and L. Clarke (1988), 'Self-employment and Training in the British Construction Industry: A Contradiction', paper presented at Colloque Europe et Chantiers, Paris, 28–30 September

12

New Competences within the French Construction Industry: their Determinants and the Strategies of Firms

Jacotte Bobroff

Introduction

Construction firms, in particular the largest firms, are presently confronting economic and social constraints that have led them to take a new look at their position within the chain of construction production, to revise the way they organise production and to re-examine their management of human resources. In fact, the French market presents a new dimension that is characterised by: a quantitative reduction in demand and an increase in competition leading to tighter price and time constraints; a reduction in the size of operations and of the proportion of new housing construction within these; and an increase in quality requirements and a greater flexibility of operations. Firms have to take these new requirements, particularly those related to flexibility, into account and they are led to redefine their strategies and the forms of labour force management they adopt. This presents a new situation for a sector which, until recently, had been based on a rigid organisation of labour, where the manual tasks of execution were distinguished from those of organisation and control. It had been satisfied with an unskilled workforce and with on-the-job training from other areas whose principal merits were those of productivity.

Some of the firms are characterised by a new approach to productivity. They are counting on a re-evaluation of qualification, based on a more flexible organisation of labour and lower numbers of workers. Site management, finding itself in charge of new responsibilities, is now delegating more tasks to the manual workers themselves. A shift in the conditions of production has come into operation: over and above productivity requirements, the labour force is expected to demonstrate the ability to organise, to oversee and to control the construction process, all this in a context where labour-force qualification has been eroded in the last decades and where a clear ageing of the workforce is evident.[1]

Thus, the labour force does not possess the characteristics required by the new conditions of production and its regeneration is made much more difficult by the fact that young people coming into the labour market have negative images of the construction trades. So nowadays firms, especially large firms, are confronted with a twofold problem, that of the rejuvenation of the labour force and that of the content of qualification and training.

The Diversity of Strategies and State Policies

In the face of these conditions and the combined effects of the economic crisis and new requirements, there is no sign of firms adopting a single approach to these questions, especially as far as dealing with labour-force problems is concerned. Different forms of organisation and of the recomposition of the labour process are being undertaken on site. The strategies, thus defined, depend on the firm's history, its characteristics, its traditions and market practices, and these elements represent the starting point for diverse combinations of the various factors of production.

The conception, preparation, realisation and management of the site are all affected by the introduction of new technologies and methods and the use of innovative materials or components. These changes lead to a number of adjustments and transformations in the economic and social relationships within firms.

Some general contractors continue to prioritise the rationalisation of the labour process (inspired by the Taylorist model of industrial organisation), based on an extremely precise description of tasks and of productivity rates. They still have a mainly unskilled, specialised labour force at their disposal and seek productivity gains from the optimal use of site materials and industrialised products, which, at the present time, are more particularly directed towards the finishing trades. Other contractors still rely on traditional trade characteristics, subcontracting the most skilled tasks if they are unable to undertake them themselves. Lastly, some firms, conscious of the need to rejuvenate their human resource management methods, attempt to consider new directions.

Diverse tendencies coexist within the sector and even within firms. Whilst some firms attempt to increase the qualification of their labour force, training existing workers and recruiting young people with a higher level of education, this does not stop them maintaining task specialisation within another section of the labour force. Sites can then be characterised by an organisation of labour that entrusts, on the one hand, simple, fragmented tasks, based on productivity, to unskilled workers, who are nevertheless capable of widening the field of their operations by increasing the number of such tasks for which they are responsible, and, on the other, reserves other activities for a group of more highly skilled workers.

The search for new solutions is still rather exceptional and attempts in this direction are concentrated on experimental sites. Thus, they concern only a small proportion of workers, most frequently those employed by large firms and who are already highly skilled or, alternatively, young people with a high level of education that the firm attempts to select, retain and even to promote to positions of site foreman or management.

The French state has played a decisive role in supporting such experiments. Plan-Construction,[2] through the medium of the 'Employment and Valorisation of the Construction Trades' programme (EVMB), offers grants to firms which choose to go in this direction and helps them gain access to state-subsidised construction markets. The construction projects undertaken within this framework over the last few years reflect professional preoccupation with the future development of construction trades and the regeneration of the manual labour force. Numerous actors are implicated in this policy, which poses the question of the transfer of qualifications: firms, trade unions and educationalists come into contact through tripartite organisations and professional consultative commissions, in order to create new diplomas and training and to discuss the classification of manual workers.

The experimental sites devoted to training have offered the opportunity to test new practices, and in particular, those based on alternance training whereby firms and educational establishments, linked either to the state education system or directly to the profession, are brought into association. These 'twin' practices have served to illustrate the shared determination of educationalists and companies to make educational instruction more relevant to professional life and to take economic and production constraints, as well as the technological developments of the industry, into account.

These site schools have enabled firms to create training programmes that make it possible to develop a new kind of manual worker with different capacities (the ability to abstract, anticipate, synthesise, etc.). Several basic tendencies characterise these experiments. Particular emphasis is placed on the integration of young people and their retention within the firm, so as to stem the ageing of the manual workforce. New competences are sought in the face of the technical and organisational changes that are occurring within the sector, with particular reference to the widening of operations, towards the preparatory stages of the production process and towards control of the finished product. There has also been an attempt to transform site management which, in view of the former conditions of mass production, had tended to emphasise leadership based on discipline and productivity. Finally, there has been an increase in the professional nature of training which relates to the objectives of the firm and aims to bring the more theoretical training closer to the actual conditions of production.

New Ways of Dealing with Labour Force Constraints

If all the firms in the sector have a vested interest in such experiments, which tend to prioritise the search for innovative solutions, numerous firms are also attempting to discover ways of dealing with production flexibility. Thus, labour force adaptability and operational flexibility are at the forefront of the preoccupations of those firms that have gained awareness of the implications of the revival of the personnel management function.

Thus, one can witness attempts to transform the management of human resources and to reorganise the labour process through the relationship between the externalisation/internalisation of labour force constraints. Some firms place responsibility for these constraints with subcontractors, reducing their own output to a minimum; these firms attempt to get around the problems of worker training by leaving direct management to the subcontractors; all their efforts are focused on mastering planning and site preparation. This option depends heavily on research and engineering, but firms cannot avoid some consideration of the types of relationship they adopt with those bodies that will be called upon to act as 'partners'. Other firms attempt to find ways of dealing with flexibility by reviewing their use of the labour force: they either attempt to adapt the labour force to new requirements, without substantially changing the qualification profile, or they attempt to regenerate the work force and give it new capabilities through training.

Amongst firms adopting the strategy of internalisation of labour force constraints, two main patterns can be identified. Firstly, some firms attempt to exercise control over uncertainty by adopting technical solutions and by laying responsibility for some of the uncertainties of production with manufacturers at the beginning of the production process. New divisions within continuous production sites are organised around the fitting of components of the finishing trades (technical pipe-lagging, breeze blocks, electric hoists) that call traditional trades and qualifications into question. Such choices enable firms recruiting a labour force trained on large sites to avoid the question of the qualification and the renewal of its manual staff. The internalisation of constraints made possible by this approach takes the potential for adaptation and the limitations of such a labour force into account. Of course, workers are required to undertake extra tasks, but these are simplified and limited to the fitting of prefabricated products: a new form of 'multi-skilling' (none the less fairly unskilled and specialised) is put into operation; the reconstruction of qualification takes place around the profile of the 'multi-skilled assembler/fitter'. This strategy does not stop firms externalising more technical tasks that require craft skills.

Secondly, a minority of firms attempt to meet the requirements of flexibility and quality control by undertaking a detailed revision of qualifications. The objective here is no longer for the firm to make decisions about the internalisation of tasks according to the capacities of the labour force at its disposal. Rather it attempts to broaden labour force qualification, to modify its content so as to make it possible to adapt the existing labour force to new technical and organisational conditions. A new profile of manual qualifications is thus sought by the firm, which attempts to achieve this by training or replacing a proportion of its manual labour force, not only in order to widen its operational field, but also in order to equip it with 'new competences'. In this instance, different characteristics are stressed (the ability to abstract, to anticipate, to be autonomous) which are directed towards the self-organisation of work, management of task boundaries and taking responsibility. Another form of multi-skilling is aimed at here, which surpasses that which characterises the 'multi-skilled assembler/fitter', whose activities are limited to the adoption of few additional, but related and simplified tasks.

This search for a new profile of manual labour gives rise to the recruitment of strictly selected young people who have attained a certain educational level and are equipped with the right attitudes to enable those 'with potential' to adhere to the values of the firm. The firms that attempt to reorganise the labour process in such a way, on the basis of an increase in qualification, are still fairly rare. Such strategies based on recruitment, training and the retention of young people with high levels of qualification, require strong management motivation and a great deal of support from the board of directors.

Amongst the major French firms,[3] some have attempted to take a new look at their management of human resources in this way; but this task is generally carried out by a few departments or services which are directly concerned with the problem.

It is more difficult to grasp the strategies of the small or medium-sized firms which have more limited resources at their disposal. However, in these firms, as amongst the larger ones, important sources of productivity can still be released through the organis-ation of tasks and regulation of the interfaces of site operations. The small and medium-sized firms that attempt to redefine their qualifi-cation requirements and to look for increased multi-skilling in their manual labour force are also numerous.

This rejuvenated workforce will later constitute a pool of labour from which the small and medium-sized firms will select the most capable members in order to replace their site management personnel.

Lastly, the more technical trades (plumbers, electricians, heating engineers) which have to confront technological developments to an even greater extent than those of main trades, declare that they can no longer limit the training of their manual labour force to special-ised technical know-how. These firms are seeking abilities that will enable the most qualified members of the labour force to progress from on-site work to the fields of engineering, methods and cus-tomer liaison.

Qualification and New Competences

The stress that firms place on the question of competence is indicative of contemporary developments. Whereas a job description that related to a series of specific and fragmented tasks was previously the norm, nowadays greater attention is paid to the ability to adapt to rapidly changing work situations. Faced with changes in the conditions of production, firms value flexibility and the need for workers to adapt to new demands, to develop and acquire new types of knowledge.

Thus, some firms have brought the traditional criteria of qualification into question not only because these are based on knowledge and know-how that relates to specific and strictly demarcated trades, but also because qualification has a social dimension. As a 'complex social relation' (Naville 1956), it is the result of negotiations and compromise between the social partners and other actors. To question this is to confront the status quo of relationships established by professional groups, the socially recognised hierarchy in the firm, the industry or even more widely, in society as a whole.

By no longer referring to existing job descriptions but to new abilities and competences, firms can thus organise new frameworks for their human resources policies and elaborate means of encouraging some workers to identify with the firm, without necessarily transforming labour relationships amongst all their other employees. In other respects the demise of traditional criteria of qualification and of knowledge linked to a trade offers the opportunity to bring other more behavioural characteristics (the internalisation of constraints, attitudes, autonomy, and responsibility) to the fore and to prioritise individuals' abilities to develop and equip themselves with skills that cut across traditional trade boundaries.

What today's firms are looking for in worker competence combines factors based on the personal qualities of the worker (aptitude, familial and professional career, practical and moral relationship to work) with the recognition of levels of education, qualification and status. A new form of professionality[4] is being created here based on professional relationships that are no longer connected to specific job descriptions. For the firms that have begun to look upon their labour force in this way this new situation leads to attempts to redefine the policies of personnel management.

The Bouygues Company[5] (the largest firm in the construction sector in the world, with a labour force over 60,000) began to pay particular attention to human resources management very early on. Nevertheless, it finds itself having to deal with the question of the transfer of skills, the reproduction of skills and the ageing of its manual labour force: in 1987 over 40 per cent of its manual workers were over forty-five years old whilst only 10 per cent were under twenty-five. This firm, whose activities are becoming more and more diversified and which is experiencing major transformations in the content of its building contractor interests, is having further to increase the efforts it has traditionally made in personnel management and in-house training.

From the beginning of the 1960s, which were characterised by a high level of manual labour turnover, the order of the Compagnons du Minorange was founded. Acting as a guild, the order's professed aim was to establish and retain a group of skilled manual workers equipped with a specific elite status guided by special regulations and given distinctive clothing. This system aimed as much at the production of a feeling of loyalty to the firm and discipline as at the reproduction of professional competence. Nowadays the number of 'Minorange' members is limited to one thousand and particular training initiatives are aimed at them, as they are all former craft-workers, of whom 10 per cent are called upon to follow advanced training courses each year.

The firm has also given priority to the mobilisation of young manual workers. At the beginning of the 1970s it created a body of 'Young Construction Builders' with this aim in mind. In order to meet the aspirations of this young labour force, a specific status and a sponsorship system were introduced here too. At the present time, two separate channels have replaced the single body, one of which is designed to increase the professionalisation of 'young builders', whilst the other is more directly oriented towards the selection and training of young people capable of progressing to supervisory level: 'the young Bouygues foreman'. In 1987 the firm allocated 3 per cent of its overall wage costs to training initiatives thus increasing threefold the amount it is legally bound to spend; half a million hours of training were given; 40 per cent of the workforce took part.[6]

Traditionally training is undertaken by the firm's management within the group but one can identify a new tendency to give greater preference to diplomas dispensed by state education and to the 'twin' initiatives undertaken in association with professional or technical colleges.

In present circumstances any firm that hopes to rejuvenate its labour force must also adopt new forms of personnel management especially as far as the younger groups are concerned. A model of urban well-educated groups is replacing that of the manual construction worker of previous decades, who was generally of rural or immigrant origin. Thus, the firm has to adopt a different form of personnel management for this young workforce to offer different ways of encouraging workers to identify with the interests of the firm, different forms of discipline and motivation, and more personalised relationships. These are the conditions that the Bouygues Company has attempted to bring together on its experimental sites[7] by emphasising certain transformations in the methods of selection and recruitment (with psychology tests and personal interviews); the definition of a level of education deemed to guarantee the development potential of the young worker; a career plan (with individual records and files); and promotions that encourage mobility and adaptability.

Although these important changes affect the human resource policies of the Bouygues Company one must not forget that they are limited to a small group of strictly selected young manual workers. They coexist with the maintenance of specialised tasks and productivity requirements as far as the less well qualified section of the workforce is concerned.

New Competences and Traditional Trades

Thus what construction firms are today referring to as 'new competences' remain closely linked to their attempts to introduce new policies in the field of human resource management and to the reorganisation of on-site labour. Although the traditional criteria for defining professions and trades are being brought into question, and stress is being put on competences that cut across several fields of technical know-how, firms still cannot neglect the apprenticeship of knowledge and practice, the experience and characteristics of traditional trades. To bring basic training in a trade into question would represent an obstacle for firms who have to face new market conditions and imperatives of quality and time.

When firms stress their need for a 'competent labour force' the content of this requirement is often vague and imprecise; but it reveals a demand that surpasses the traditional characteristics of manual workers. Of course to talk of multi-skilling and of autonomy is to refer to the ability to adapt to new tasks, to take responsibility for and to deliver a product within favourable conditions of quality, time and even price. However, first and foremost it refers to the technical mastery of a craft or trade, mastery that can later be extended to the carrying out of other operations.

The traditional building trades are in fact, characterised by those qualities that are at the present time demanded by firms as 'new'. Of course the contours of these qualities were somewhat blurred during the period of the large prefabricated sites, where the image of the skilled manual worker, especially within large firms, was brought into question and the sector now finds itself faced with a crisis as far as the reproduction of the qualification of its workforce is concerned. The capacities and aptitudes that need to be brought into play represent the foundation of certain construction trades and are particularly essential to the craftworkers who control their use: organising the supply, work, time and control of the finished product. Thus, through the acquisition of knowledge and technical know-how and through the technico-professional culture on which they depend, the traditional trades remain the bedrock of developments expressed in terms of 'new competences'.

Over and above basic technological knowledge and the individual dimension of qualification, professions and trades are founded on qualities of a more social nature. Indeed, by also calling for a more collective dimension which enables workers to take their place within a collective work unit and to become rapidly productive within that group, the 'new competences' have a social element. Here too the notion of apprenticeship to a trade and the respect of rules that this implies are at the basis of the system of values and professional relationships. It is this technico-social culture that can not be avoided and that firms express in the following way: 'progress from practical *"savoir-faire"* to behavioural *"savoir-être"*'.[8]

Multi-skilling and Autonomy: What Competences?

Thus multi-skilling and autonomy are the two characteristics sought by firms which identify in this interpenetration of skills from diverse trades, a means of adapting their labour force to the transformation and future development of the conditions of production. Not all forms of multi-skilling lead to an increase in qualification: the multi-skilled builder-fitter, whose tasks on continuous sites (cf. Bobroff and Campagnac 1987) are limited to the assembly and fitting of prefabricated products divided up into 'packages', retains a fragmented work profile and will not benefit from additional autonomy. The work cycle is extended to cover new activities, but through the simple addition of manual interventions of the same kind that do not call upon more complex forms of knowledge.

This type of multi-skilling which characterises the profile of the manual worker on continuous sites does not permit a reconstruction of the labour process. It is limited to extension of tasks, i.e. to the regrouping of manual operations previously spread over several successive posts in such a manner that workers complete whole groups or subgroups of operations (cf. CEREQ, 1976; Bobroff and Le Goff 1987). Furthermore, as far as the workers are concerned, this profile does not in itself correspond to a qualification, as it is limited to the acquisition of just one form of know-how, whilst the technological and organisational knowledge of these practices does not figure in the transfer of knowledge.

However, other forms of multi-skilling that are founded on trades, professional and technical knowledge and know-how, are appearing. The reconstructions based on a recognition of traditional trade skills are of quite a different kind and would seem to represent an obligatory stage from which efficiency and quality factors may be generated within the context of modern sites.

Even in the case of sequential sites, the sequential multi-skilled worker must have a different role to play. As skilled manual workers with responsibility for carrying out all the tasks within their specialism, with the help of technical knowledge and know-how, but also with the general knowledge over and above that specific to a single trade, such workers should be able to extend the field of their activities to new tasks. This represents a new field of competence, organised through a different reconstruction of various trades. Of course, only some aspects of skill are directly adopted from each trade, but this reconstruction is based on a previously acquired trade and on the ability to attain an understanding of the entire production process. Thus, the worker has to master a whole series of tasks undertaken in this way, covering the production process from beginning to end: supply of raw materials, reading plans, site preparation, control over the sequence of tasks and schedules, work organisation, control over task execution, delivery and reception of the finished product.

This new specialisation, which exists at the boundaries of several trades, surpasses the specific knowledge of each of these and requires the ability to abstract and generalise. Past experience can only be capitalised upon and transferred to other products on other sites with the aid of a more theoretical training programme.

Thus multi-skilling represents a great variety of concrete situations and covers a range of competences which vary according to markets, stages of production, types of firm and personnel management policies. It ranges from a straightforward job enlargement through widening operations to several related fields, the aim of which is usually limited to getting skilled manual workers to make better use of slack periods, to a situation where it can also enable true job enrichment through the addition of tasks of a totally different kind to those that define the traditional trade speciality. In this case, the acquisitions of the practices and tricks of the trade is not enough, new technological knowledge and formalised data also have to be called upon.

It is from this basic principle, the distinction between enlargement and enrichment, that we have attempted to approach the diversity of the existence of multi-skilling on various construction sites. Of course we came across numerous intermediate levels and the types of multi-skilling are rarely this 'pure'; but in most cases job enlargement only enables firms to reach a 'low' level of multi-skilling, whilst job enrichment, based on trade characteristics, allows 'high' levels. The latter may be defined by the ability to master new products but also new materials and techniques and to adapt to, or even to design and implement, new forms of work organisation. Thus, 'enriching' multi-skilling cannot be distinguished from the characteristics it implies that cut across traditional trade and knowledge boundaries and, in particular, that of autonomy.

Taking all of the constraints (technical, organisational and economic) into account, thus refers to another competence; that of autonomy. It is without doubt this quality, the basis of the traditional trade and the independence of the craftworker, that has been most eroded by the specialised practices of large construction sites. This explains its reappearance in the modernising discourse of firms, under the term 'new competences' associated with other themes like responsibility, motivation and initiative. The content of the term 'autonomy' seems to be even more general than that of multi-skilling in the sense that it not only concerns the professional field, but also refers to individual psychology and to the socio-cultural context.

In particular the desire for autonomy at work expressed by young workers represents a new cultural situation that is manifested in the rejection of the hierarchical and paternalistic relationships habitually associated with the sector and by the desire to 'control one's own experiences'. As far as firms are concerned this term implies certain requirements, linked to the need to increase educational standards, but also to reorganise the labour process on a new basis, where responsibility and an awareness of the constraints and objectives of the firm occupy a central position.

As with multi-skilling a certain number of capacities go to make up autonomy: the ability to reflect upon, to analyse, to anticipate and to organise one's own work, the management of unforeseen circumstances and quality control. These represent several different dimensions of the capacity for autonomy (Bobroff and Le Goff 1987), including, firstly, general knowledge and the ability to understand, which make it possible to deal with plans and technical drafts. The ability to read plans to interpret them, and even to be able to modify them in the event of unforeseen circumstances, would seem to be a preliminary requirement for autonomy within work, the minimal basis for an understanding of the whole of the production process. Secondly comes the ability to plan and organise work and time. This refers to the mental reconstruction of operations which depend on the capacity to formalise and abstract. This is a necessary stage on the path to anticipating, articulating and regrouping the various forms of operation, from a single activity to a global task. Lastly comes a dimension more in the order of 'responsibility': the faculty of workers to master their own interventions, operating methods, safety constraints and unforeseen circumstances they may come across and the ability to exercise some form of control over the finished product. New criteria appear at this stage, those that take account of clients' demands, in terms of quality, time and even cost.

The highest level of autonomy would require workers to elaborate their own methods of adaptation and adjustment on the basis of their perception of the initial stages and the final completion of the production process, and for them to do so at each intermediary stage of production. These characteristics of abstraction, anticipation and adaptation surpass practical know-how. Although they characterise craftworkers and often improvers, manual workers have never had the opportunity to develop them, all the more so because the development of such forms of autonomy is often dependent on conditions of freedom, the delegation of power and the bringing of hierarchical relationships into question.

Will the firms that are currently demanding such abilities be willing to follow this path and to undermine traditional relationships and the hierarchical network of construction sites? The question is all the more important when it comes to the replacement and the rejuvenation of the labour force, as the young people with higher levels of qualification who some firms are eager to recruit are even less likely to accept past working conditions and forms of authority.

Developments are taking place, both within the vocational educational system and within the profession itself. New qualifications (professional baccalauréats) have recently been elaborated in order to establish a link between the levels of realisation and execution and more analytical and abstract processes. A privileged position, on the boundaries of the execution, organisation, research and management spheres, exists for this type of professional category, in a profession where the necessary condition for recruiting and retaining young manual workers lies in a re-evaluation of diplomas and classifications.

The National Federation of Construction (representing the profession), which until now had refused to renounce the old table of manual classifications organised on the basis of job description, today accepts that other criteria may be given priority. Thus, four levels of manual qualification are to be introduced, which value the possession of multi-skills, the capacity to organise work, autonomy and the ability to take responsibility for a small team.

Types of Human Resource Management to Motivate Young Workers

In the past, firms preferred to count on on-the-job apprenticeships as a means of training and retaining young people. Disciplinary considerations and training in low-level, specialist skills that effectively made the young person a 'prisoner' within the firm, were given priority. Today firms recognise that a higher level of general education and of qualification is needed if they are to develop the abilities they require.

All of the technical and organisational characteristics that may be used to define this new manual population are also based on different behavioural elements that distinguish them from those that characterised previous generations of workers: motivation, new modes of relation to and identification with work, the firm, the matching of a personal and a professional career plan. The young construction worker who is taking the place of the previous model is defined by different expectations and aspirations.

The firms which are aware of these developments attempt to introduce new working conditions and types of training. To retain young people within the profession, firms are required to take things much further than isolated experiments and to guarantee some form of continuity. Few firms have attempted to do this. However, some that we may qualify as innovative in the field of human resource management are paying particular attention to the recruitment of young people. Observation of the sites where attempts in this direction have taken place enables us to draw the following conclusions (Bobroff 1987a and 1987b).

These policies tend towards a new model of the organisation of the construction site and of relationships. These 'new' sites have several objectives attributed to them. Firstly, to demonstrate to young people the existence of new opportunities and qualification options by confiding intermediate management tasks to them within a fairly short space of time. Secondly, to bring the normal division of labour into question by widening the scope of their operations. For labourers in the main trades, skills are extended to the tasks of the finishing trades and this option represents a favoured means of motivating workers and improving the over-specialised image of the trade. Thirdly, to give young people a certain number of competences, as a necessary requirement for the mastery of production costs and quality control. The development of multi-skilling represents, in fact, an opportunity to see new know-how and organisational capacities emerge and to improve autonomy and the sense of responsibility. Fourthly, to improve the social climate and instigate new relationships within the work environment, based on improved communications policies with young workers being personally assessed and, finally, to improve working environment on the construction site (modern and adapted materials, more comfortable quarters and working clothes).

Many conditions of this kind must be brought together in order to improve recruitment and especially to retain the young workers who have been strictly selected for their capacities to progress towards new responsibilities. For these young people, a re-evaluation of the trades cannot take place without there being some change in the traditional division of labour, without some thought being given to working conditions and relationships on site and without some guarantee of promotion. All of these elements need to be taken into consideration in a formalised management policy for the young labour force. Training may be essential in directing this labour force towards the required abilities and competences, but it will only make sense and be effective if it takes place within the framework of such developments.

The fact that the traditional division of labour has been brought into question and tasks have been extended to the finishing trades, illustrates how strongly committed young people are to diverse forms of multi-skilling and shows the value of their interest in these so-called 'new competences'.

The training given under the dual form of theoretical classroom learning and practical experience on site also seems to be important to young people who see this as an opportunity to build upon their achievements within the education system and to extend their technical knowledge, whilst obtaining the means to a more abstract comprehension of each activity and of the production process as a whole. The reading and interpretation of construction plans occupies a central position within such training programmes, as does the practical apprenticeship of various operations within structural and finishing work. Young workers are extremely responsive to this type of learning directed towards multi-skilling. They see it as an opportunity to acquire a useful basis on which to widen their competences.

Finally, it will be all the more easy for a collective work unit, based on young workers, to come into existence if the latter represent an important group on site, if a good working atmosphere is created and if they are thus able to prove their ability to run a site successfully from beginning to end.

In view of all the constraints that the construction industry today has to face, there is no evidence of a single direction being taken either towards requalification or towards deskilling in the Taylorist mode, but rather of great diversity in the way labour-force questions are being dealt with. Nevertheless, most firms are attempting to redevelop their attitudes towards productivity and cost management through a reconstruction of the labour process. In so doing, they stress the need for flexibility in production and for the labour force to adapt to the uncertainty of operations.

There are indications of great diversity in the strategies they adopt, in particular, as far as decisions about integrating labour-force constraints or, alternatively, externalising them are concerned. Those that attempt to increase qualification, or even to modify its content, are usually characterised by innovations in the field of human resource management policies. Although they do not represent a majority within the sector, it is from reflexions undertaken by these firms that a definition of a problem of qualification in terms of 'new competences' has begun to emerge. It is this tendency and the reconstruction of the labour process that it implies that we have attempted to present in this chapter.

Notes

1. 16 per cent of the employees in the construction and public works sector (Bâtiment et Travaux Publics (BTP)) are between 18 and 24 years old, but they represent only 13 per cent of the skilled manual work force, as against 30 per cent of unskilled labour. The under-25s only represent 3.4 per cent of skilled manual numbers. Among employees of the construction sector, 58 per cent are considered 'skilled' in the manual classification tables. But this category is not at all homogeneous as far as real levels of skill are concerned (see Centre d'Information et de Documentation Jeunesse, March 1988 and 'Les chiffres-clés du BTP', Comité Central de Coordination de l'Apprentissage du Bâtiment et des Travaux Publiques, Paris, September 1987).

2. Organisation that is linked to the Ministry for Town Planning and Housing. For a review of its activities in the training field, see 'Formation en chantier, des expérimentations pour projeter des métiers', Plan-Construction, March 1988.

3. In France, 93 per cent of the construction and public works firms employ fewer than 10 people and of these firms 95 per cent are craft-based. So this sector is dominated by small firms. Over the last fifteen years there has been a bipolarisation of activity within the sector between large and small firms, to the detriment of medium-sized firms which have almost disappeared. The weight of the 8 largest firms in the sector is significant: they account for 10 per cent of turnover and 250,000 employees, 16 per cent of the population working in the construction sector (*Le Moniteur*, November 1988).

4. On the question of professionality see Zarifian (1985).

5. For an historical overview of the group see Campagnac and Nouzille (1988).

6. In 'Bilan 1987' published by the Bouygues enterprise.

7. Cf. the description of an experiment of this type aimed at the training and recruitment of young people on a Bouygues site (Bobroff 1987a: 82–7).

8. Phrase quoted by the President of the Pont-à-Mousson firm in *L'Usine Nouvelle*, 26 June 1986.

Jacotte Bobroff

Bibliography

Bobroff, J. (1987a), 'Chantier: Attention Jeunes!', Plan-Construction/
EVMB, Collection Expérimentation Paris
—— (1987b), 'La qualification: des politiques d'entreprise face aux aspirations des jeunes et leurs stratégies professionnelles', in *L'Emploi des
jeunes dans le bâtiment*, Plan-Construction/EVMB. Paris
Bobroff, J. and E. Campagnac (1987), 'La démarche sequentielle de la
SGE-BTP: quels atouts pour les travailleurs et les PME?', Centre d'En-
seignement et de Recherche Techniques et Sociétés, Plan-Construction/
EVMB Paris
Bobroff, J. and J. P. Le Goff (1987), 'Polyvalence et autonomie dans le
bâtiment: quelles compétences?', results of a seminar organised and
written with the aid of Plan-Construction/EVMB. Paris
Campagnac, E. and V. Nouzille (1988), *Citizen Bouygues*, Éditions Bel-
fond. Paris
CEREQ, (1976), 'L'Organisation du travail et ses formes nouvelles',
Centre d'Études et de Recherches sur les Qualifications, Internal note.
Paris
Naville, P. (1956), *Essai sur la qualification du travail*, Éditions Marcel
Rivière, Paris
Zarifian, P. (1985), 'A la recherche des groupes professionnels', Research
Report CEREQ, Paris

13

Organised Interests and Vocational Training in the West German Construction Industry

Wolfgang Streeck and Josef Hilbert

Introduction

The term 'vocational training system' in the Federal Republic of Germany refers to any public or private institutions or activities that directly or indirectly serve to provide occupational qualifications. While general education is provided by public schools, in vocational training the public and private sectors collaborate. Vocational training takes place primarily in the so-called 'dual system'. For one or two days a week apprentices attend a public vocational school where both general subjects and more theoretical occupational subjects are taught. The rest of their weekly working time apprentices spend at the workplace where practical skills are acquired in the ongoing working process.

The term 'dual system' denotes a combination of two different training locations within the same training programmes. Vocational training follows general schooling and precedes actual working life. As a rule, vocational training programmes have a duration of three years. Workplace training is based on training regulations that under the federal Vocational Training Act are negotiated among the organised social partners (labour unions and business interest associations), decreed by the Federal Government, and supervised by the chambers.[1] In contrast to this centralisation of authority with respect to workplace training, vocational schools are institutions of the Länder. The standing Conference of the Länder Ministers of Education passes general curricula in an attempt to harmonise the school components of initial training and to coordinate them with the subjects of workplace training.

In other countries of the European Community, institutionalised efforts to provide occupational qualifications in a separate training phase after general schooling and prior to working life are the exceptions rather than the rule. In the Federal Republic, training in the 'dual system', the so-called apprenticeship, is the classic way of entering the employment system. In total, there are about 380 officially recognised training programmes. 60 per cent of young people complete a training programme in the dual system.

Unlike other countries, vocational training is treated in Germany primarily as an educational activity, with the boundaries between training and the employment system being more sharply drawn than between the training and the school system. As a consequence, vocational training in the Federal Republic is comparatively unaffected by the ups and downs of political or business cycles, and its encompassing and securely established organisational structure is in strong contrast to countries whose vocational training system consists primarily of a set of individual programmes specialising on the specific, imminent problems of particular sectors or regions.

On the other hand, vocational training in the Federal Republic is, in spite of its institutionalisation as a branch of the educational system, densely intertwined with industrial practice. This contributes to both the closeness of training curricula to practical needs, as well as the employment prospects of apprentices, whose transition from training to industrial practice has become, under the concept of the 'dual system', the trade mark of the German vocational training system. Organising this connection across the boundary between the economic and the educational system, while at the same time preserving the relative autonomy of training *vis-à-vis* short-term economic needs and interests, requires stable and highly differentiated institutions of regulation, resource mobilisation, implementation and control. Both state agencies and, as representatives of the practical interests related to training, the social partners share in these institutions, which extend across several levels from the individual firm providing training, to the region and the industrial sector, up to the level of the country as a whole.

In the following[2] we will describe the role of the social partners in vocational training by focusing on the situation in the German construction industry, not only because of the focus of the present volume but also because the social partners of this sector initiated and run a vocational training scheme and some further training schemes which are of a comparatively high standard and sometimes serve, in some way or other, as examples for reform initiatives in other sectors.

The Need for Reform

In the late 1960s the political parties and the relevant interest groups agreed that the German system of vocational training was in a state of 'crisis' and in need of 'reform'.[3] Three internally connected reform goals were debated. First, the traditional boundaries separating different vocations were to become less rigid. Related trades were to have a common initial training period, with specialisation being introduced gradually at later points. The idea was to equip apprentices with greater flexibility to cope with changing tasks and technical requirements. Second, the portion of vocational training provided outside the firm was to be increased. It was assumed that the average firm, whether because of small size or increasing specialisation, was no longer in a position to provide the kind of general training that was envisaged, particularly for the initial training period. Third, the financing of vocational training – to the extent that it was not directly controlled by the state – was to be restructured in order to compensate firms for the (rising) costs of apprenticeship programmes. Particularly important in this respect was the proposal of a committee of experts reporting to the Federal Government to levy a general training fee from all firms which would then be used to reimburse firms with apprentices. This was conceived as a means of increasing the number of apprenticeships as well as the quality of training.

While the Social Democratic Party and the trade unions pressed vigorously for broader basic training and more integrated training curricula, an enlarged role for external training centres and some form of training levy, the employers had strong objections, especially against the training levy. But even on this subject a measure of disunity remained among employers' associations. Within the Federation of German Employers' Associations (BDA), the two affiliates that were most inclined to find positive elements in the government's reform plans were the employers' associations of the construction industry. In part, this was due to certain peculiarities of technology and industrial structure which spoke strongly in favour not only of more integrated and externalised training but also of new forms of funding.

Apart from the requirements created by increasingly rapid technological change, the narrow specialisation of traditional construction industry occupations had always been in conflict with the need for different trades to cooperate closely on the building site. Productivity increases if workers skilled in one building trade can be used temporarily to perform tasks of other trades, or at least to prepare the ground for the specialist workers. Joint basic training of workers can thus facilitate the management of building sites and improve the organisation of work.

Construction firms at any given time are usually engaged in only a small number of large-scale and lengthy projects. As a result, it is possible that apprentices are never exposed to certain jobs during their entire apprenticeship. External training institutions are therefore a useful device to ensure that all apprentices do in fact pass through a common basic curriculum. Further points in favour of a large training portion outside the firm are the great dependence of construction work on weather conditions; the increasing use of piece-rates for construction teams, which leaves little time for instructing apprentices; and the constant pressure of deadlines on construction sites which may negatively affect the quality of training (Kath 1981: 326).

Compared to other industries, construction firms are usually small. Training costs therefore may become a heavy burden, particularly if more stringent regulations impose higher training standards. Moreover, the fluctuation of skilled workers between construction firms traditionally has been high, which makes the amortisation of training costs for individual firms even less probable than in other industries. Both factors speak for a financial scheme above the firm level which distributes the costs of training more equally.

Another reason why the construction industry was more receptive than other industries to the reform proposals of the early 1970s was its deteriorating position in the market for skilled labour. The number of apprentices in the construction industry had declined almost continuously from 1950 to 1972. While in 1950 there had been 93,000 apprentices, only a decade later this figure had been cut to 52,000. By 1972 the lowest point was reached with 26,100 apprentices. Although other sectors in manufacturing also suffered from a decline due to demographic changes as well as the expansion of secondary education, the construction industry was hit much more seriously. According to its associations, in order to provide for a constant stock of skilled workers, a ratio of 9 apprentices per 100 skilled workers has to be maintained. Around the year 1970, however, there were only 3 apprentices to every 100 skilled workers.

Thus, when in the late 1960s the modernisation of vocational training moved onto the political agenda, this was immediately perceived by the industry as an opportunity to improve the attractiveness of the skilled construction trades. But while the employers were quite willing to pursue the reform ideas that were being floated at the time, they were clearly not prepared to accept greater influence on vocational training by the state. In part, this was because direct state regulation would inevitably have meant a general transsectoral solution, particularly with respect to financing. Only a sector-specific approach, however, could give the construction industry a competitive advantage over other sectors in the market for apprentices. This view was shared by the trade union which was no less concerned about the declining numbers of apprentices and skilled workers than the employers.

Interest Organisation in the German Construction Industry

Firms in the construction industry are organised by two employers' associations, both of which at the same time function as trade associations. Artisanal firms are represented at the federal level by the Zentralverband des Deutschen Baugewerbes (ZDB, Central Association of the German Building Industry).[4] Non-artisanal firms are represented by the Hauptverband der Deutschen Bauindustrie (HDB, Association of the German Construction Industry). Both associations negotiate jointly with the industrial union for the construction industry, Industriegewerkschaft Bau-Steine-Erden (IG BSE, Industrial Union of Construction Workers). These three organisations played the decisive role in the reform of vocational training in the construction industry.

There were about 50,000 artisanal construction firms in West Germany in the early 1980s. About 90 per cent of these were organised in 686 local guilds that were affiliated to 29 regional guild associations. These, in turn, were joined at the national level in the ZDB (Figure 13.1). Together with other artisanal trade and employers'

Figure 13.1 Employers' and trade associations in the West German construction industry

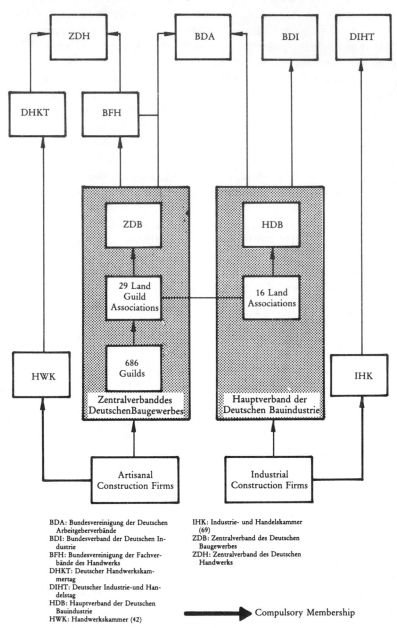

BDA: Bundesvereinigung der Deutschen Arbeitgeberverbände
BDI: Bundesverband der Deutschen Industrie
BFH: Bundesvereinigung der Fachverbände des Handwerks
DHKT: Deutscher Handwerkskammertag
DIHT: Deutscher Industrie-und Handelstag
HDB: Hauptverband der Deutschen Bauindustrie
HWK: Handwerkskammer (42)

IHK: Industrie- und Handelskammer (69)
ZDB: Zentralverband des Deutschen Baugewerbes
ZDH: Zentralverband des Deutschen Handwerks

➤ Compulsory Membership

associations, the ZDB forms the Federation of Artisanal Associations (Bundesvereinigung der Fachverbände des Handwerks, BFH) and, ultimately, the Central Association of German Artisans (Zentralverband des Deutschen Handwerks, ZDH).

Of the 10,000 non-artisanal construction firms in 1980, about one-third (almost exclusively the larger ones which specialise in civil engineering) were organised in the 16 regional associations of the HDB. Four of these also organise artisanal firms and are therefore at the same time affiliated to the ZDB. The HDB, just like the ZDB, is a member of the BDA. It is also affiliated to the Federation of German Industry (BDI) which is the non-artisanal counterpart of the ZDH.

The differences between the domains of the two main employers' associations explain their different interests in, and contributions to, vocational training. Although in 1970 non-artisanal firms employed about 33 per cent of all workers in the industry, they accounted for only 13 per cent of the apprentices. Artisanal firms, by contrast, with 67 per cent of the workforce, were training 87 per cent of the industry's apprentices. This unequal distribution was due to a variety of factors. Training in the artisanal sector typically takes place in firms with close paternalistic ties between employer and employee. Since these firms are mostly located in rural or small town labour markets of limited size, the internal amortisation of training costs is comparatively more likely.

The condition is different in non-artisanal firms. Originally they either provided informal, on-the-job training or relied on the training efforts of the artisanal sector whose skilled workers they absorbed in large numbers. This became less than satisfactory with technical change (e.g. the introduction of armoured concrete) and growing mechanisation. Large firms increasingly began to look for a type of skilled worker who was more flexible and able to cope with a variety of tasks, who had comprehensive qualifications, and in particular was capable of acquiring additional skills. The kind of training required for this was both costly and difficult to provide on the construction site. When in addition the number of apprentices in the artisanal sector began to decline dramatically in the 1960s, the HDB as the representative of the large firms realised that a comprehensive reform of vocational training in the construction industry, artisanal as well as non-artisanal, was inevitable.

The reform of vocational training in construction in the 1970s was promoted jointly by the two large employers' associations.

Given the different problems and interests of the two associations and their members with regard to training, this common effort appears quite extraordinary. There were of course structural factors favouring a joint approach, such as the fact that many of the firms represented by the HDB and ZDB operate in the same local labour markets. But at least as important was the existence of a single trade union for the entire industry which strongly supported the introduction of an integrated, unified training scheme. This union, the IG BSE, is one of 17 industrial unions belonging to the West German trade union federation, the DGB.

Trade union and employers' associations in the German construction industry have a long history of cooperation (Streeck 1981). In the 1960s in particular, the industry's growing recruitment problems gave rise to an elaborate sectoral social policy based on collective agreements which as a rule were declared binding on all workers and employers in the industry by the government. Out of these common efforts grew the 'Social Funds of the Construction Industry' which are jointly controlled by the union and the two employers' associations (Sperner et al. 1976). In 1980, the funds collected what in effect amounted to a legally enforceable payroll tax of 20 per cent of total wages from each employer in the industry. The money is paid to construction workers under a number of social policy programmes aimed at compensating the various disadvantages construction workers suffer in comparison to workers in other industries as a result of casual employment. Apart from their main functions, the funds provide an institutional opportunity for informal meetings and cooperation between employers and trade union. From the perspective of the latter, they also offer a form of parity codetermination adapted to the specific conditions of the construction industry.

The vocational training reform in the 1970s was a remarkable event for a number of reasons. Not only was it one of the first such projects to be started after the passage of the Vocational Training Act of 1969. In addition, it was one of the most comprehensive and innovative, and it was pursued with unusual speed and strategic determination. For the most part, this was due to the close cooperation of the social partners at the sectoral level who between them developed the project and defended it against resistance from both their own rank and file and powerful employers' associations outside the industry. Moreover, the two sides successfully worked together to ensure that the reformed training system, and the considerable resources that came to be invested in it, remained under their joint control rather than that of the state.

The Vocational Training Reform of 1974

The reform project that was negotiated in the early 1970s between the three associations had three main elements: (1) the introduction of a new, integrated training curriculum; (2) the creation of a levy system to finance training activities; and (3) the establishment of a network of training centres to provide training outside individual firms.

The Integrated Training Scheme

The strategy of the three associations was to produce complete and mutually agreed draft regulations that without modification would then have to be accepted by the government.[5] The objective was to exclude as far as possible outside interference. This was directed as much against the state as against the BDA and ZDH, which were hostile to significant elements of the reform project.

Concerning the substance of the new training scheme, there was agreement among union and employers that in order to increase the attractiveness of the industry for young people, the duration of apprenticeships had to be reduced, a large portion of the training had to be shifted from the construction site to training centres outside the firm, and standards had to be raised. The latter was to be achieved by reorganising the training curriculum on the model of what is called in German *Stufenausbildung*, a training concept that was new and considered rather daring at the time. It involved essentially two things:

1 A curriculum starting with broad basic training in the first year and leading gradually, with an intermediate level of specialisation in the second year, towards specific occupational qualifications. An examination was to be taken and passed not only at the end of the apprenticeship but also after the second year.
2 The integration of as many construction industry occupations as possible in the same training scheme, with common basic training in the first year and only limited differentiation between occupations in the second. This implied integration also of artisanal (e.g.

tilers) and non-artisanal (e.g. concrete workers) construction occupations, as well as identical curricula for identical occupations regardless of whether training was provided in artisanal or non-artisanal firms – something that was almost revolutionary especially for the artisanal sector.

Working closely together, trade union and employers' associations produced a first draft of a new training regulation, complete for the Minister to decree. Several other such drafts had to follow, however, in successive attempts to accommodate as many as possible of the objections that were raised by other interested parties. For example, one cause of delay was opposition of employers' associations of other sectors and of the national associations such as the BDA and the ZDH which had to be heard formally by the Minister.

The final version of the Integrated Training Scheme for Construction Industry Occupations (*Stufenausbildung für Bauberufe*) which was transformed into a governmental decree in May 1974, provided for one year of common basic training for no less than 14 construction trades, artisanal and non-artisanal (Figure 13.2).[6] In the second year, apprentices were to be divided in three groups, building, finishing, and civil engineering. Having passed their first examination, they would then proceed to nine months of training in one of the 14 specialised occupations. The final examination was to certify their status as skilled workers in these occupations.

Another innovative aspect of the training scheme was the way in which it divided training time between the workplace, the (public) vocational school, and external training centres. The construction industry was the first to rely extensively on a 'third training location' in addition to the workplace and the vocational school system. Since this seemed to undermine the dual system, it added to the controversy between the construction industry and the national employers' associations. Construction industry apprentices in their first year today spend only six weeks at the workplace, and as much time in the training centre as at school. While later this relationship changes, in the second year the training centre still occupies more than one-third of the time an apprentice spends outside the school.

The Levy System

A foremost concern of the authors of the Integrated Training Scheme were its effects on firms' willingness to train. The larger

Figure 13.2   Integrated training scheme, 1974

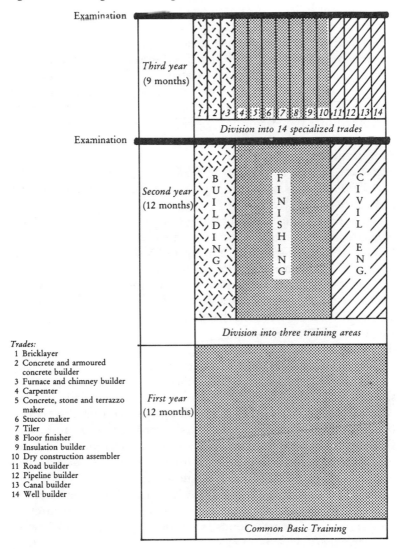

Examination

Third year
(9 months)

1 2 3 4 5 6 7 8 9 10 11 12 13 14

Division into 14 specialized trades

Examination

Second year
(12 months)

B
U
I
L
D
I
N
G

F
I
N
I
S
H
I
N
G

C
I
V
I
L

E
N
G.

Division into three training areas

Trades:
 1 Bricklayer
 2 Concrete and armoured
   concrete builder
 3 Furnace and chimney builder
 4 Carpenter
 5 Concrete, stone and terrazzo
   maker
 6 Stucco maker
 7 Tiler
 8 Floor finisher
 9 Insulation builder
10 Dry construction assembler
11 Road builder
12 Pipeline builder
13 Canal builder
14 Well builder

First year
(12 months)

Common Basic Training

training period outside the firm both increased training costs and
reduced the productive contribution of apprentices. Moreover, the
introduction of the scheme coincided with a deep recession in the
construction industry. For these reasons, the inevitable next step
had to be a reorganisation of the financing of vocational training

with the aim of reducing the costs for firms that provided training.

In September 1975, the union and the employers' associations of the construction industry signed a 'Collective Agreement on Vocational Training'. It stipulated that each firm in the industry had to pay a levy of 0.5 per cent of its payroll into a central fund out of which firms were to be compensated for part of their training expenses, especially for the costs of external training. Payments were to be collected by the Social Funds of the Construction Industry using the established procedure. The agreement was declared legally binding on all construction firms regardless of association membership, by government decree. In successive years, the levy was raised to 1.5 per cent in 1979 and 1.7 per cent in 1986 due to the ensuing increase in training activities and a declining wage bill as a result of the recession.

Given the unequal distribution of training between artisanal and non-artisanal firms, any system that finances training by a payroll levy inevitably redistributes funds from HDB to ZDB firms. Since the share of non-artisanal firms in the industry's wage bill clearly exceeds their share in the number of apprentices, such firms under the Industrial Agreement in effect subsidise training in the artisanal sector. There are indications that this was seen by the artisanal firms and their association as a *quid pro quo* for their agreement to the integrated curriculum.

The introduction of the training levy in the construction industry coincided with plans by the government to establish a comprehensive national training levy by legislation. For the associations of the construction industry, this coincidence was both an asset and a liability. Since the national employers' associations were at the time fighting an intense political battle against the government proposal, the emerging agreement in the construction industry was a dangerous precedent for them. As a consequence, the ZDB and HDB came under heavy attack inside the BDA and the ZDH, even more so than over the integrated training curriculum. To defend themselves, they argued that separate funds for individual industries run by the 'social partners' were more acceptable than one comprehensive fund controlled by a state bureaucracy. In this sense, they presented their solution as an alternative to the government's plans. In any case, while the national associations ultimately defeated the government proposal, they were unable to make the construction industry associations withdraw from their collective agreement, or to prevent the agreement being declared generally binding by the government.

The Establishment of Training Facilities outside Firms

The next problem on the agenda after the introduction of the levy system was the provision of adequate facilities for training outside the firm. Since it had been one of the motives of the reform to prevent such training taking place in state institutions, these facilities had to be created and operated by the industry itself through its employers' associations and chambers. There was agreement that artisanal and non-artisanal firms had to provide for training facilities in proportion to their share in the number of apprentices. This was not difficult for the non-artisanal firms represented by the HDB which were responsible for only a minor fraction of the apprentices. The situation was different in the artisanal sector whose existing external training capacity was small in comparison to its number of apprentices and to the requirements of the Integrated Training Scheme. It was because of this problem that the decree of 1974 provided for a transition period of four years during which the Integrated Curriculum was obligatory only in regions with sufficient external training facilities.

For obvious reasons, the creation and management of the new external training centres had to be the responsibility of local and regional associations. The ZDB therefore had to wait for its affiliates, or the Chambers of Artisans, to take the initiative. This, however, was not forthcoming. In part, the reluctance of local associations reflected the high initial investment costs. Under the demanding Integrated Training Scheme, there needs to be one external training post for every four apprentices. Although the government was willing to contribute up to 90 per cent of the initial investment costs as a subsidy, external training capacity in the artisanal sector of the construction industry grew only slowly. It was not until the middle of 1982 that, after eight years, the decree on the Integrated Training Scheme finally became effective in the entire country.

The main reason why even large government subsidies failed to induce local artisanal associations to set up external training facilities was growing opposition on the part of artisanal firms to the Integrated Training Scheme. When the new scheme was gradually implemented, it turned out that many of the firms represented by the ZDB had not been quite aware of its implications when it was passed. The ZDB went through a critical period in the second half of the 1970s when its members were demanding in growing numbers that the new training system be revised or abandoned. But due to the 'consensus principle', modification of what was by then already a ministerial decree was possible only with the agreement of both the union and the HDB, and this is an important reason why the system has remained essentially unchanged up until now.[7]

The Consequences of the Reform

During the time the new training regulations were gradually introduced, the number of apprentices in the construction industry increased strongly. Between 1974 and 1980 it grew by more than one half to 62,000. Apprentices in the construction industry workforce grew from 2.4 to 4.9 per cent, and in 1980 there was one apprentice to every nine skilled workers which exactly represented the necessary reproduction ratio. The increase in the number of apprentices in construction was significantly higher than the general increase in apprenticeships that occurred in the 1970s. According to both the union and the employers' associations, the quality of training also improved. The construction industry now has an extensive system of external training centres operated and financed by its associations. Although there continues to be a considerable degree of discontent among employers with the Integrated Training Scheme, especially among small firms, there is not likely to be any significant 'reform of the reform' in the near future.

It is of course difficult to say whether the considerable gains of the construction industry in the intersectoral competition for apprentices were indeed caused by the greater attractiveness of the new Integrated Training Scheme. Many other factors have undoubtedly played a role. According to the union and the employers' associations, the most important effect of the reform seems to have been that the levy system made firms more willing to take advantage of the higher demand, due to demographic factors, by young people for training opportunities. It needs to be emphasised that the disproportionate increase in the number of apprenticeships in construction took place in a period in which the industry underwent a more serious economic crisis than any other sector, and in which its total number of employees declined sharply.

The suggestion that the reform had greater effects on the behaviour of firms than on the preferences of young people looking for training opportunities, is borne out by subsequent developments.

As the number of school leavers entering the dual system began to decline for demographic reasons in the mid 1980s, the first industry that was affected was construction. Between 1984 and 1985, the number of new apprenticeship contracts in the construction industry decreased from 21,000 to 13,000, to the alarm of the unions as well as the employers' associations. In the future, all sides expect the number of apprentices to fall far short of the 1984 peak of 72,100.

Outside the industry, the new training scheme had only limited repercussions. In part, this was because the national employers' associations did their utmost to prevent a further 'sectoralisation' of training policy. Thus, the use of collective agreements to establish a levy finance system remained more or less confined to the construction industry. Moreover, the proportion of vocational training time spent outside the firm is in all other economic sectors far lower than in construction. On the other hand, it is true that it has generally increased. Also, while no other industry has embraced the idea of integrated curricula and common basic training for a large number of occupations quite as enthusiastically as the construction industry, at least the division between basic and specialised training has today become generally accepted.

The Social Partners in Further Training

In line with their tradition of innovative joint initiatives to increase the governability of their unwieldy industry, the social partners in the construction sector have been engaged in various efforts to extend the scope and improve the quality of further training. Leaving aside the *Meister*[8] training in the artisanal part of the industry (Streeck et al. 1987: ch. 3), these initiatives were, just as the reform of initial vocational training, motivated by the need to alleviate the disadvantages of casual employment for both workers and employers. They were also a reaction to changing technical and economic requirements in an industry whose labour force had become comparatively unskilled during the period of expansion in the 1950s and 1960s, resulting in considerable skill deficits that were impossible to remedy just by expanding initial vocational training.

In particular, the main incentive for the employers to extend and upgrade further training was that this was expected to facilitate efficient utilisation of ever more expensive machinery through reduction of downtime and swifter repairs. Moreover, further training was seen as a way of attracting and keeping a core labour force of German skilled workers at a time when heavy reliance on unskilled foreign labour was creating growing management problems on the building site. For the union, the primary objective was to increase employment stability by making employers invest in human capital; to enlarge the opportunities of workers in the external labour market through certification of acquired skills; and to improve the social security status of redundant construction workers (unskilled workers are expected to accept any job offered to them by the labour administration whereas skilled workers have certain rights to reject employment outside their occupation without losing unemployment benefit).

In close parallel to their activities in other areas, trade union and employers' associations in the German construction industry have created, by industrial agreement, a separate, sector-specific system of further training and certification adding to and complementing the three transsectoral systems: the artisanal *Meister* training, the further training for other artisanal occupations under the supervision of the Chambers of Artisans, and the system of further training organised by the Chambers of Commerce and Industry. All three 'general' systems are available to the construction sector as well; but there are also qualifications that are certified exclusively by special examination boards for the construction industry that are set up by the social partners. The respective certificates are valid only inside the industry; they do, however, carry an entitlement to be grouped in a particular wage category under the collective agreement.

Again apart from the artisanal *Meister* training, there are four main areas of further training in the construction industry: the training of machinists; the training of foremen (*Poliere*); a further training scheme in the scaffolding industry; and the further training of skilled building workers in restoration work. To illustrate the regulation and the practice of further training the following section will focus on restoration work.

Further Training in Restoration Work

In recent years a growing share of the workload of the building industry was related to the restoration of historical buildings. As postwar needs for reconstruction and infrastructural investment have abated, a new concern has developed with the preservation of historical monuments. In the 1970s, local and regional governments have begun to extend protection not just to churches, castles and monasteries but also to a large number of more recent buildings. Today, it is estimated that about 1.5 million buildings are in some way or other protected, which amounts to about 15 per cent of all buildings in the country.

Restoration work has thus become a new growth area for an industry that is otherwise undergoing secular decline and contraction. However, restoration requires traditional skills and knowledge of traditional materials and techniques which have no longer been provided in the era of 'modern', 'industrialised' building work. One result was that many restoration projects in the 1970s had to be carried out by foreign specialists, in particular from Poland, in spite of high and rising unemployment among German building workers. In the early 1980s, the union and the employers' association of the artisanal building sector, the ZDB, recognised that in order to open up and serve this potentially sizeable market, they had first to invest in recreating the required skills. A number of Further Training Regulations were negotiated between the social partners in 1984 and 1985, creating various certified occupations in restoration that were based on the vocational education and experience of building occupations such as bricklayer, painter and carpenter.

Two main categories of Further Training Regulations for restoration work can be distinguished. The first regulates access to the occupation of 'Restorator' and requires that participants have passed their *Meister* examination. In 1985, regulations of this kind existed for painters, stone masons, bricklayers, carpenters, and stucco workers. The approximate training time required to pass the examination is estimated at 900 hours of course work. The second category concerns the further education of journeymen and skilled workers who can be trained to become masons, stone masons, carpenters, etc. 'for restoration work'. To be admitted, applicants have to have at least two years of practical experience in their occupations.

Further Training Regulations are negotiated between the union and the artisanal employers' association of the sector where they apply. They are then finally approved by the respective national associations, the DGB and the ZDH. Under the Statute of Artisans (*Handwerksordnung*), they have to be formally adopted by each individual Chamber of Artisans which administers the respective examinations. IG BSE and ZDB have also developed nationally standardised curricula for the courses leading up to these examinations.

For many of the further training occupations in the construction industry, especially at the skilled worker level, training courses are offered not just by employers' associations or third parties but also by the union. Among other things, these serve to intensify the commitment of workers to the union. The IG BSE has also successfully insisted that at least for a transition period, practical experience on the building site is recognised as a substitute for participation in formal training with respect to admission to examinations. This applies in particular to those occupations that were introduced by the social partners through collective agreement, outside the control of state agencies or Chambers.

Apart from the industry's labour needs, union and employers in construction have another reason to be interested in intensified further training. As the demographic structure of the population changes, the external training centres created in the 1970s for the new vocational training scheme find it increasingly difficult to utilise their capacity. Extending their activities into further training would appear to be a logical way of avoiding rising deficits that would have to be covered by higher fees or out of the budgets of Chambers and employers' associations. However, because of the demanding curricula and since most training centres serve large geographical regions, attendance concurrent with work is often impossible. As a consequence, the industry's social partners have a vested interest in public support for workers attending further training courses, and they have in fact jointly objected to the respective cuts in the budget of the Federal Labour Office.

Notes

1. Chambers are regional, sector unspecific business interest associations with compulsory membership (see Groser et al. 1986).
2. This article is a revised version of ch. 5 in Streeck et al. (1987).
3. A detailed case analysis of the reform of vocational training in the West German construction industry during the 1970s is presented in Streeck (1983).
4. On the distinction between artisanal and non-artisanal firms in Germany, see Doran (1984) and Streeck (1986).
5. Appendix B in Streeck et al. (1987) gives a brief outline of the Procedure for the Development of Training Regulations.

6. Detailed inspection of the list of occupations included, and not included, in the Integrated Training Scheme reveals its impact on the building industry (as distinguished from civil engineering) and on the small firms. Most of the firms that engage in building are small and the vast majority of them have artisanal status. The law recognises seventeen artisanal construction trades, or occupations. This includes chimney sweepers and painters, but not plumbers or electricians, who in Germany are not classified among the construction industry. Five of the seventeen trades, including the chimney sweepers, painters and roofers, are not represented by the ZDB but by separate artisanal associations, and significantly enough these were not covered by the reform and the integrated curriculum.

All 12 construction trades organised by the ZDB but one were merged in the Integrated Training Scheme. The one exception was baking-oven building which is a highly specialised, traditional occupation.

Before the reform, formal training in some of these occupations, especially concrete and road building, was also provided in the non-artisanal sector, albeit under different curricula. The reform eliminated these differences, and training in the respective occupations was standardised for artisanal and non-artisanal firms.

Finally, in addition to the eleven artisanal and 'mixed' occupations, three more occupations were included in the Integrated Training Scheme that were, and continue to be, trained only in the non-artisanal sector. These were the pipeline builders, the canal builders and the dry construction assemblers (*Trockenbaumonteur*). All non-artisanal manual construction occupations were thus included. Later in the 1970s, another non-artisanal building occupation of the track construction worker (*Gleisbauer*) was created and also fitted into the Scheme.

7. Since 1974, there have been a series of minor changes in the system all of which were negotiated between the three associations. Most important among these was the extension of the training period to a full three years, upon pressure from the ZDB. Many other demands of the artisanal firms were rejected. At the time of writing, the HDB has served notice of its intention not to prolong the levy system, but it appears that this is only a tactical move.

8. Further training in West Germany appears in a great diversity of forms and most of the opportunities for further training are not formalised and standardised (see Streeck et al. 1987). The area of artisanal Meister (*Handwerksmeister*), however, is an important exception to this evaluation of the situation in general. Under the statute of artisans (*Handwerksordnung*) federal regulations are in force for virtually all artisanal occupations. In addition to specific occupational skills, they require economic and legal knowledge as well as vocational teaching skills. Passing the *Meister*-examination is a precondition for setting up a new firm in the artisanal sector. A relatively new further training occupation in the non-artisanal sector is that of the Certified Foreman (*Industriemeister*). The need in the non-artisanal sector to create a career occupation as in the artisanal sector resulted in the decreeing of an equivalent standardised regulation.

Bibliography

Doran, A. (1984), *Craft Enterprises in Britain and Germany: A Sectoral Study*, Anglo-German Foundation for the Study of Industrial Society, London

Groser, M., J. Hilbert and H. Voelzkow (1986), *Die Organisation von Wirtschaftsinteressen im Kammersystem der Bundesrepublik Deutschland*, Materialien zur sozialwissenschaftlichen Planungs- und Entscheidungstheorie No. 9, Universität Bielefeld, Fakultät für Soziologie

Kath, F. (1981), 'Umfang und Bedeutung der überbetrieblichen Ausbildung', *Gewerkschaftliche Bildungspolitik*, 319–39

Sperner, R. et al. (1976), *Die Sozialkassen in der Bauwirtschaft: Kommentar*, Selbstverlag Dr. Blumensaat, Hamburg

Streeck, W. (1981), *Gewerkschaftliche Organisationsprobleme in der sozialstaatlichen Demokratie*, Athenäum, Königstein

—— (1983), *Die Reform der beruflichen Bildung in der westdeutschen Bauwirtschaft 1969–1983: Eine Fallstudie über Verbände als Träger Öffentlicher Politik*, Discussion Paper 83–23, Wissenschaftszentrum Berlin

—— (1986), *The Territorial Organization of Interests and the Logics of Associative Action: The Case of the Artisanal Interest Organizations in West Germany*, Discussion Paper 86–24, Wissenschaftszentrum Berlin

Streeck, W., J. Hilbert, K.-H. van Kevelaer, F. Maier and H. Weber (1987), *The Role of the Social Partners in Vocational Training and Further Training in the Federal Republic of Germany*, CEDEFOP (European Centre for the Development of Vocational Training), Berlin

Part V

---

*The Completion of the
Internal Market*

14

The Completion of the Internal Market and its Impact on the Building Sector in Europe

Jürgen Koch

Some Aspects of the Building Industry in the European Community

The building industry is one of the key sectors of the twelve countries of the European Community (EC). There are approximately 8.8 million people working in it, of which 7 million are wage and salary earners (Hauptverband der Deutschen Bauindustrie 1988: 11). Building workers formed 7.2 per cent of the gainfully employed in 1985 (Hauptverband der Deutschen Bauindustrie 1988: 11).

In the postwar years until the 1970s, the building industry was a motor of growth in Western Europe. At the end of the 1970s it underwent a decline due to the saturation of traditional markets and the drastic reduction of state construction orders. Since then the level of unemployment in the building sector has been higher than the level of unemployment in the economy as a whole in nearly all member states of the EC. Even the construction boom of the last couple of years in some of these states has not altered anything in this respect. Conservative estimates assume 1.5 million reported unemployed workers in the building trade in 1987. However, this level appears to be too low because the proportion of self-employed is currently increasing in many member states. When unemployed, they are not usually registered in the unemployment statistics. This group now forms one-third of total employment in the building trade in Great Britain and the trend towards self-employment is increasing in other member countries too.

Table 14.1 Large construction firms in EC countries, 1987

	Orders in million dollars		
	Domestic	Abroad	Total
1 Bouygues, France	7,160.0	1,910.0	9,070.0
2 SAE Société Auxiliaire d'Entreprises, France	2,774.0	1,696.0	4,4700
3 Philipp Holzmann AG, Federal Republic	2,509.2	1,941.6	4,450.8
4 SGE Groupe, France	2,935.0	765.0	3,700.0
5 George Wimpey PLC, Great Britain	2,519.2	1,118.6	3,637.8
6 Spie Batignolles, France	2,601.0	1,020.0	3,621.0
7 Dumez, France	1,674.0	1,731.0	3,405.0
8 GTM Entreprise, France	2,714.5	303.8	3,018.3
9 Hochtief AG, Federal Republic	1,960.0	810.0	2,770.0
10 Bovis Intl. Ltd, Great Britain	1,222.0	974.8	2,196.8

Source: Hauptverband der Deutschen Bauindustrie 1988: 39–42.

In 1987 the volume of construction work within the EC amounted to £290 billion. Between them the Federal Republic of Germany, France and Italy produced 60 per cent of the total construction volume. The proportion of building investments to gross domestic product varies considerably between the different member states of the EC. It stood at 7.8 per cent in Great Britain in 1987, whilst it was 11 per cent in the Federal Republic of Germany.

To analyse the consequences of the completion of the internal market for the construction industry it is important to look at some of the industry's characteristics which clearly differentiate it from other sectors of national economies. Small and medium-sized firms are preponderant in all the member states of the EC, though the trend to firm concentration has increased considerably in recent years. Differences in size structure are significant in the large EC member states: in 1983 there were 242 firms with more than 500 employees in Great Britain, 154 in France but only 105 firms of this size category in the Federal Republic of Germany. The dominating role of French and British construction firms in Europe is also shown in Table 14.1, which lists the 10 largest European construction firms (construction orders in millions of dollars in 1987).

The composition and organisation of the construction industry is heterogeneous. For example, the placing of orders with subcontractors is much higher in Great Britain and France than in the Federal Republic of Germany. The Statistical Office of the European Community data show that from 1983 the ratio of inputs were about 70 per cent in Great Britain and France, but only 50 per cent in the Federal Republic. In addition, there is considerable variation in the size distribution of companies. Although there are no exact statistics on establishments with fewer than 20 employees, the smallest establishments form a large proportion of firms in Italy while medium-sized establishments are underrepresented. In contrast, there are proportionately more large firms in France and in Great Britain.

The completion of the construction market is not only complicated by the preponderance of small and medium-sized firms in the construction industry. In addition, construction works are usually performed at the building site, i.e. the location of production is fixed and the costs of transporting machines and people are high. The use of different construction materials and the existence of different styles of architecture are not only attributable to different conditions of climate but also to the fact that buildings are an expression of cultural development and regional variety. The demand of the population for a certain quality of housing is dependent not just on income but on the value attached to housing in the scale of priorities of citizens throughout the EC. Building will never be mass-produced but usually remains a one-off item of production. Some economies of scale are not expected even with a total opening of the market.

The Internal Market

The euphoria of the founding years of the European Economic Community disappeared in nearly all the member states in the 1970s because of the stagnation of the process of political integration and economic recession. The term 'Eurosclerosis' was applied to the economic and political decline of the old continent against its main rivals Japan and the United States, and it was assumed that this decline could not be halted. As a result, in the mid 1980s the Commission proposed the revival of the objective of the completion of the internal market to the governments of the 12 EC states. The Commission argued with the member governments that only the total abolition of frontiers for products, services, capital and people

Figure 14.1 Comparison of the economic development of the EC, the USA and Japan

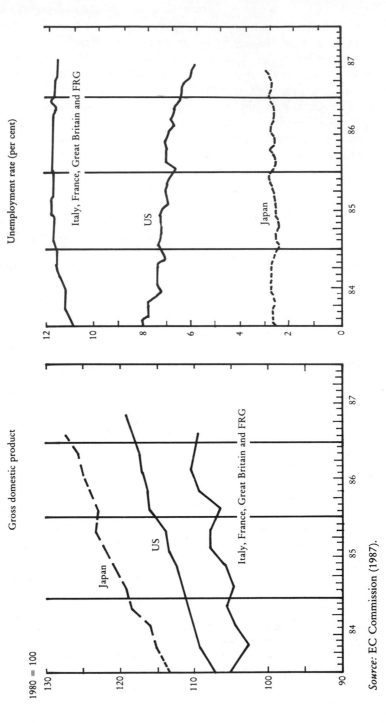

Source: EC Commission (1987).

within the EC would allow the Community to compete against its main economic rivals in world markets. The Commission supported this argument with the findings of the Cecchini report, a study which calculated the economic costs to the Community of failing to harmonise the EC internal market.

The Cecchini Report

The Cecchini report is a study of several thousand pages to which dozens of scientists, consulting firms and economic research institutes contributed. The basis of the calculations of the costs of the 'non-realisation of Europe' were existing data, forecasts and surveys of firms. With an effective publicity campaign the Commission publicised the optimistic forecasts of the study that it had, itself, commissioned. The report assumes that the completion of the internal market will increase economic growth by 4.5 to 7.5 per cent with a simultaneous reduction of inflation of between 5 and 4.4 per cent. It considers that up to 5 million new jobs could be created if suitable accompanying politico-economic steps are taken (Cecchini 1988: 134).

The Commission assumes a margin of error of about 30 per cent in its calculations. At the same time it shows that the positive effects will be obtained if *all* existing limitations of the domestic market are eliminated. Finally the study emphasises that the adaptation of the market participants to the requirements of the internal market will lead to significant job losses in certain regions and sectors at the outset. On the other hand, the social costs of necessary structural adaptation at both the micro-economic and at the macro-economic level are not shown in detail in the Cecchini report.

Whilst the abolition of customs barriers has led to a huge increase in cross-border inter-European trade, national markets for public procurement have remained relatively closed. The total volume of public procurement orders in the Community reached 530 billion ECUs in 1986. It was therefore higher than the volume of cross-border trade within the Community (500 billion ECUs) and constituted 15 per cent of the gross domestic product of the member states (Cecchini 1988: 37). The public sector made cross-border procurement orders with a value of 0.14 per cent of GDP in 1986. Obviously, all efforts by the EC Commission to liberalise public procurement had failed.

Figure 14.2 Development of employment in the EC

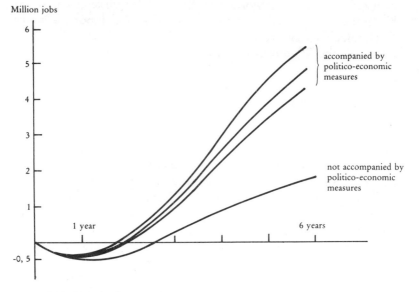

Source: EC Commission (1988).

The Character of Public Procurement

The system of public procurement varies between countries. For example, in the Federal Republic and Italy procurement in energy and road construction are largely decentralised, whilst in France and Great Britain they are centralised. Different legal frameworks of conditions, for example, on the form and extent of state shareholdings in firms, are important factors influencing the liberalisation of procurement in construction all over Europe.

Even assuming that many products and services will not be required to compete all over Europe, or are used in such small batches as to make community-wide tendering unrealistic, the Cecchini report estimates the volume for community-wide tenders to be 240–340 billion ECUs, i.e. 7 to 10 per cent of total GDP. About 25 per cent of public procurement was in the construction sector in 1984.

The macro-economic significance of public procurement markets is very different in individual member states. Whilst public procurement forms nearly 22 per cent of the GNP in Great Britain it is only

Figure 14.3 Breakdown of public purchases by supplying sector –
Belgium, France, West Germany, Italy and United
Kingdom, 1984

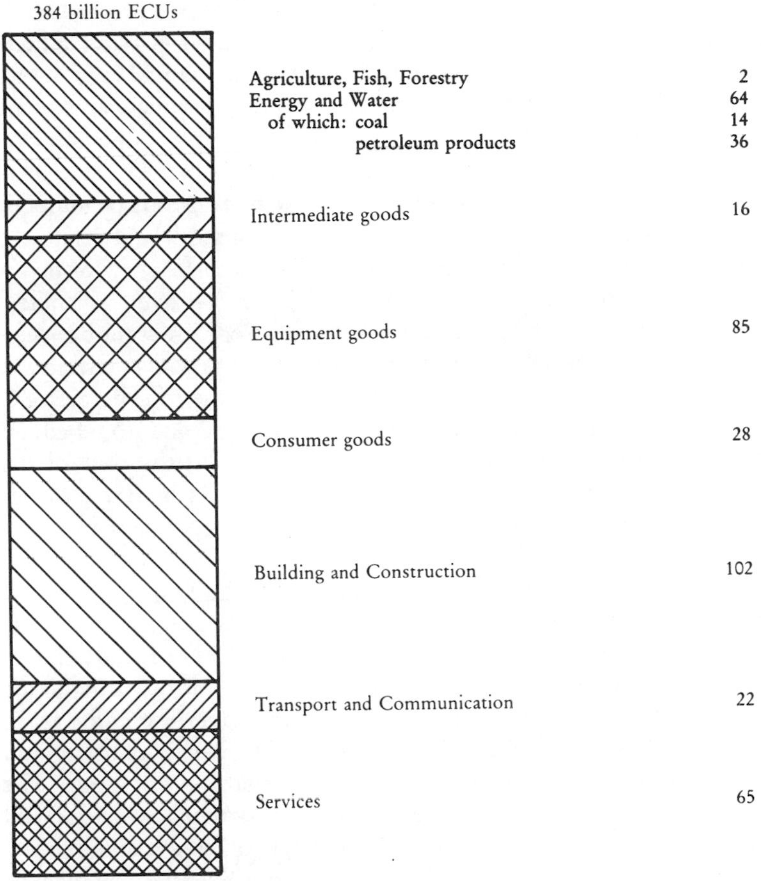

384 billion ECUs

Agriculture, Fish, Forestry	2
Energy and Water	64
of which: coal	14
petroleum products	36
Intermediate goods	16
Equipment goods	85
Consumer goods	28
Building and Construction	102
Transport and Communication	22
Services	65

Source: Atkins Management Consultants (1987: 89).
NB. These figures should be treated with caution. The data have been
supplied from a variety of sources including Eurostat, National Accounts,
contract data compiled by ministries and local government representative
bodies, company accounts and the consultants' own estimates.

11.8 per cent in the Federal Republic of Germany. In fact, potential
price savings through liberalising the domestic market in the building sector are limited, but the huge extent of construction orders
makes even relatively small price reductions profitable. According
to Cecchini potential savings are to be expected especially in the

following fields: in border regions; in technically advanced building operations, airports and new innovative methods of construction; and if the difference between regions with high and low levels of construction activity leads to different margins of profit, producing a stimulus for firms with low order books to tender in areas of high construction activity (Atkins Management Consultants 1987: 92–4).

The EC cross-border market for construction products amounted to £37 billion in 1985. This corresponded to nearly 30 per cent of total building production (BIPE 1988: 451). Of this, 43 per cent is made up of the construction materials, which are goods of mineral, non-metallic origin. Many of them are heavy materials of relatively low cost which makes transportation inefficient. The costs of many construction products double with transportation over 100 miles. Finally, clients' demand and taste in styles is very different between regions. Given these facts, trade in construction products within the Community is amazingly high. On average, in the four biggest EC member countries, Italy, France, Great Britain and the Federal Republic of Germany, it comes to 22 per cent. At the time of the research, the ratio of imports came to 15 per cent in Italy, 20 per cent in Germany, 30 per cent in France and 50 per cent in Great Britain (Cecchini 1987: 89).

Cecchini reports on the results of a survey of 200 firms in the 12 EC member states which shows that different national standards form a decisive barrier to commerce for 70 per cent of trade. There were difficulties in adapting to currently required foreign standards with 60 per cent of products. France and the Federal Republic act in a particularly protective way. German and French construction clients tend to prefer national producers regardless of price. The regulation of standards in these countries is particularly strong and not clear to outsiders. An additional barrier to foreign competitors is that product licences are difficult to obtain, since every single unit of the product has to be approved. Many producers of construction products try to overcome these nearly insurmountable non-tariff obstructions to commerce by setting up production branches in the country in which the product is to be marketed.

According to the study, labour costs in building production do not differ from other sectors of industry. The comparison of hourly labour costs in ECUs for 1986 shows they were 15.3 in the FRG, 15.1 in France, 13.4 in Belgium, 11.8 in Italy and 9.3 in Spain. Many employers reported in the survey that they assume that differences in labour costs will disappear as a result of the total integration of

Figure 14.4 National markets for building products, 1985
(total 110 billion ECUs)

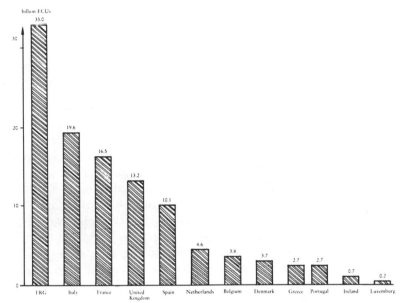

Personal requirements of firms and households included

Source: BIPE (1988: 4).

the market and competitive pressure.

The standardisation of construction materials (e.g. fire resistance, stability, health standards) which is recommended by the report will still take some time to achieve. It will lead to important cost savings through improved economies of scale for producers. Those countries whose domestic markets are currently still protected by strong non-tariff barriers of trade will have to prepare for considerable pressures of adaptation. The reduction of transportation costs by improvements in infrastructure and the abolition of border formalities will intensify the pressure on prices for domestic products. The Cecchini report assumes direct savings for 820 million ECUs all over the EC. The four big EC states alone can anticipate dynamic cost savings of a further £500 million through larger batch production.

The proportion of industrially produced building products might accelerate as a consequence of the completion of the internal market. Obviously this sector, which employs a total of 1.7 million

271

people in the EC, will experience important structural alterations. The firms surveyed estimate that there will be a decrease in building product prices of between 0 and 4 per cent because of intensified competition and improved transportation, alongside an increase in demand for construction products of between 2.5 and 10 per cent (BIPE 1988: 473).

The Strategy of the EC Commission for the Building Sector

The EC Commission has tried from the outset to guarantee European competition for public construction orders. A directive from 1971 planned that all public construction projects with a volume of more than 1 million ECUs should be advertised all over Europe. Especially innovative and expanding sectors, such as armaments, power, transport, telecommunications and water supply were excluded. However, this directive failed miserably. An inquiry of the Commission showed that only 2 per cent of public construction orders were given to firms from other member states in 1986. These were largely firms which were working on both sides of an inland border, so they were 'native' firms after all (ESC 1987: 2).

A number of factors have contributed to the failure of the directive: projects have been fragmented intentionally to stay below the threshold of 1 million ECUs; the direct placing of public construction orders with contractors now accounts for one-third of orders; procedures for awarding contracts have not been clear; and the excluded sectors (energy, transport, telecommunications) have been broadly interpreted by contractors.

The Commission presented a new proposal for a directive in 1986 as a result of this failure (COM (86) 679 final). This tried to overcome the loopholes in the 1971 directive. It proposed that contractors who exercise public functions or whose construction orders come directly or indirectly from public funds should be included in the provisions. It also proposed that the Commission should be informed of planned construction orders six months before the issuing of a tender and that a negotiation procedure would replace direct procurement from a contractor. In addition, provisions have been made for the exclusion of obviously low tenders, for example those which do not observe social insurance regulations. The response in most member states of the EC was negative. The state authorities fear the interference of European bureaucrats in their public procurement practices and the employers are afraid that Brussels will be 'bureaucratically top heavy' in inspecting adherence to the directive. Member states and construction firms have argued that the requirement to provide early information about planned building operations cannot be met in practice since it will lead either to the publication of inappropriate information or to a reduction in building investment. The requirement to provide written reports on order-placing and notification of orders would need additional staff, and small administrative units with relatively few orders on a European level would be totally overburdened by this. As a result of this debate, it is expected that the desired aim of stimulating competition will be counterbalanced by these clauses in the directive.

The Attitude of the Trade Unions

In June 1988 the European Federation of Building and Woodworkers, a union of 23 member trade unions out of 10 EC countries, explicitly welcomed the initiative of the Commission in opening the European construction market. At the same time, they criticised the failure to reach an agreement on social criteria in the first draft directive on construction coordination.

The European Federation of Building and Woodworkers made their agreement conditional on the observation of a number of conditions. These are: the observation of local regulations on health and safety at work; the observation of local collective agreements; the exclusion from tendering lists of companies breaking these criteria; the prohibition of labour-only subcontracting and the placing of orders with chains of subcontractors; the retention of existing rights of employees to information and participation; and the protection of employees by national collective agreements when firms have contracts in foreign countries (EFBW 1988). The West German construction union, the Industriegewerkschaft Bau-Steine-Erden (IG BSE),[1] elaborated the following demands into the discussion:

1 *Prohibition of subcontractor chains.*
   The prohibition of subcontractor chains currently effective in the Federal Republic of Germany could be undermined by the directive draft. This will increase the difficulties of controlling illegal working practices. However, if it is impossible to control

the black economy and illegal forms of employment, it is obvious that firms which do comply with the law will be at a competitive disadvantage. This forms the basis of the demand for the prohibition of subcontractor chains and the requirement that main contractors name potential subcontractors.

2 *The exclusion of firms unable to guarantee standards of work and employment.*
Employers who do not observe labour-related laws, for example regulations and collective agreements concerning health and safety, should explicitly be excluded from tendering lists.

3 *Improved powers to examine exceptionally low tender prices.*
If it is obvious that firms' tenders do not observe social legislation the awarding of contracts to them should be prohibited (IG Bau-Steine-Erden 1987: 2–5).

In September 1987 the Economic and Social Council of the EC almost unanimously agreed that the observance of social legislation and collective agreements at all levels in all companies involved in a single contract should be guaranteed and that offers which failed to observe these conditions should be excluded from tendering processes. It also requires main contractors to publish the works they want to place as subcontracts at the tendering stage (ESC 1987: 11). The European trade unions as a whole did not expect the full observation of their own demands or of the formal statements of the Economic and Social Council in detail. Rather, they sought acknowledgement of the principle that social criteria should be considered in the award of construction contracts (Koch 1988: 10–11). In the ensuing months the struggle over the construction coordination directive continued. While the employers' organisations and the Conservative governments tried to get the European Parliament to reduce the bureaucracy in the construction coordination draft, the trade unions focused on enforcing social criteria alongside administrative simplification. As an example of what is meant by this, in the Federal Republic of Germany the IG Bau-Steine-Erden requires companies tendering for public contracts to deliver a statement of adherence to the collective agreement. In this way only companies which adhere to locally effective construction safety and health regulations and to collective agreements are allowed to participate in public tenders. An appropriate declaration of the company has to be countersigned by the workers' council. Until now this regulation is only effective for the city state of Hamburg

(Baubehörde Hamburg 1987). The European trade unions also base their argument on the regulations in the United States which prevent 'social dumping' in public construction orders through importing low paid workers (US Department of Labor 1986). The Davis Bacon Act requires construction workers to be paid at 'locally prevailing wages' in building operations where the US Federal Government provides 25 per cent finance or more. In 1964 a clause explicitly stated that 'fringe benefits' were included in this. Construction firms which break the law can be suspended from public tenders for three years.

At the first reading of this directive the European Parliament agreed that there should be a threshold of 5 million ECUs for the procurement of construction orders. In May 1988 an overwhelming majority of the Parliament confirmed the opinion of the trade unions that main contractors should have unrestricted responsibility for every subcontract. Support was also given to the idea that contractors should have a duty to notify parts of the order to be subcontracted and be obliged to fix local employment conditions in the contract documents. Public contractors have also been authorised to give consideration to the employment of the long-term unemployed and young people in regions of high unemployment if this is covered by approved programmes of the Commission.

The EC Council of Ministers made important administrative simplifications to the directive in a statement of October 1988 (EC, Council of Ministers 1988). However, the Council gave up any consideration of social criteria in construction order placing as a result of pressure from the British, German and Dutch governments. Even the observance of labour safety regulations and the notification of subcontractors were written in as discretionary clauses which are not binding.

Parliament Confirms the Demands of the Trade Unions

In February 1989 a second reading of the draft directives took place in the European Parliament. By a qualified majority of its members, the social criteria introduced in the first reading were agreed. This refers to the unlimited responsibility of the main contractors for all kinds of work, to the designation of the parts of the order to be subcontracted as well as to the observance of local employment conditions and health and safety regulations.

In response to questions from the Parliament, Vice-President Martin Bangemann, who is responsible for the domestic market, explained that 'working conditions' are to be understood in the terminology used by the International Labour Office. In the opinion of the Commission this includes laws and generally binding collective agreements. The Commission explained explicitly that 'social dumping' should be avoided by the construction coordination directive. Bangemann stated: 'This formulation has the aim that the bidder does not make an offer without reference to local labour costs' (European Parliament, 14.2.1989: 50). The Commission refers in this way to the ILO agreement No. 94 concerning labour clauses in the contracts negotiated by public authorities. Six EC countries are party to this 1952 convention. Great Britain originally ratified this agreement, but cancelled it with a series of deregulatory measures.

The Free Market for Building Products

In May 1985 the EC Council of Ministers followed the suggestion of the Commission and agreed a new draft proposal on technical harmonisation and standardisation to which they gave the term 'New Approach'. As a result, areas in which harmonisation is indispensable and areas in which it is possible to rely on mutual acknowledgment of national regulations and standardisations will be clearly distinguished. The harmonisation of legal orders will now confine itself to enforcing health and safety requirements, and will allow a product to be traded freely. This strategy is to be welcomed in principle. However, it contains significant drawbacks. From the point of view of the employees affected, three questions have to be answered unconditionally:

1 Who decides what is to be standardised at a European level?
2 Who decides on the standards, i.e. who defines the requirements for health and safety?
3 Who guarantees the strict use of European standards in all the member states?

The so-called 'building product directive' was finally decided in December 1988. Within the next two and a half years it will be transposed into national law. Based on harmonised technical rules it will guarantee an unhindered exchange and use of building products in the European Community. The directive does not only concern building products (building materials and components of construction and civil engineering), but is also the basis for the exchange of technical services, the description of the works in tender documents and for the form of building contracts.

In the coming years it remains to be seen if the conferences of the Comité Européen de Normalisation (CEN) and the Comité Européen de Normalisation Électrotechnique (CENELEC) are capable of agreeing harmonised European standards and will succeed in maintaining and improving the level of protection for employees.

Social Progress by the EC

The spirit of the EEC Treaty proposes social progress and the levelling up rather than the levelling down of conditions of employment. Article 118a states that member states shall pay 'particular attention to encouraging improvements, especially in the working environment, as regards the health and safety of workers and shall set as their objective the harmonisation of conditions in this area, while maintaining the improvements made . . .' However, these provisions do not prevent individual states from maintaining or introducing more stringent measures for the protection of working conditions. Many initiatives harmonising regulations in the field of health and safety at work in the building sector are now under negotiation or have already been agreed. These include regulations for the use of mobile construction plant, protective clothing and minimum requirements for health and safety in workplaces, to name but a few.

Other aspects of the building industry are also being examined by the EC institutions. The European Centre for the Development of Vocational Training (CEDEFOP) carried out an analysis of tests of occupational competence for skilled workers in the construction sector in July 1987 (CEDEFOP: 1987). The study compared qualifications in selected construction trades. In 1988, the Commission ordered a study comparing collective agreements in the construction sector covering payment, working time and training in Belgium, the Federal Republic of Germany, France, Italy, Spain and Greece. The long-term aim of the EC is the adaptation of vocational training systems.

Jürgen Koch

Construction Trade Unions in the Internal Market

The European Federation of Building and Woodworkers was established in 1973. According to its constitution, the main task of the EFBW is the representation of interests of the EC building and wood trade unions on EC institutions. Moreover, the EFBW promotes the exchange of opinions and information between its member associations on questions of economic and social development in the building and woodworking sectors and the development of wage negotiations in these sectors. For this purpose the EFBW regularly conducts surveys among its member associations.

By 1989 24 trade unions in 10 member states had joined the EFBW representing more than 2 million organised members. The Secretary's office of the EFBW is situated in Brussels. The EFBW is also attached to the European Trade Union Confederation (ETUC) with which it cooperates closely. For years the EFBW was only able to fulfil basic personnel and administrative duties and affiliated unions were not prepared to provide sufficient finance to represent their European interests. This has been primarily because of the characteristics of the building industry, and traditionally low levels of union organisation. Apart from Denmark, where more than 90 per cent of employees are unionised, the level of organisation in the other EC member states reaches a maximum of 30 per cent.

The recession in the building industry, rationalisation of investments and the steady growth of self-employment have led to a decrease in membership of the building trade unions in many member states. At the same time, political pressure on employee representation has been increased by the decisive anti-union policies of many Conservative governments. Since they were fighting for economic and political survival locally and at national level, most of the trade unions were even less prepared to make commitments of money and personnel to apparently absurd international activities. The EFBW is weakened by the fact that the CGT, the biggest trade union in France, is not a member of it and that, until now, no unions from Portugal and Greece have been admitted.

The completion of the internal market has produced a common fear of declining standards of health and safety and social security provision at national level, and has led the European building unions to place greater value on international cooperation, at least at the EC level. The last general meeting of the EFBW at the end of

1988 agreed the doubling of membership contributions in order to increase staffing at the Secretary's office in Brussels.

Conclusion

The internationalisation of construction production is increasing in Europe and this development will only be accelerated by the EC initiatives for opening European building markets. Competition between the big building firms of the EC member states will intensify through procurement policies for large public construction orders. The same is true for the pressure of competition on companies operating near EC domestic borders. The extent to which the objective of achieving equal opportunities for all competitors in the internal market is reached depends not only on the translation of the EC building coordination directive into national law but also on its practical application. Finally it should be noted that only 10 per cent of construction production is covered by the actual directive.

Intensified competition will also result in closures of firms. This is particularly the case in border regions where medium-sized firms are affected by cross-border competition. Von Ameln argues that the consequences are incalculable in respect of social and labour market policy for the cities and communities which are handicapped from the outset by their border position (1989: 13). The creation of jobs expected overall in the Cecchini report by the completion of the internal market will not be achieved, at least for the building sector.

Moderate economies of scale can only be expected with some specific construction products and services which are not fixed by location. Apart from this, the improved access of foreign companies to neighbouring markets within the EC must be considered. This will increase the attraction of the European building market not only for European but also for Japanese and South Korean building companies. Already a process of mergers and acquisitions has been occurring to an extent never previously experienced in the construction industry as well as in other industrial sectors of the EC in preparation for the internal market. The large building companies are preparing for the internal market by buying medium-sized firms in neighbouring countries. The process of concentration not only creates new demands on European laws on the formation of cartels, but also endangers existing institutions of codetermination and employees' rights to information.

The European trade unions will be able to respond to these new demands only if they can represent their interests at national and European level. At the same time they must not miss the possibilities for achieving their objectives through workplace representation, even if they are limited. In the long run, it will be necessary for building unions in the EC to improve information exchange both bilaterally and through the EFBW. It will also be necessary for them to coordinate trade union strategies to avoid being played off against one another in the European arena.

At building sites the control of existing standards of labour safety and the control of illegal forms of employment will become even more difficult. The observance of the regulations, laws and existing collective agreements will only be guaranteed if staffing is increased in the appropriate supervisory authorities; that is to say, if sanctions for offences are increased and the trade unions cooperate closely, especially in the EC domestic border regions.

The debate about the location of enterprises which is now being held by the employers' associations and the Conservative politicians in many EC countries in order to reduce social standards has even less justification in construction than in other industrial sectors. Apart from this, existing differences in labour costs may be counterbalanced by higher levels of productivity (Hauptverband der Deutschen Bauindustrie 1988). The specificities of this sector, for example, in the high level of regionalisation of markets and the highly location-bound nature of production have been discussed above.

The completion of the internal market will lead to an important increase in building volumes in the coming years. In the building sector, as elsewhere, companies are preparing for European competition by investing. In addition, an increased volume of trade between member states will only be possible if infrastructure in the EC can be developed quickly and this will require programmes of construction work. Finally, community-wide pressure is growing to begin investment in the field of environmental protection. In the protection of water resources alone, huge investments are necessary to protect the North Sea, the Baltic and the Mediterranean from ecological disaster. In addition, investments are to be expected in urban renewal and housing.

Note

1. The German construction union, the Industriegewerkschaft Bau-Steine-Erden (IG BSE) organises all employees in the construction industry (main trades and finishing trades), in civil engineering, the building materials industry, architectural firms and housing companies which administer large building complexes.

References

Ameln, R. von (1989) 'Öffentliche Auftragsvergabe im Gemeinsamen Markt aus kommunaler Sicht', *Der Städtetag*, 1, 7–14
Atkins Management Consultants (1987), *The 'Cost of non-Europe' in Public Sector Procurement*, Epsom
Baubehörde Hamburg (1987), *Fachliche Weisung der Baubetriebe z 2/87 zur Änderung der Fachlichen Weisung 1/84 vom 10.5.1984 über die Vergabe von Bauleistungen*
BIPE (1988), *Le 'Coût de la Non-Europe' des Produits de Construction*, Note de synthèse, Bureau d'Information et de Prévisions Économiques, Neuilly-sur-Seine
Cecchini, P. (1988), *Europa '92, Der Vorteil des Binnenmarktes*, Baden-Baden
CEDEFOP (1987), *Entsprechung der Berufsbefähigungsnachweise von Facharbeitern auf dem Sektor Bau*, CEDEFOP, Brussels
EC Commission (1987), *Jahreswirtschaftsbericht 1987–1988*, Brussels
—— (1988). *Europäische Wirtschaft*, Nr. 35, Luxembourg
EC Council of Ministers (1988), *Gemeinsamer Standpunkt des Rates zur Genehmigung der Richtlinie des Rates zur Änderung der Richtlinie 71/305/EWG über die Koordination der Verfahren zur Vergabe öffentlicher Bauaufträge (870/88)*, Brussels
EFBW (1988), *Entschließung zur Baukoordinierungsrichtlinie der EG (679/86)*, European Federation of Building and Woodworkers, Brussels
ESC (1987), *Stellungnahme zu dem Vorschlag für eine Richtlinie des Rates zur Änderung der Richtlinie 71/305/EWG über die Koordinierung der Verfahren zur Vergabe öffentlicher Bauaufträge (Dok. KOM (86)679 endg.)*, Economic and Social Committee of the EC
European Parliament (1989), *Ausführliche Sitzungsberichte*, 14.2.1989
Hauptverband der Deutschen Bauindustrie (1988), *Die Bauwirtschaft in der Europäischen Gemeinschaft*, Wiesbaden/Bonn
IG BSE (1987), *Stellungnahme zum Vorschlag für eine Richtlinie des Rates zur Änderung der Richtlinie 71/305/EWG über die Koordinierung der Verfahren zur Vergabe öffentlicher Bauaufträge – KOM (86) 679 endg.*, Industriegewerkschaft Bau-Steine-Erden, Frankfurt

Koch, J. (1988) 'Arbeitnehmer – Fünftes Rad am EG-Wagen?' *EG-Magazin*, 5/88, 10–11

US Department of Labor (1986), *Construction Wage Determination, Manual of Operations*, Employment Standards Administration Wage and Hour Division, Washington, D.C.

Index